Palgrave Macmillan Series in Global Public Diplomacy

Series Editors
Kathy Fitzpatrick
University of South Florida
Tampa, FL, USA

Philip Seib
University of Southern California
Los Angeles, CA, USA

At no time in history has public diplomacy played a more significant role in world affairs and international relations. As a result, global interest in public diplomacy has escalated, creating a substantial academic and professional audience for new works in the field.

The *Global Public Diplomacy* Series examines theory and practice in public diplomacy from a global perspective, looking closely at public diplomacy concepts, policies, and practices in various regions of the world. The purpose is to enhance understanding of the importance of public diplomacy, to advance public diplomacy thinking, and to contribute to improved public diplomacy practices.

More information about this series at
http://www.palgrave.com/gp/series/14680

Nicholas J. Cull · Michael K. Hawes
Editors

Canada's Public Diplomacy

Editors
Nicholas J. Cull
Annenberg School for
Communication
University of Southern California
Los Angeles, CA, USA

Michael K. Hawes
Canada-US Canada Fulbright
Commission
Ottawa, ON, Canada

Palgrave Macmillan Series in Global Public Diplomacy
ISBN 978-3-319-62014-5   ISBN 978-3-319-62015-2   (eBook)
https://doi.org/10.1007/978-3-319-62015-2

This Palgrave Macmillan imprint is published by the registered company Springer Nature Switzerland AG
The registered company address is: Gewerbestrasse 11, 6330 Cham, Switzerland

For John W. Holmes (1910–1988), a great Canadian Diplomat.

Acknowledgments

This book is the product of a one-day symposium in September 2017 at the Center on Public Diplomacy, Annenberg School for Communication and Journalism at the University of Southern California. That conference drew together the past recipients of the Fulbright chair in Public Diplomacy at USC. The editors—who also organized that symposium—owe thanks to the colleagues who assisted especially Jay Wang, director of the Center on Public Diplomacy and Stacy Ingber, CPD's indefatigable Assistant Director for Programming & Events. The US-Canada Fulbright commission provided support in celebration of 70 years since the passage of the Fulbright Amendment, 30 years of its own work, and the 10th birthday of the USC Fulbright chair. The symposium was also supported by the Annenberg School, the Master's Program in Public Diplomacy and by the Center For International Studies, located in the USC Dana and David Dornsife School of Letters, Arts and Sciences.

We appreciate the willingness of the contributors to this boot to revise their spoken remarks and update their perspectives as the production schedule was overtaken by events.

In compiling the book the editors have been well assisted. Nick Cull acknowledges the help of Anna Loup, Shelby Bolen, and especially Rachel McKenzie, who brought a Canadian eye to the final stages of the manuscript. The completion of this book was supported by the Centre for Communication Leadership at USC Annenberg, and Nick Cull is pleased to be able to acknowledge the help of Professor Geoff Cowan, who coincidentally was the Dean of Annenberg behind the foundation of the Fulbright Chair.

Michael Hawes wishes to acknowledge the ongoing support of the US State Department, the program's core sponsor, Global Affairs Canada, the core Canadian partner, and all of those persons and organizations that support the Fulbright program. The Canadian Consulate in Los Angeles has been especially supportive, both of this event, and the program more broadly. He would also like to acknowledge the assistance of Rebecca Dixon.

Both editors have appreciated the enthusiasm of series editors Philip Seib and Kathy Fitzpatrick, of our patient editor at Palgrave, Anca Pusca and project coordinator Ashwini Elango.

Defects are wholly homegrown.

May 2020   Nicholas J. Cull
                                                           Michael K. Hawes

CONTENTS

NOTES ON CONTRIBUTORS

Andrew F. Cooper is University Research Chair in the Department of Political Science, and Professor at the Balsillie School of International Affairs, University of Waterloo, Canada. From 2003 to 2010 he was the Associate Director and Distinguished Fellow of the Centre for International Governance Innovation (CIGI). He teaches in the areas of the Theory and Practice of Diplomacy, National Perspectives on Global Governance, International Political Economy, and Comparative and Canadian Foreign Policy. Holding a Doctor of Philosophy (D.Phil.) from Oxford University, he has been a Visiting Professor at Harvard University, The Australian National University, Stellenbosch University in South Africa, and Shiv Nadar University, India. He is the author of eleven books and editor/co-editor of 21 collections including *The Oxford Handbook of Modern Diplomacy (OUP, 2013)*. In 2000 he was Fulbright Scholar in the Western Hemisphere Program at the School of Advanced International Studies (SAIS), Johns Hopkins University, Washington, DC. In 2019 he received the Distinguished Scholar Award from the Diplomacy Section of the International Studies Association. He held the Fulbright chair at USC in 2009.

Daryl Copeland is an educator, analyst, consultant, and former Canadian diplomat. He is the author of *Guerrilla Diplomacy: Rethinking International Relations*, a Research Fellow at the Canadian Global Affairs Institute, a Policy Fellow at the University of Montreal's Centre for International Studies and Research (CERIUM), and Senior Advisor, Science

Diplomacy at the International Institute of Applied Systems Analysis (IIASA) in Austria. Mr. Copeland specializes in the role of science and technology in diplomacy, international policy, global issues, and public management. He has won several awards and has published 12 book chapters and over 200 articles in the popular and scholarly press. His twitter handle is @GuerrillaDiplo. He is a long-term contributor to the blog associated with the USC Center on Public Diplomacy and is a Senior Fellow of the Center.

Nicholas J. Cull is professor of Public Diplomacy at the University of Southern California where he is affiliated with both the Center on Public Diplomacy and Center for Communication Leadership. Originally from the UK, he is a widely published historian of the role of media and culture in foreign affairs. His most recent books are a survey text: *Public Diplomacy: Foundations for Global Engagement in the Digital Age* (Polity, 2019) and (with Nancy Snow as co-editor) *The Routledge Handbook of Public Diplomacy (2nd edition)* (2020). Cull has delivered training and/or advice at many foreign ministries and diplomatic academies around the world including those of the United States, UK, Canada, Switzerland, Netherlands, South Korea, Japan, and South Africa. He has held visiting appointments with Universita Cattolica del Sacro Cuore, Milan and Beijing Foreign Studies University. In 2019 he was a visiting fellow at the Reuters Institute for the Study of Journalism at Oxford University.

Bernard Duhaime is Professor of International Law at the Faculty of Law and Political Science of the Université du Québec à Montréal (UQAM), where he teaches mainly international human rights law and specializes on the Inter-American System of Protection of Human Rights. He also serves as a Member of the Working group on enforced or involuntary disappearances reporting to the United Nations Human Rights Council. Bernard Duhaime is a Fellow of the Pierre Elliott Trudeau Foundation (2017–2021). Previously, Prof. Duhaime was a lawyer at the Inter-American Commission on Human Rights of the Organization of American States. He is a member of the Quebec Bar in Canada. He is the author of more than fifty publications. He founded the Clinique Internationale de Défense des Droits Humains de l'UQAM and was its first director. He held many international fellowships including the Canada-US Fulbright Visiting Chair in Public Diplomacy at USC in 2011.

Michael K. Hawes is Chief Executive Officer of the Foundation for Educational Exchange between Canada and the United States of America and Executive Director of Fulbright Canada. Since 1985, he has been a professor of international relations (currently on leave) in the Department of Political Studies at Queen's University in Kingston. He holds a Ph.D. in political science from York University in Toronto. He is a member of the Editorial Board at the *Canadian Foreign Policy Journal*. He also co-convenes the Canada Colloquium Series at the University of Hawaii at Manoa. His most recent book, with Christopher Kirkey, is *Canadian Foreign Policy in a Unipolar World* (Oxford, 2017). He is himself an alumnus of the Fulbright program at Berkeley (1999/2000) as well as the Fulbright chair at USC in Spring, 2010.

Mark Kristmanson is a scholar, producer, and administrator. From 2014 to 2019 he served as Chief Executive Officer of the National Capital Commission after directing its public programs and national events for a decade. He holds a Ph.D. from Concordia University in Montréal, an M.A. from City University in London, as well as executive training at Harvard University's Graduate School of Design. Previously, he served as founding Executive Director of the New Brunswick Arts Board and expert adviser to the Cultural Capitals of Canada Program. He is the author of *Plateaus of Freedom: Nationality, Culture, and State Security* (Oxford, 2003) as well as numerous scholarly articles. He founded the Capital Urbanism Lab and speaks regularly at conferences on environmental sustainability, urban design, national commemorations, and indigenous reconciliation. He is a consultant with Larry Beasley and Associates. He held the Fulbright chair at USC in 2011.

Camille Labadie is a lecturer at Université du Québec à Montréal (UQAM). She holds a degree in History from the University of Strasbourg (France), as well as a degree in International Relations and International Law, and a master's degree in International Law. Camille Labadie has carried out several missions with the Parliamentary Assembly of the Council of Europe. She has also been a project assistant at the International Bureau for Children's Rights and acted as case manager at UQAM's International Human Rights Defence Clinic (CIDDHU). She is the recipient of several scholarships for excellence from the Faculty of Political Science and Law at the UQAM, where she is currently completing her doctoral studies under the supervision of Professor Bernard Duhaime.

Her research focuses on reparations for cultural damage in international law, and she acts as coordinator of the *Chaire de recherche sur la gouvernance des musées et le droit de la culture.*

Evan H. Potter is associate professor in the Department of Communication, University of Ottawa. He is the founding editor of the *Canadian Foreign Policy Journal* and an author of booked including *Branding Canada: Projecting Canada's Soft Power Through Public Diplomacy* (2009). His other work includes *Transatlantic Partners: Canadian Approaches to the European Union* (1999) and (as editor) *Cyberdiplomacy: Foreign Policy in the 21st Century* (2002). Potter received his B.A. in political studies at Queen's University at Kingston, his M.A. in international affairs at The Norman Paterson School of International Affairs at Carleton University, and his Ph.D. in international relations at the London School of Economics in the UK. He held the USC Fulbright chair in 2008.

Sarah E. K. Smith is Assistant Professor in Communication and Media Studies, and affiliated faculty in the Bachelor of Global and International Studies program at Carleton University, Ottawa. She is a Fellow of the Canadian Global Affairs Institute and a founding member of the North American Cultural Diplomacy Initiative (NACDI), a multi-disciplinary partnership of academics, policymakers, and practitioners interested in interrogating and advancing cultural diplomacy. Smith completed her Ph.D. at Queen's University and subsequently worked as Curator of Contemporary Art at the Agnes Etherington Art Centre. She held a post-doctoral Fellowship with the Transnational Studies Initiative at Harvard University and a Banting Postdoctoral Fellowship in the Department of English and Film Studies at the University of Alberta. Smith's research addresses visual culture, contemporary art, and museums. Her writing has been published in journals including *TOPIA: Canadian Journal of Cultural Studies*, *Journal of Curatorial Studies*, and *Journal of Canadian Studies*. She is the author of *General Idea: Life & Work*, published in 2016 by the Art Canada Institute. She is currently completing a book on culture and free trade in North America to be published by the University of British Columbia Press. She held the Fulbright chair at USC in 2015.

Stéfanie von Hlatky is an associate professor of political studies at Queen's University in Kingston, Ontario and the former Director of the Queen's Centre for International and Defence Policy (CIDP). Her research focuses on NATO, armed forces, military interventions, and defense policy. She has published in the *Canadian Journal of Political Science*, the *Canadian Foreign Policy Journal*, *Defence Studies*, *International Journal*, *European Security*, *Études internationales*, *Asian Security*, as well as the *Journal of Transatlantic Studies*. She is the author of *American Allies in Times of War: The Great Asymmetry* (Oxford University Press, 2013). She has also published two edited volumes: *The Future of US Extended Deterrence* (with Andreas Wenger) (Georgetown University Press, 2015) and *Going to War? Trends in Military Interventions* (with H. Christian Breede) (McGill-Queen's University Press, 2016). She held the Fulbright chair at USC in 2016.

Ira Wagman is an associate professor of Communication Studies at Carleton University, with a cross-appointment between the School of Journalism and Communication and the Institute for the Comparative Study of Literature, Art, and Culture. He is also a Research Associate at the Max Zelikovitz Centre for Jewish Studies, the Carleton Centre for Public History, and the Centre for European Studies. He researches, teaches, and writes on media history, communication theory, and the study of the cultural industries. He uses historiographical and interpretive research methods including archival work, policy analysis, and media criticism. His work covers a range of geographical settings, including Canada, France, and Italy as well as international political institutions such as the European Union and UNESCO. His publications include *Cultural Industries.ca: Making Sense of Canadian Media in the Digital Age* (coedited with Peter Urquart). He has held visiting professorships and research fellowships at the University of Freiburg, Erasmus University Rotterdam, the University of Amsterdam the University of Arhus, SUNY-Plattsburgh, and Universita Cattolica del Sacro Cuore, Milan as well as USC where he was the 2013 Canada-US Fulbright Visiting Research Chair in Public Diplomacy.

CHAPTER 1

Canada and Public Diplomacy: The Road to Reputational Security

Nicholas J. Cull

The Mountie looked inordinately tall as he stepped forward to pose for photographs. His Red Serge jacket caught the eye from a distance, even though the knots of visitors gathering at the entrance to the building. Up close, his medal ribbons indicated that he was the real deal and not just a handsome actor in a hired costume. Off to one side, a stilt walker in the glittery Cirque du Soleil costume had attracted her own following, but a line formed regardless and pairs of visitors waited politely for their own private moment with an enduring visual icon of Canadian-ness. It could have been a scene from a parade in the shade of the parliament in Ottawa, but it was not. It was Shanghai in the summer of 2010 and Canada was just one of 190 countries seeking to present themselves to the ordinary people of China as participants in what was to be the largest mass participation event in history to date, the Shanghai Expo. Canada had embraced the opportunity, committing over forty million dollars to build a pavilion

N. J. Cull (✉)
Annenberg School for Communication, University of Southern California, Los Angeles, CA, USA
e-mail: cull@usc.edu

© The Author(s) 2021
N. J. Cull and M. K. Hawes (eds.), *Canada's Public Diplomacy*, Palgrave Macmillan Series in Global Public Diplomacy, https://doi.org/10.1007/978-3-319-62015-2_1

1

and becoming the first country to formally commit to exhibiting at the fair. The Mountie stood at the gate of an impressive whole—there was the Canadian pavilion building with its eye-catching angular steel and cedarwood flanks created by the firm of Saia Barbarese Topouzanov of Montreal; there was an interactive exhibit entitled The Living City which showcased ideas of sustainable civic development; there was a film from the National Film Board which edited images from multiple Canadian cities to produce a hybrid Canadian urban experience; there was a restaurant which introduced fairgoers to both Poutine and Moosehead beer. Cirque du Soleil were integral to the operation, as was the honorary chairman of the pavilion, a Canadian familiar to every Chinese household, Mark Roswell. Known by his stage name Darshan (big mountain), Roswell was noted for his mastery of Mandarin and traditional Chinese comic form. In some ways, it was a moment of well-staged entertainment, but it was also a moment of diplomacy as complete as any moment attending that summer's other Sino-Canadian milestones—Premiere Hu Jintao's State Visit to Canada or Governor General Michaëlle Jean's visit to China—except in that it was not designed to engage a foreign government, but, rather, a foreign public. It was a moment of public diplomacy and a step towards ensuring that aspect of security that comes from being well thought of in the world: reputational security.[1]

This book will explore the contemporary Canadian experience of public diplomacy. It is intended for two audiences: students, scholars, and practitioners with an existing interest in Canadian foreign policy who seek to understand its public dimensions, and for a second audience familiar with public diplomacy from a literature which has tended to focus on United States or British cases, who are interested to better understand the Canadian experience. This introduction will attempt to serve both audiences.

Public diplomacy is an essential component of contemporary foreign relations. The term originated in the mid-1960s, when theorists in the United States sought a way to speak about out-reach to foreign publics that would leave the term 'propaganda' free to be thrown at the Communist Bloc. Its first use was in the title of the Edward R. Murrow Center of Public Diplomacy at Tufts University near Boston, founded as a memorial to the former journalist who had exemplified the practice while running global outreach for President Kennedy. It has since evolved through use by practitioners and scholars into a convenient portmanteau phrase for the range of instruments used by an international actor to conduct foreign policy by engaging a foreign public. Whatever its coiner's intent, public diplomacy is no longer synonymous with propaganda because propaganda is always conceived as a mechanism for getting to a particular result. Public diplomacy has the capacity to be a two-way street, to benefit both sides of a relationship and to allow for growth. Yet it is clear from the practice of public diplomacy that some elements (perhaps all, in the hands of some actors) risk tumbling back into propaganda. This is part of the reason why scholarship and public discussion of public diplomacy are so important. The term jumped beyond its US origin only in the 1990s as part of the process of understanding the mechanism by which the Cold War had come to an end. As the role of the media in international relations grew, so interest in public diplomacy increased. The attacks on the United States of September 11, 2001, sealed its relevance. Suddenly, the western world needed a frame to understand how to reach out to public opinion as part of a campaign against terrorism. Public diplomacy became a key part of that discussion. As my co-editor **Michael Hawes** argues in his chapter, Canada has an admirable tradition of public diplomacy but has allowed that to slip. It is essential that the country learn all it can to revive the best in its past global engagement. A restoration requires a full understanding of the nature of public diplomacy.

While the term 'public diplomacy' is new, its practice is as old as organized statecraft. In its classic form, public diplomacy may be divided into five essential components: listening, advocacy, cultural diplomacy, exchange diplomacy, and international broadcasting. Each element has its relevance in the world today and its own place in Canada's approach.

Listening is an international actor's attempt to engage an international audience by systematically collecting information from and about them and feeding what is learned into the policy-making process. While the greatest diplomats seem to do this instinctively, many larger powers seem to forget to listen. The work is typically conducted within embassies, though in some circumstances, independent agencies such as market researchers or media analysts may be employed to inform a particular policy. Canadian listening in the past has included attention to the position of the country in national brand and soft power indices. Significant players in contemporary listening include the Swiss, who, since 2001, have operated a research-driven approach under the auspices of a unit within the foreign ministry called *Présence Suisse/Präsenz Schweiz*. Listening in public diplomacy is sometimes focused narrowly on the process of evaluating a campaign; proof of effectiveness is always helpful at budget time and, hence, this kind of listening is a growing preoccupation for public diplomacy agencies around the world. The need for a genuine culture of listening in Canadian public diplomacy is one of the issues raised by veteran Canadian diplomat **Daryl Copland**.

Advocacy is an international actor's work to explain a particular policy to an international audience. It includes a wide range of methods including speeches, press releases, and—in recent years—online campaigns. Trends within advocacy include large-scale, single-country campaigns promoting national brands, such as the Indian tourist ministry's Incredible India campaign, which began in 2002, or the UK's GREAT campaign, launched in 2011. We are also seeing multi-actor advocacy collaborations around particular issues—for example, the alliance between non-governmental organizations and nations which mobilized so successfully against landmines in the 1990s. Contemporary challenges in advocacy include the problem of credibility in a world segmented by social media. Credibility is boosted when the speaker and audience are linked by similarity. Social media has allowed people to receive much of, if not all of, their information about the world from people very similar to themselves in terms of ideology or demography. Thus, the challenge public diplomats face—communicating with an audience necessarily not like them—is greater than ever. For some countries, advocacy is the most important element of public diplomacy, and indeed, during the premiership of Stephen Harper, the entire process of foreign ministry public engagement was known as advocacy. Major campaigns during the Harper years included work to rally US opinion behind the Keystone XL pipeline program. Some recent Canadian cases of advocacy using digital tools are addressed in the chapter by **Evan Potter**.

Cultural diplomacy is an international actor's engagement of a foreign public by facilitating the export of some element of that actor's artistic or public life or to accomplish a foreign policy project through work in the cultural realm. Historical forms of cultural diplomacy have ranged from missionary activity to complex networks of international schools. Many countries have sought to teach their language to foreigners; others have set up agencies to promote their arts or sporting attainment internationally. Most western powers have long-established specialized agencies for cultural diplomacy, such as Germany's Goethe Institute, Britain's British Council, and Japan's Japan Foundation. Exceptions include the Republic of Ireland, which found that people tended to like the country anyway and felt that the government could do little to top the impact of Irish bars and annual St Patrick's Day festivities. The great advantage of cultural diplomacy is that it can function and win friends in situations when direct political contacts are all but impossible. Its disadvantage lies in the necessity of working in the medium-term and of delivering demonstrably politically useful results through cultural avenues. The chapter by **Sarah E. K. Smith** considers the evolution of Canada's arts diplomacy in New York City. Other significant elements of Canadian cultural diplomacy have included the export of films created by the National Film Board of Canada, Canadian hosting of and participation in international expositions, and promotion of Canadian attainment in the field of literature. The Canada Council for the Arts works to assist with translation and travel through its Arts Abroad grants program.[2] Complications in cultural work are addressed in the case study of the Dead Sea scrolls presented by **Bernard Duhaime and Camille Labadie**. It is encouraging to see a renewed Canadian government interest in this approach, as evidenced by a report from the Senate published in June 2019 entitled: *Cultural Diplomacy: At the Front Stage of Canada's Foreign Policy*.[3]

Exchange diplomacy is an international actor's attempt to cultivate a foreign public by arranging for representatives of that public to spend time experiencing the actor's way of life or vice versa. Countries commonly offer both educationally oriented exchanges and exchanges with a more explicit policy objective which might seek out leaders, like the International Visitor Leadership Program launched by the United States following the Second World War, or the UK's Chevening Scholarships. There are also military-to-military exchanges which support cooperation within alliances like NATO and build relationships beyond. Exchanges differ from other forms of public diplomacy in the extended time frame necessary to show results; conversely, they pay off in terms of the strength of the bonds created and the ease with which they support mutual learning. Canada has a variety of exchange mechanisms including the Canadian Education Exchange Foundation (CEEF), a not-for-profit corporation which arranged international exchanges for the country's students and teachers, with support from provincial governments and the national Department for Canadian Heritage.[4] There are also exchange organizations dedicated to promoting a single bilateral relationship. This volume is a project of Fulbright Canada: the Foundation for Educational Exchange between Canada and the United States of America. Its authors have all served as Fulbright professors at the University of

Southern California's Annenberg School for Communication and Journalism in Los Angeles, and thereby played a part in building US/Canada understanding. Canada has been part of exchange programs within the Francophonie and English-speaking international communities, including Oxford University's venerable Rhodes Fellowships. Its alumni include the former Canadian Minister for Global Affairs and current Deputy Prime Minister, Chrystia Freeland.

International broadcasting has historically been a distinct element of public diplomacy, separated both by its need for infrastructure and the ethical journalistic approach needed to ensure long-term credibility. Even before the rise of the electronic media, international actors sought to engage foreign publics by providing a construction of the world's events, from the newsletters put out by the Holy Roman Emperor Frederick II to entire newspapers created for foreign consumption by belligerent powers in the Great War. Radio opened almost unlimited horizon, giving nation-states and other actors, such as the Vatican, an opportunity to speak directly to audiences around the world. The work initially relied on the technology of shortwave radio by which signals could be bounced off the underside of the ionosphere to reach audiences thousands of miles away. In the era of the satellite and internet, international broadcasting remains an important element of the public diplomacy of the largest actors, including the BBC, France 24, Deutsche Welle, and the US government stations overseen by the Broadcasting Board of Governors (Voice of America, Radio Free Asia, and so forth). Recent years, moreover, have seen new initiatives in the broadcasting field by powers seeking to redress the domination of a western perspective on the air, including Qatar's *Al Jazeera* and multiple language channels created by China's CCTV and Russia's *RT* (formerly *Russia Today*). There is not only a clash of perspective but also a clash of news culture, with western stations emphasizing ethical practices and balance in their news while some other players show a willingness to broadcast disinformation. Canada now plays little role in this battle despite a long history of work in the area. In 1945, Canada launched its own 'Voice of Canada' as the international service of the Canadian Broadcasting Corporation. In 1970, it took the new name Radio Canada International (RCI) and was part of the lineup of international stations which broadcast a democratic and balanced view of world news into fourteen languages into the Eastern Bloc and other regions during the Cold War. RCI has declined dramatically since the end of the

Cold War. In 2012, it sustained an 80% budget cut, ceased all broadcasting on the shortwave, and reduced its services to just five languages carried out only on the internet. The possibility of reviving Canadian international broadcasting is explored in the chapter by **Ira Wagman**.

The relationships between these core elements of public diplomacy have been subject to various conceptualizations—one of the most helpful of which originated at the Canadian foreign ministry in 2005. The public diplomacy pyramid imagined the nation's public diplomacy as an up-ward pointing equilateral triangle divided into three equal bands: advocacy at the top, profile-raising in the middle, and relationship-building at the bottom. Vertical axes on either side indicated time—short, medium, and long-term—and level of government control from high to un-mediated/people-to-people. Advocacy was therefore the sharp end; short-term and highly controlled; cultural diplomacy maps onto profile-raising with a medium-term and a medium level of government intervention; exchange diplomacy maps onto relationship-building, requiring a long time frame but functioning without government mediation. The triangular shape implied that the elements needed one another, and indeed that a broad investment in relationship-building was a necessary foundation for the other elements.[5] This was not the Harper-era strategy, rather, Canadian engagement became like spear on a wobbly shaft: advocacy with minimal lines of cultural and government-supported exchange. The Harper years are discussed in detail by **Andrew Cooper**.

The dominant concept in theorizing the application of public diplomacy is the notion of 'soft power,' as coined in the closing months of the Cold War by the Harvard-based political theorist Joseph Nye. In Nye's conception, soft power is a type of international leverage which comes from recognition of an international actor's values and culture. It supplements the better understood hard power mechanisms of financial or military pressure. Most actors integrate hard and soft approaches into a cohesive package, which Nye dubbed 'smart power.' In addition to the instruments of public diplomacy, its tools include the practical contributions of international aid or the positive example of participation in mechanisms of global citizenship. The concept of soft power was especially embraced in China, where it was seen as a mechanism to further the country's peaceful rise. China invested in mega-events, language programs, and media expansion in an effort to win admirers. These seem to have worked best in legitimizing governments domestically. Its most effective tool internationally actually seems to have been engaging foreign countries through trade. The coinage of soft and smart power had considerable significance for Canada, given the country's generally positive reputation and long-term involvement with international government. Canada is an ideal case for a soft power analysis, especially since the election of Prime Minister Justin Trudeau, a leader known for his personal charisma and public displays of ethics. Trudeau's impact is addressed in the essay by **Stéfanie von Hlatke**'s case study of his first year.

Public diplomacy has evolved since the end of the Cold War. Technological and political forces have combined to multiply the number of players seeking to engage foreign publics. Provinces, cities, and even well-known individuals can act in the international information space, sometimes as single actors and sometimes as partners in coalitions. In the world at large, Scotland, Catalonia, California, and many other regions are engaging foreign publics in their own right. Subnational actors with a bearing on Canada's global profile include Quebec, which has a number of cultural outposts around the world. Canadian cities also sometimes operate as international actors. The mega-events hosted by Montreal—the expo of 1967 and Olympics of 1976—were public diplomacy on behalf of the city as well as the country, and in years since, the ranks of Canadian cities with a global profile have grown. Toronto's film festival is well enough established as a piece of civic diplomacy to have its own crisis— the 2009 debacle over its decision to feature a special strand linked to Tel Aviv.[6] The civic public diplomacy case explored here is a treatment of the city of Ottawa and the issue of gifts by **Mark Kristmanson**.

What, then, is the future of Canadian public diplomacy? As these essays make clear, the field is complex and Canada faces many challenges, not a few of its own making. In the wider field of public diplomacy, the potential for transnational regions becoming actors in their own right is being explored. It may be that the next Canadian place to play for the world's attention is shared with the United States—Niagara or Detroit/Windsor—rather than Canadian alone.[7] All countries have to remember that just as a single good citizen can enhance a reputation, so a single bad citizen can damage it. Canada has been helped by single citizens who were unrepresentative of their times. Sino-Chinese relations have benefited from the memory of Norman Bethune, the Canadian doctor who served on the Long March in the 1930s. Conversely, Canada has weathered a few villains, including its chemically enhanced athlete Ben Johnson and Toronto's chemically enhanced mayor Rob Ford. It is not a country immune from scandal. Interestingly, the scandals around

Justin Trudeau made little impact on Canada's international reputation. In 2019, the country reached the unprecedented height of third place in the Anholt nation brands index (now known as the Anholt-Ipsos Nation Brands Index), runner-up to Germany and France.[8]

Canada plainly enjoys immense reserves of international admiration, which endured even when the country downplayed its global citizenship role. Its rising status in the Anholt NBI is evidence of this. Yet, it is no longer enough to look good. A country must also *be* good. In the West, the debate around soft power is shifting from an emphasis on perception to a discussion of reality. Joseph Nye's work on US presidents now considers the underlying morality of their foreign policy.[9] Simon Anholt now argues that for the long-term, countries should focus on actually being good countries rather than just courting a good image. To this end, he has created a Good Country Index in which countries are ranked based on a range of actual contributions to global good across a range of areas including culture, science, environment, and the nation's well-being. These contributions are adjusted to account for GDP, which puts the contribution of some of the wealthier countries into perspective. Canada still does well. In the 2017 version it ranked 10th, but the 2018 index, published in the summer of 2019, placed Finland in first place and Canada at 11. Canada's best score—in the health and well-being category—was 4th. Even if the usual comparator of Canadians—the United States—is presently languishing at 40th in terms of its aggregate good, Canada still has room to improve and move closer to where its citizens would wish it to be.[10]

The viral pandemic of 2020 has the potential to upend perceptions of international reputation. Countries which are managing well in the crisis have a certain coherence and high levels of trust in central government and a record of investment in healthcare. In the world in which reputation is based on relevance to an audience, countries which take the lead in building a collective response through organizations like the World Health Organization and wider UN will be more appreciated than those that insist of working unilaterally. Canada is one of the countries best placed to emerge with an enhanced reputation and well suited to shine in the world of Covid 19. The United States, in contrast, is extremely badly positioned.

Canada has an admirable heritage as a participant in the global conversation that is public diplomacy. Going forward, it is essential that the government continues to invest in the infrastructure on which sound public diplomacy rests, and by extension, ensure its ongoing reputational security. Rule one of public diplomacy will always be to listen first, but rule two is to show up. Canada sometimes falls short. Canada did not show up at the Milan Expo of 2015, and the Senate report of 2019 documents other programs that have fallen by the wayside. However, the challenges of the future will call for more than the familiar resources and approaches. Public diplomacy in the twenty-first century is not just about a government asking 'what can I say' to a foreign public to advance my interests, but also about asking 'who can I empower' to advance the issues that I care about. The most credible partners in global conversations are unlikely to be nation-states, and Ottawa would do well to look to empower Canada's provinces, cities, universities, museums, artists, indigenous and diaspora groups, and even individuals, to engage as widely possible. In an interdependent world, Canada also has a role to play in helping other nations to be heard, understood, and to develop their own reputational security, making their own contributions to the global good. Developing media literacy and defusing the victim narratives are, for example, an essential part of the process of lifting the world out of the dysfunctional media environment of the second decade of this century. Canada is turning again towards public diplomacy. The bottom line is that reputation is part of twenty-first-century security and for all Canada's advantages it has to work to ensure success in this field. This volume is offered as a contribution to the process.

NOTES

1. For further discussion of the concepts outlined in this introduction see Nicholas J. Cull, *Public Diplomacy: Foundations for Global Engagement in the Digital Age*. Polity: Cambridge, 2019. Reputational Security is introduced pp. 166–167.
2. http://canadacouncil.ca/funding/grants/arts-abroad.
3. https://sencanada.ca/content/sen/committee/421/AEFA/Reports/Report_CulturalDiplomacy_e.pdf.
4. http://www.frenchstreet.ca/canadian-education-exchange-foundation-ceef-2/.
5. See Cull, *Public Diplomacy*, p. 7.
6. https://www.theguardian.com/film/2009/sep/07/toronto-film-festival-boycott.
7. For an experiment with transnational branding in Scandinavia see https://www.oecd.org/cfe/regional-policy/publicationsdocuments/

Oresund.pdf and Jesper Falkheimer, 'Place Branding in the Øresund Region: From a Transnational Region to a Bi-national City-region,' *Place Branding and Public Diplomacy*, August 2016, Volume 12, Issue 2–3, pp 160–171. https://link.springer.com/article/10.1057/s41254-016-0012-z.
8. https://www.ipsos.com/en-us/news-polls/Germany-Retains-Top.
9. Joseph Nye, *Do Morals Matter? Presidents and Foreign Policy from FDR to Trump*. Oxford University Press: New York, 2020.
10. https://www.goodcountry.org/index/results (as published in July 2019).

CHAPTER 2

"We're Back": Re-imagining Public Diplomacy in Canada

Michael K. Hawes

For Canada, the predisposition toward diplomatic options, as well as the projection of Canada's soft power through a series of programs and policies that utilize the principles and practices of public diplomacy, have been the hallmark of its foreign policy since the end of World War II. Canada played a disproportionately large role in shaping and defining the postwar world order, while, at the same time, consciously portraying itself as a peacekeeper, helpful fixer, and honest broker. Canada was the arch-typical middle power, especially during the so-called golden age of Canadian foreign policy (most notably the Pearson era),[1] through the Pierre Trudeau years,[2] and (briefly) again in the late 1990s, when Jean Chretien was the Prime Minister and Lloyd Axworthy was the Foreign Minister. Pearson virtually invented peacekeeping as a diplomatic instrument and was instrumental in bringing the development agenda to the attention of the world. Similarly, Minister Axworthy was all about defining Canada as a leader in values and principles, mainly through his campaign

M. K. Hawes (✉)
Fulbright Canada, Ottawa, ON, Canada
e-mail: mhawes@fulbright.ca

© The Author(s) 2021
N. J. Cull and M. K. Hawes (eds.), *Canada's Public Diplomacy*,
Palgrave Macmillan Series in Global Public Diplomacy,
https://doi.org/10.1007/978-3-319-62015-2_2

13

to reduce the number of land mines in the world and his commitment to bringing to an end the practice of using children as soldiers.

These values, along with the policies, practices, and instruments that accompanied them, including the Understanding Canada program, the existence of Academic Relations Officers from Canadian embassies and consulates around the world, and the existence of high-end cultural programs—all viewed as core elements of Canada's traditional public diplomacy strategy—were considerably less evident during the Harper years. By the end of the Harper decade, it had become clear to many Canadians that Canada had lost its way and that Mr. Harper and his Conservative government were increasingly at odds with the core values of Canadians. Indeed, this 'drift' was one of the key contributing factors in the defeat of the Conservative government and the convincing victory of Justin Trudeau and his Liberal party—so much so, that just one day after the October 2015 election, Justin Trudeau noted that, *"Many of you have worried that Canada has lost its compassionate and constructive voice in the world over the past ten years .... Well, I have a simple message for you: on behalf of 35 million Canadians, we're back."*[3]

Others in this volume have provided a more detailed assessment of Canada's postwar public diplomacy strategy and offered several compelling case studies that help us to more fully understand the arguments (made both here and elsewhere) about the vagaries of public diplomacy in Canada. The purpose of this chapter, by contrast, is to examine the claim, "we're back." More specifically, this piece focuses on the claim that the Trudeau government has re-committed itself to a broad and enduring strategy of public diplomacy, traditional Canadian values, and principles and practices of multilateralism. To do this, it is incumbent upon the author to offer a critique of the underlying principles of the Harper government concerning its foreign policy strategy and their decision to scale back on Canada's public diplomacy efforts, most notably by discontinuing the Understanding Canada[4] program and cutting back on funding for embassy-based public diplomacy initiatives. In the end, this paper will argue that, while the intentions of the Prime Minister and his government were both genuine and well-intentioned, the reality is: the election of President Trump in 2016 and his commitment to follow through on his election promises to kill the Trans-Pacific Partnership (TPP) and 'cancel' the North American Free Trade Agreement (NAFTA) posed an existential threat to Mr. Trudeau's new government and, in effect, put the Canadian government in a position where they had no choice but to focus their attention on the negotiation of the trade agreement with the United States at the expense of most other issues.[5] Further, this paper argues that the 'new public diplomacy,' such as it is, has a particularly strong bias toward situating Canada and its values within the North American context and that these core values reflect the priorities outlined by the Trudeau government in the early days of its first mandate. In short, while there was a genuine interest in re-invigorating Canadian public diplomacy, what we have witnessed, with some key exceptions, is better seen as a systematic and careful redefinition and some repurposing of Canada's existing public diplomacy tools.

Before the primary analysis, it is crucial to differentiate between 'public diplomacy' and 'public affairs.' While the two are both critical terms for this analysis, the difference is both nuanced and modest. Still, there is good reason to make the distinction clear. What follows is a short history of Canadian foreign policy, followed by a specific discussion of the Harper government's foreign policy priorities, along with a focus on why America still matters to Canada, and, finally, an analysis of the current government and its attempt to re-imagine Canada's public diplomacy.

Public Diplomacy and Public Affairs

Public diplomacy is the conduct of international relations by governments through public communications media and through dealings with a wide range of non-governmental entities (political parties, corporations, trade associations, labor unions, educational institutions, religious organizations, ethnic groups, and influential individuals, among others) to influence the politics and actions of other governments.[6]

Public diplomacy is also distinct from, though related to, a foreign ministry's public affairs role. The latter often uses similar activities and techniques but directs them at its citizens to help them interpret the outside world from a national perspective and raises awareness of their country's international role and that of their diplomatic service. In Canada, a considerable number of the activities identified as 'public diplomacy' in official government documents are, in fact, communications and consultation programs directed at domestic audiences. More often than not, these activities strengthen partnerships with other federal government departments and different levels of government on international issues of mutual interest. The challenge in communicating Canada's global role is in demonstrating that Global Affairs Canada is linking its actions to broader national priorities.[7]

Interestingly, with the re-election of the Trudeau government in the fall of 2019 and the appointment of Global Affairs Minister Chrystia Freeland to the role of Deputy Prime Minister and Minister of Inter-governmental Affairs, this distinction may become somewhat blurred.[8]

On a side note, while public diplomacy has always been important and public affairs have always been necessary, both are more critical today than ever before, given the realities of technology and the prevalence of disinformation strategies. Understanding what others feel, think, value, and experience is increasingly valuable and dangerous to ignore. The simple act of 'living in someone else's shoes' or 'seeing the world through someone else's eyes' is so powerful, so transformative, and so neces-sary, that it hardly bears repeating.[9] Public diplomacy helps address the disinformation problem and offers a path to mutual understanding.[10]

Public diplomacy is a little bit like cholesterol. There is the 'good' kind, and there is the 'bad' kind. The human body needs cholesterol to build healthy cells. Cholesterol is essential to all human life. However, too much cholesterol, the 'bad' type, in particular, can lead to heart disease and other life-threatening illnesses. So too is the case with public diplomacy. The 'good' kind is all about supporting people's ability to experience the world, speaking truth to power, sharing best practices, and mutual understanding. However, the 'bad' kind is about disinformation and interference and has nefarious motives. While bad public diplomacy may not pose any immediate danger, it can, among other things, subvert democracy, interfere with good intentions, and distort reality.

A SHORT HISTORY OF CANADIAN FOREIGN POLICY

A country's foreign policy typically reflects deeply held national pref-erences, both philosophical and ideological, while, at the same time, remaining sensitive to current goals, ambitions, and priorities. Foreign policy is predicated on some understanding of the national interest, and should, all other things being equal, help to ensure national secu-rity, encourage economic prosperity, and promote social justice. In other words, foreign policy is about maximizing influence abroad while simul-taneously maximizing the physical, economic, and social security of a state.

Foreign policy is shaped, among other things, by the long-term habits of its citizens, demographic realities, previous policies and practices, personal preferences of leaders and the priorities of political parties, institutional facts, and, to a very significant extent, structural realities—whether systemic, regional, or domestic.[11] Canadian foreign policy has been shaped in significant ways by all of the factors identified above. Students of foreign policy typically look for patterns that characterize how a country interacts with the rest of the world and for fundamental changes to those patterns and priorities. For Canada, as we have argued elsewhere, *"two basic and interrelated facts have shaped and subsequently characterized Canada's role in the world. The first is the disproportionately large role that the United States has played in the economic, social, cultural, and political lives of Canadians. The second is a significant commitment to the principles and the practice of multilateral diplomacy and multilateral management."*[12]

Canadian foreign policy has traditionally been defined by the country's historical relationship with the UK, the understanding that we have a role in shaping and maintaining peace, and a relatively enthusiastic commitment to international organizations. Beginning in the postwar era, Canada increasingly saw its foreign policy priorities defined and shaped by Washington, in terms of both its security and its prosperity. The so-called continentalization of Canada's foreign policy did, however, have its ups and downs. In 1972, a newly re-elected Liberal government (with a very narrow margin) chose to pursue what they described at the time as 'the third option strategy' ... a strategy specifically designed to diversify Canada's trading partners and thereby reduce our vulnerability to the United States. That strategy failed, at least insofar as our trade numbers go, as Canada's dependence on the US market rose through the next two decades.[13]

Canada's foreign policy (and, in particular, its foreign economic policy) shifted dramatically back in a direction that privileged the United States. After a reasonably significant national debate, Canada signed a free trade agreement with the United States, which came into force on January 1, 1989, followed by a North American free trade agreement, which officially became law on January 1, 1994. In real terms, all three signatory nations experienced increased trade, economic output, foreign investment, and better consumer prices. NAFTA created jobs and dramatically increased foreign direct investment. Some would argue that NAFTA played a role in suppressing wages in the manufacturing sector in the

United States, but others contend that foreign competition and other factors played a much more significant role.

Canada continues to be deeply influenced by the United States, and, beginning in the early 1990s, by a growing commitment to North America. The trilateral agenda was most notably advanced when Mexico joined Canada and the United States as a full partner in continental free trade (via the North American Free Trade Agreement), and, more recently, through the creation of the Security and Prosperity Partnership (SPP).[14] While there has been a relatively significant attenuation concerning the broader commitment to multilateralism, Canada has not entirely lost sight of specific issues that affect global order. While the preference for order, broadly defined, remained somewhat constant during this period, the geographic focus shifted away from the postwar preoccupation with Europe and the larger global order. It has been replaced with the notion of a North American Community,[15] and, to a somewhat lesser extent, with an increasing interest in Asia, in terms of both security concerns and economic issues.

However, the 1990s brought profound political and economic change and equally profound challenges for internationalists. The decade which began so full of promise, with the collapse of the Soviet Union and a near-universal commitment to democratic principles (what many heralded as the great moral and ideological victory of the West), ended with social malaise, economic uncertainty, and financial crises. The most disconcerting economic event of the decade, the so-called Asian financial crisis, was, in fact, anything but a regional phenomenon. It was a global crisis affecting emerging markets in Asia, Latin America, Eastern Europe, and Russia. Moreover, the crisis wreaked havoc on the seemingly invincible Japanese economy, the world's second largest at the time, and contributed to China's rising economic importance as well as hastened the economic reordering of Asia.

Prime Minister Harper and the Dismantling of Canada's (Modest) Public Diplomacy Infrastructure

On May 2, 2011, Stephen Harper secured the parliamentary majority that he had been seeking since 2006. Among other things, this victory allowed the Prime Minister and his new Foreign Minister to pursue a series of policies and practices that had the potential to alter the direction of Canadian foreign policy fundamentally. These new priorities were driven by a clear focus on prosperity and an abiding interest in emerging markets. In particular, the new Canadian foreign policy appeared to be focused on the high-growth markets of East and South Asia and the Western Hemisphere. The central element of this strategy was an interest in enhanced relations (political, social, scientific, educational, and economic) with China, India, Brazil, and other emerging economies. The Department of Foreign Affairs, newly trimmed down and with a more definite sense of purpose, was reorganized such that it could focus on economic opportunity as opposed to international organizations, diplomatic activity, and political priorities. Foreign Minister Baird, along with other members of the Harper team, spent much time in these priority regions and much time and energy informing Canadians of their importance.

Concerning our argument here, it is critical to note that this strategy suggested a diminished role for Canada's traditional partners and allies and, hence, a reduced need for the policies and instruments used to cultivate and sustain those relationships. More specifically, there was a sense that Canada was looking for markets, not partners, and economic opportunity, not political stability. As such, the underlying logic of public diplomacy was, to say the least, muted.

There is a strong argument to be made that the primary drivers of Canada's foreign policy effective changed in 1989, long before Mr. Harper arrived, and that the end of the Cold War was the key factor. First, Europe was no longer essential to global security or economic prosperity. Second, multilateral organizations were no longer vital to the management of international affairs. Finally, the importance of military alliances was less evident to countries like Canada. The liberal governments of the '90s and early 2000s moved slowly to accept these changes and even more slowly in terms of reorganizing Canada's foreign policy strategy. De facto, prosperity became an increasingly important part of Canada's foreign policy in the 1990s, while security (borders, terrorism, and the like) dominated the agenda after 9–11. Security, as they say, trumped trade.

The 'new conservative government' of Stephen Harper, elected in the Spring of 2006, remained cautious through their minority government period (2006–2011). I might argue that this cautiousness was simply a reflection of the fact that they worried about the electoral consequences of any dramatic change in policy. They maintained a healthy relationship and worked closely with Washington on border issues, except where those negotiations stood in the way of prosperity. A case in point is the Western Hemisphere Travel Initiative (WHTI),[16] which required that Canadians and Americans carried passports to traverse the border. In principle, this should not have been an issue. However, Canadians were accustomed to traveling to the United States without the need for a passport; the initiative seemed to go against the international trend and appeared to suggest (likely with good reason) that the special relationship between the two countries was effectively dead.

On the foreign policy front, Canada did host the G8 and G20, though not without incident. Canada also made a failed bid to secure a seat on the United Nations Security Council. There is reason to believe that this disappointment was one reason why the Harper government moved away from Canada's longstanding commitment to multilateral management. However, the real sea change came with the election of 2011 and the realization of a majority government for Prime Minister Harper. With the exception of unqualified support for Israel, the new majority government moved quickly on their prosperity agenda, dramatically moving away from traditional markets (though, at least officially, not the United States) and worked tirelessly to insinuate themselves in the emerging markets in the Americas and Asia. The following official statements from DFAIT speak directly to this trend.[17]

> The Harper government will never forget that one in five Canadian jobs is directly or indirectly dependent on exports and that trade accounts for almost 60 percent of our GDP.
>
> That is why we are committed to securing and deepening access to traditional markets—like the United States—and broadening and expanding access to more markets—like the European Union, India, and the other fast-growing countries of Asia, and the Americas.
>
> …the Minister emphasized that the Harper government will not sit idle and is committed to building on and intensifying Canada's pursuit of new and better trading relations.
>
> The government is also working on completing an agreement with India—one of the world's fastest-growing and largest economies, with one billion customers—which has the potential to provide a $6-billion boost to Canada's economy.

Canada announced in 2010 that it was interested in joining the Trans-Pacific Partnership (the TPP) and, at that time, became an official observer. The Harper government, at the time still in a minority situation, indicated that it would not join. Moreover, the bid to join was reportedly blocked by the United States and New Zealand, who had concerns with Canadian agricultural policy and its lax Intellectual Property laws. The business community in Canada lobbied hard for inclusion, arguing that the Obama administration was playing the Harper government and that Canada's interests in the APEC region would be compromised if it was excluded. The ill-fated TPP would be the world's largest free trade zone (including America, Australia, New Zealand, Malaysia, Singapore, Brunei, Chile, Peru, and Canada). Canada officially joined the negotiations on June 19, 2012, a day after Mexico was asked to join the negotiations.

Assuming that the TPP came to fruition, which it did not, it would have accounted for nearly half of global output and nearly half of all world trade. Critics of the TPP argued that the net advantage of joining was minimal, as Canada already had agreements with most of the countries involved. Critics also argued that, *"the Harper government ... has completed only six free trade deals since coming to office. All tolled, those six agreements amount to less than $1.5 billion worth of Canada's annual exports - around 0.4 percent. The United States accounts for 75% of Canada's 475 billion dollars in worldwide exports in 2010."*[18]

In the end, as we now clearly know, this strategy was not one that had legs. The focus on emerging markets, the pre-eminence given to trade agreements, and the movement away from traditional partners and priorities would all prove to be out of synch with broader trends and, ultimately, with political realities in the United States.

The Trudeau Government, Canadian Values, and Public Diplomacy

In 2015, Mr. Trudeau and his Liberal party won a clear majority with 184 seats. The results of that election were surprising to some, but not to others. All administrations have a life span; voter fatigue is real; Mr. Harper was increasingly out of touch with Canadians; discouraging global trends and failed Canadian policies (most notably, as they negatively affected the Canadian economy) all grated on the Canadian voter.[19]

Mr. Trudeau arrived in office with a clear agenda, focused on addressing issues related to indigenous persons, providing a level playing field, offering support for women and girls, and focusing on the youth. He spent that first fall at summits, most notably the Paris Climate Summit and the ASEAN meetings. Canadians were more than impressed and more than a little proud to have a leader that was a household name around the world and who spoke passionately and eloquently about Canada's role in the world. The values that he espoused and his commitment to realizing them seemed both genuine and manageable in the heady early days of the first Justin Trudeau government. In particular, his commitment to accept significant numbers of Syrian refugees was a substantial public diplomacy victory and a public affairs victory. Moreover, it played a significant part in highlighting a real Canadian success story, which is immigrant reset-tlement and integration.[20] He also put in place a feminist development assistance strategy and a feminist foreign policy.

Mr. Trudeau seems to have done an excellent job on the public diplomacy front, as he is recognized as a progressive leader and trusted ally, a proponent of gender equality and women's empowerment, and a committed partner in dealing with climate change.[21] Interestingly, there is rising concern in some circles that action does not entirely match up with rhetoric. On climate change, the Trudeau government signed the Paris Agreement and instituted a federal carbon tax, but they have been slow to address emissions at home. Canada's role as a peacekeeper, once the world leader, was at best limited, with Mali being the only major initiative in the first four years. Concerning the government's feminist foreign policy and development assistance policy, the record is mixed. The government has done an excellent job of addressing the gender imbalance in the upper reaches of the foreign service, as well as set an ambitious target of 95% of development assistance being dedicated to women's equality and empow-erment by 2022. However, the reality is that Canada spends only 0.26% of gross national income on development assistance, as compared to the U.N. target of 0.7%.

Nevertheless, given the circumstances, it is somewhat difficult to judge the record of this government. Shortly after the 2015 election in Canada, and, arguably, long before they could realistically put many of the Prime Minister's promises in place, Americans elected a President who campaigned on an America-first strategy, and a promise to 'terminate' the North American Free Trade Agreement. Quite simply, this repre-sented an existential threat to the Canadian economy and required that the Trudeau government deploy the majority of its human resources and dedicate much of its attention to the renegotiation of the trade agree-ment. The USMCA (or CUSMA, as it is called in Canada) was eventually passed by the US Congress, but only after the 2019 election, and with some cost in terms of the relationship.

On the public affairs front, the Trudeau government has been somewhat less successful. On balance, while the Canadian public generally remained supportive of the Prime Minister and his government, some issues were harder to sell in 2019. In fact, by the time we arrived at the fall of 2019, the wheels seemed to have come off. The Liberals lost 27 seats, including two high-profile cabinet members from the West. The Bloc in Quebec seemed reborn, capturing 32 seats in Quebec (up from 10 in 2015); the Conservatives won 121 seats (up from 95); the NDP dropped from 39 to 24, and the Greens were up one from 2 to 3. In the end, Mr. Trudeau formed a minority government and stated that he had no interest in any kind of formal coalition. Instead, he pledged to move forward one vote at a time.

During the election, there were some public relations[22] issues that harmed the Prime Minister's brand. There was a picture circulated where Mr. Trudeau was attending an 'Arabian Nights' party dressed in robes and a turban and had visibly blackened his face and hands. The picture received considerable attention, both at home and abroad. The story mainly took hold in the mainstream media in the United States.[23] The story received considerable attention for a short time but did not seem to impact the Prime Minister too negatively. Bad press is an issue under most circumstances, but especially when both the public diplomacy strategy and the public affairs strategy are tied so closely to the Prime Minister's personal brand.

There were other issues, though, that were more concerning—both from an electoral perspective and concerning the government's broader public diplomacy and public affairs strategy. In particular, there was considerable ongoing negative press before and during the campaign involving the so-called SNC-Lavalin Affair. The 'scandal' involved allegations that the Prime Minister or someone at the PMO attempted to interfere in the corruption and fraud case against the Montreal-based engineering firm by pressuring then Justice Minister and Attorney General Jody Wilson-Raybould to interfere in the case.[24] In the end, the affair had considerable political costs. Jody Wilson-Raybould was demoted in a cabinet shuffle in January of 2019, then resigned from her post as Minister of Veterans Affairs weeks later on February 4. Jane Philpott, then President of the Treasury Board, resigned from her cabinet post on March 4, publicly stating that her reasons for leaving the cabinet related to the government's handling of the SNC-Lavalin Affair. On August 4, Ethics Commissioner, Mario Dion, released his report, which concluded that Prime Minister Trudeau did, indeed, try to influence then Justice Minister, Wilson-Raybould. What followed were two more high-level resignations, specifically, Clerk of the Privy Council, Michael Wernick and Principal Secretary to the Prime Minister, Gerald Butts. Trudeau was apologetic, but the damage had been done.[25]

In the end, the Canadian federal election turned out to be a referendum on the Prime Minister, who won the election and returned to power with a minority government. The direct political cost of the SNC-Lavalin scandal was, at minimum, two high-profile cabinet ministers, the Clerk of the Privy Council, and his trusted long-time friend and advisor, Gerald Butts. One might argue that it also cost him his majority. The most concerning part of the whole affair relates to how it impacted the Trudeau brand, both at home and abroad.

In some ways, the outcome of the 2019 Canadian federal election was predictable, or, at least, it seemed so. In the Canadian context, it is commonplace to win a majority the first time out, followed by a minority government in the second term. Pierre Elliot Trudeau, who won a very clear majority in 1968, barely scraped by in 1972, winning by only two seats over Robert Stanfield's Progressive Conservative Party. The principal explanation seems to be some combination of changing economic realities and a perceived failure to realize the many promises that they had made just a few short years earlier.

In Justin Trudeau's case, and again, while the press likes to point to his predilection for 'dressing up,' the perception that he views the job in mainly ceremonial terms or the SNC-Lavalin scandal, the more significant issue seemed to be one that relates to his brand. Specifically, Mr. Trudeau had built an incredibly successful brand based on progressive ideas and, in particular, on gender and indigeneity, and then got into a very pubic confrontation with his only female indigenous cabinet minister and lost the confidence of another very senior female cabinet minister.

Conclusions

This paper has argued that during the tenure of Stephen Harper, the Canadian government systematically moved away from traditional Canadian principles and practices in foreign policy and pursued what they chose to call the prosperity agenda. It further argues that Justin Trudeau was swept to power in 2015 based on his brand and on a commitment that Canada would once again play a constructive and engaged role in global affairs. The question that the paper asks, most directly, is whether a specific public diplomacy strategy emerged and to what extent that affected the 2019 election.

The evidence suggests that the election of President Trump in 2016, his decision to 'terminate' NAFTA, and the delicate negotiations that followed and led to the USMCA/CUSMA, diverted the priorities of the Trudeau government away from the plan laid out in the 2015 election campaign and year one of the administration to a more reactive strategy, which focused on the relationship with the United States and on 'rescuing' the trade relationship. It is fair to say that the record is at best mixed, but with a very significant asterisk. As we can see from many of the soft power surveys, Canada continues to rank very highly, and the Prime Minister seems to have retained much of his luster outside of North America. However, there are issues in the United States and at home.

The chapter will conclude with several observations about the lessons learned as they relate Canadian foreign policy and to Canada's role abroad.

To begin with, the second Justin Trudeau government would be well advised to invest more fully in public diplomacy and to use it more effectively. An excellent start was to move Minister Freeland from Global Affairs to Intergovernmental Affairs. She became Minister of Global Affairs specifically to deal with the trade debacle. Having succeeded, her stature and her skills can be brought to bear on the crucial issues relating to internal divisions in Canada. Mr. Champagne, the new Global Affairs Minister, has little baggage and is better positioned to pursue a progressive outward-looking strategy. Instead of giving priority to the diplomat-technicians, those who have mastered the art of responding immediately to expectations, this government needs to privilege the diplomat-thinkers, those who can decode future trends and help Canada find its path. In short, restore balance, stimulate debate, listen to those on the ground, consult the experts, and increase our diplomatic presence on some continents, particularly in Africa, where Canada's footprint is slowly fading.

Moreover, in the end, this government should not be afraid to be bold. It was, after all, Mr. Trudeau's progressive views and his commitment to global issues that helped to get him elected in the first place. The reality, of course, is that the United States will remain Canada's most important economic, diplomatic, and military partner for the foreseeable future. Disrespecting that fact is not the best strategy. Instead, there is merit in taking concrete steps to support the rules-based international order and to promote and encourage strategies, like combatting global warming, that resonate with Canadians. The world is in constant flux; Canada needs to provide its own perspective.

NOTES

1. Andrew Cohen, *While Canada Slept: How We Lost Our Place in the World*, Toronto, McClelland and Stewart, 2003. See, especially, chapter 2, "The Renaissance Men: The Golden Age of Canada's Foreign Policy."
2. See Robert Bothwell, *Alliance and Illusion: Canada and the World, 1945–1984*, Vancouver, UBC Press, 2007.
3. "We're Back, Justin Trudeau Says in a Message to Canada's Allies Abroad," *The National Post*, 20 October 2015. https://nationalp ost.com/news/politics/were-back-justin-trudeau-says-in-message-to-can adas-allies-abroad.
4. Stephen Brooks, ed., *Promoting Canadian Studies Abroad: Soft Power and Cultural Diplomacy*, London, Palgrave, 2018.
5. "Trump Will Formally Cancel NAFTA to Press Congress to Approve a New Trade Deal," *USA Today*, 2 December 2018. https://www.usa today.com/story/news/politics/2018/12/02/donald-trump-formally-cancel-nafta-make-way-new-deal/2181399002/.
6. See Alan K. Henrikson, "What can Public Diplomacy Achieve?," *Discussion Papers in Diplomacy*, Netherlands Institute of International Relations, Clingendael, 2006.
7. See Evan Potter, "Canada and the New Public Diplomacy," *International Journal*, 58(1), Winter 2002–2003, pp. 43–63.
8. "Chrystia Freeland: Canada's New Deputy Prime Minister Who Could Prove Crucial for Trudeau," *Guardian*, 21 November 2019. https://www.theguardian.com/world/2019/nov/21/chrystia-freeland-canada-deputy-pm-trudeau.
9. The Fulbright Program, often cited as the flagship program in America's postwar public diplomacy strategy, was explicitly designed to allow this kind of mutual understanding and cultural appreciation.
10. For an interesting discussion of these matters, see James Pamment, "Countering Disinformation: The Public Diplomacy Problem of Our Time," USC Center on Public Diplomacy Blog, 13 August 2018. https://www.uscpublicdiplomacy.org/blog/countering-disinform ation-public-diplomacy-problem-our-time.

11. See Michael K. Hawes and Christopher Kirkey, "Structure Matters: The Impact of the Unipolar World on Canada's Foreign Policy," in Michael K. Hawes and Christopher Kirkey, eds., *Canadian Foreign Policy in a Unipolar World*, Toronto, Oxford University Press, 2018.

12. Michael K. Hawes, "Managing Canada-U.S. Relations in Difficult Times," *The American Review of Canadian Studies*, 34(4), Winter 2004, p. 595.

13. Gordon Mace & Gerard Hervouet, "Canada's Third Option: A Complete Failure?," Canadian Public Policy, 15(4), December 1989, pp. 387–404.

14. Greg Anderson & Chris Sands, "Negotiating North America: The Security and Prosperity Partnership," The Hudson Institute, White Paper, Updated Edition, September 7, 2008.

15. Robert A. Pastor, *Toward a North American Community: Lessons from the Old World to the New*, Peterson Institute for International Economics, 2001.

16. Department of Homeland Security, U.S. Customs and Border Protection, "Western Hemisphere Travel Initiative." https://www.cbp.gov/travel/us-citizens/western-hemisphere-travel-initiative.

17. http://www.international.gc.ca/media_commerce/comm/newscommu niques/2011/151.aspx.

18. Barrie McKenna, "Canada Eyes Access to Dynamic Markets," *Globe and Mail*, 20 June 2012, A3.

19. "It Was Not Just Harper: Why the Conservatives Lost, and How They Can Win Again," Editorial, *Globe and Mail*, 23 October 2015. https://www.theglobeandmail.com/opinion/editorials/its-wasnt-just-har per-why-the-conservatives-lost-and-how-they-can-win-again/article26957 781/.

20. "Canada Resettled More Refugees Than Any County in 2018, U.N. Says," *Canadian Press*, 20 June 2019. https://www.cbc.ca/news/pol itics/canada-resettled-most-refugees-un-1.5182621.

21. Domenik Tolksdorf & Xandie Keunning, "Trudeau's Foreign Policy: Progressive Rhetoric, Conventional Policies," *Green European Journal*, 25 September 2019.

22. 'Public relations' are distinct from public diplomacy and public affairs, in that this is a much narrower concept which has to do with the state of the relationship between the public and a company or other organization or the public and a famous person.

23. See Anna Purna Kambhampaty, Madeleine Carlisle and Melissa Chan, "Justin Trudeau Wore Brownface at a 2001 'Arabian Nights' Party While He Taught at a Private School," *Time Magazine*, 18 September 2019. https://time.com/5680759/justin-trudeau-brownface-photo/.

24. Mark Gollom, "What You Need to Know About the SNC-Lavalin Affair," *CBC News*, 13 February 2019. https://www.cbc.ca/news/politics/tru deau-wilson-raybould-attorney-general-snc-lavalin-1.5014271.

25. John Paul Tasker, 'I Take Full Responsibility,' Trudeau Says in Wake of Damning Report on SNC-Lavalin Ethics Violation, *CBC News*, 14 August 2019. https://www.cbc.ca/news/politics/trudeau-snc-ethics-commissioner-violated-code-1.5246551.

CHAPTER 3

Is Canada "Back"? Engineering a Diplomatic and International Policy Renaissance

Daryl Copeland

We are in **Terra incognita**. As end the second decade of the twenty-first century, one thing is clear: this is not the world envisioned by the signatories of the Atlantic Charter, or even the post-Cold War triumphalists. As a result of continuing globalization (the defining historical process of our times) and *heteropolarity* (the emerging world order model), the operating environment for diplomacy is undergoing profound transformation. Under pressure from a staggering array of vexing, science and technology-driven transnational threats, state-centricity in international relations is

Some elements of the analysis which appears below have been presented elsewhere in other formats.

D. Copeland (✉)
The Montreal Centre for International Studies, Université de Montréal, Montréal, QC, Canada
e-mail: daryl.copeland@guerrilladiplomacy.com

International Institute of Applied Systems Analysis (IIASA), Laxenburg, Austria

Fellow, Canadian Global Affairs Institute, Calgary, Canada

© The Author(s) 2021
N. J. Cull and M. K. Hawes (eds.), *Canada's Public Diplomacy*, Palgrave Macmillan Series in Global Public Diplomacy, https://doi.org/10.1007/978-3-319-62015-2_3

waning fast. The lack of an effective institutional response has revealed a global governance gap of striking magnitude.

Donald Trump, abetted by a clutch of retreaded generals and assorted other barbarians inside the gates at 1600 Pennsylvania Ave, has accelerated the decline of America's global prestige and influence. This has created a vacuum; rising Asia, particularly in China, India, and ASEAN, has emerged as the primary beneficiary. Brexit, internal divisions, and the rise of xenophobic, right-wing populism in many parts of Europe has preoccupied the EU. Just when the world most needs the moderating influence of a strong and united Europe, both the organization and its members are looking inwards at precisely the time that they should be looking out. Shaky institutions, toxic politics, and a wavering commitment to democracy and the rule of law have prevented a number of potentially significant powers from achieving anything close to their promise. Brazil, South Africa, Mexico, Egypt, Nigeria, and a host of other countries remain on the sidelines as the status quo crumbles. All of this has been complicated by the persistent machinations of a cunning, calculating, and increasingly bold Russia intent upon reasserting itself as a great power. The bear is wide awake and hungry. Bottom line? Analysts and decision-makers today face the daunting challenge of navigating in uncharted spaces, identifying and managing multiple vulnerabilities, and responding to the strategic imperative of converting adversity into opportunity. There is scant sign that this message has resonated, or even registered faintly, within Global Affairs Canada, or, for that matter, anywhere else in the government of Prime Minister Justin Trudeau.

THE WAY WE WERE

Canada once contributed imaginatively, energetically, and generously to the cause of broadly based international security and prosperity. That commitment, and the stature which it produced, was not merely conjured by spin doctors. It was earned, grounded demonstrably in action and fact. From the late 1940s through the early 2000s, Canada enjoyed a well-deserved reputation as an innovative international policy entrepreneur. Lester Pearson and the current Prime Minister's father, Pierre, for instance, were renown for their commitment to development and peace. Canada played a central role in the design and construction of the United Nations and Breton Woods institutions. Through the Suez Crisis and the invention of peacekeeping, to the Colombo

Plan, North-South Dialogue, establishment of the Canadian International Development Agency (CIDA) and the International Development Research Centre (IDRC), and late Cold War Peace Crusade, Canada's vigorous diplomacy of the deed—including the resettlement of several hundred thousand Indochinese "boat people" in 1979–1980—translated into practical political influence and an oversized place in the world.[1]

Under PM Brian Mulroney's Conservative government, from the mid-1980s to the early 1990s Canada brought home an acid rain treaty with the USA, concluded the Montreal Protocol on Ozone Layer Depletion, played a central role in orchestrating the legendary 1992 Earth Summit in Rio de Janeiro (UNCED), and led the Commonwealth's campaign against apartheid in southern Africa. Canada was also very active in trying the shape the Asia Pacific security architecture, launching the (ultimately unsuccessful) North Pacific Cooperative Security Dialogue and playing a constructive role in Track II diplomacy related to territorial disputes in the South China Sea.[2]

Public diplomacy began to come into its own during that period, and, under Prime Minister Jean Chretien, was a central feature in both the prosecution of the successful 1995 "fish war" (also known as the Turbot War) with Spain/EU, as well as the founding of the Arctic Council in 1996. Public diplomacy reached its soft power[3] zenith during the second half of the 1990s with Foreign Minister Lloyd Axworthy's *Human Security Agenda*.[4] Even after giving up on global order mega-projects such as ending poverty, resolving conflict and bringing distributive justice to all mankind—due largely to severe resource reductions imposed in the late 1990s—Axworthy pressed on.[5] Cleverly retrofitted by officials to appear rationally sequenced and coherent, this rapid-fire string of achievements—including the treaty banning land mines and initiatives on blood diamonds, small arms, children in conflict, the International Criminal Court, and the Responsibility to Protect doctrine (also known as R2P)—was nonetheless impressive. The sense of active international engagement was reinforced by Finance Minister Paul Martin's central role in the establishment of the G-20 in 1999.

In short, during the last two decades of the twentieth century, even in the face of significant international policy financial constraints, Canada was able to make a difference. Multilaterally, the country played a central part in UN and NATO operations in the former Yugoslavia.[6] Although marred to some extent by General Romeo Dallaire's debacle in Rwanda and the disgraceful performance of the Airborne Regiment in Somalia, Canada's performance was for the most part well-received.[7]

Can that leadership be restored, as has been directed by Prime Minister Justin Trudeau in his ambitious "to do" list set out in the Foreign Minister's Mandate Letter?[8] Not easily. Since 9/11, Canada's record has been mixed, with visionary international enterprise notably absent. During the tenure of Liberal PMs Chretien and Martin, participation in the disastrous invasion of Iraq was avoided, but ultimately the ill-starred engagement in Afghanistan was embraced.[9] In 2003, Foreign Minister Bill Graham brought Canadians the innovative, interactive Foreign Policy Dialogue, using the Internet for the first time to ventilate and democratize the foreign policy development process.[10] His successors, John Manley and Pierre Pettigrew, despite high expectations, delivered few new initiatives, although Pettigrew did sign off on the expansive 2005 International Policy Statement.[11] There was much to admire in this pathfinding inter-departmental effort to integrate diplomacy, defence, commerce, and development, but all traces of that epic undertaking disappeared with the election of Stephen Harper's Conservative government in 2006.

Although the pace of Canada's progressive international engagement had already slowed appreciably by the mid-2000s, and a break with the past was to be anticipated, it has been the last ten years that spoiled Canada's brand. Little of the widely admired internationalist legacy survived the Harper Conservatives' attack dog mentality and visceral contempt for all that came before. On Harper's watch, the one-time leading peacekeeper and Boy Scout to the world became unrecognizable, regarded as a liability, the country that others preferred to ignore.[12] The UN and its activities were devalued: ideology was substituted for science, diplomats and public servants were muzzled, support for international NGOs slashed and the Pearson Peacekeeping Training Centre and Rights and Democracy shuttered.[13] The revolving-door legacy of Foreign Ministers Peter Mackay, Maxime Bernier, David Emerson, Lawrence Canon, John Baird, and Rob Nicholson is faint. Even the otherwise commendable provision of increased assistance for maternal and child health was marred by its exclusion of support for family planning.[14]

By the fall of 2015, the foundations of Canadian internationalism had been reduced to rubble, and public diplomacy, honed by Ambassador Allan Gotlieb in Washington 1981–1989 and elevated to priority status by Prime Minister Paul Martin 25 years later, had become a distant memory.[15]

Reaping the Whirlwind

Fast forward to the present. During its first year in office, the Trudeau government showed itself remarkably adept at harvesting a wide variety of low-hanging fruit, both political and public administrative. Some gestures were symbolic, others more substantive. In the wake of a lengthy parade of largely indifferent foreign ministers, the PM chose to appoint former Liberal Party leader Stephane Dion, a thoughtful and experienced former academic. Dion's 2008 Green Shift electoral platform, although successfully tarred by the Tories as a carbon tax, if adopted, would have placed Canada in the forefront of efforts to address the drivers of climate change.[16] Dion, who was replaced by Chrystia Freeland on 10 January 2017, though not a natural communicator, read his briefs and often wrote his own speeches. On key files such as multilateralism, climate change, carbon pricing, and environmental protection,[17] directions were changed and real progress achieved. So, too, in Canada's relations with the USA, Mexico, the BRICS countries, the opening to Iran, and, after much prevarication, a return to peacekeeping operations.[18] Although there has not been any fundamental rebalancing of Canada's position on the key issues of Middle East peace, funding was restored to UNRWA. Diplomats, like scientists, were "unmuzzled" and are once again afforded the confidence, trust, and respect required to engage in unscripted conversations.[19] The foreign ministry was re-christened Global Affairs Canada (GAC), and the curiously conceived "Sovereign's Wall" in the lobby of the Pearson Building decommissioned, with the oversized portrait of the Queen removed and the magnificent Pellan canvasses returned.[20]

How to interpret this compression of activity? For starters, it must be framed and contextualized. In 2015, the new government inherited a disturbingly diminished international space. After a decade of diplomatic retraction, with the foreign ministry largely sidelined and marginalized by efforts to promote Canada as a "warrior nation", almost any action was bound to seem significant.[21] Yet changing the amalgamated department's name—not unlike attending summits and offering a comforting range of international assurances—has been the easy part. The early gains have been registered, but the real work has yet to begin. More specifically, restoring the country's place in the world will take more than a good showing at the Conference of the Parties (COP 21) Climate Change Conference in Paris, turning up at various multilateral meetings (such as the G20, Commonwealth of Nations, APEC, G-7, NATO, NAFTA, etc.), hosting the UN Secretary General, resettling several tens of thousands of Syrian refugees, and upbeat references to Canadian diversity and resourcefulness in Davos and elsewhere.[22] By my reckoning, Canada is adrift and has been for over a decade. Years of accumulated cuts under both Conservative and Liberal governments, exacerbated by negligence and incompetence in the management of Canada's international relations, have been costly. Support for public diplomacy programming was reduced by some $40 million 2006–2014. With the termination of its short-wave broadcasting activity and reduction to an on-line rump of its foreign language services, Radio Canada International has been gutted, and except for marginal participation in the consortium contributing to French language TV-5, Canada is effectively without a voice in international broadcasting.

Capacity has been reduced across the board—spending on official development assistance, despite the marginal increase in the last Budget, remains below 2011 levels.[23] Canada is not paying its share and is seriously lagging as a contributor to collective effort.[24] Trudeau is now staring into an unmistakable performance gap, which means that Minister Chrystia Freeland faces a difficult task. Although it has not been reflected in the faltering NAFTA negotiations and the deteriorating trading relationship, she has done a commendable job of upping Canada's ground game in the USA.[25] Yet apart from the thin gruel served up in her address to Parliament in June 2017, remarkable mostly for its emphasis on hard power and the military, the Minister has offered few indications of any kind of new thinking on other major issues.[26] That said, the bar was placed very low to the ground for the incoming government. Under the auspices of the "deliverology" approach to public management imported from the UK, Cabinet members and senior officials have been instructed to measure and produce results.[27]

Things certainly began on an encouraging note. In marked contrast to its finger-wagging, petulant, hectoring predecessor, Trudeau's team showed itself more interested in listening than lecturing, in lingering rather than leaving. The first months provided some evidence of a change in orientation and direction. The PM's exceptional global profile and widespread media adulation created high expectations regarding Canada's return to liberal internationalism, and between Trudeau's frequent statements and the indications offered by his advisors, Canadians were given some idea of what might be in store.[28]

That said, if policy constitutes the poetry of international relations, then diplomacy represents the plumbing. In this respect, when it comes to converting ambition into action, we have to date heard far more about the international policy "what" than the diplomatic "how". Apart from a removal of the gag order, the reinstatement of high-level science advice [but not in the foreign ministry] and a widely anticipated return to mainstream practices in public and digital diplomacy, remarkably little been said about the mechanics and retooling which will be necessary to underpin a return to progressive global activism.[29] Lacking is a readiness to reinvest in international policy institutions and to reconstruct. Dion was unable to deliver on those files, recent federal budgets have brought almost no relief, and Trudeau and Freeland are running out of time to turn the trick.

That is the essential background, but... where to now? The situation—and, for that matter, the argument—is not straightforward. Drilling down, de-layering, and some further conceptual unpacking are required.

Not the Same Old, Same Old...

Power is restless, and, especially since the end of the Cold War, it has been on the move. Foreign ministries, for their part, have lost a good deal of their turf to cabinet offices, central agencies, and other government departments. Much has been made of the re-emergence of the China and India on the world stage and the migration of the dynamic centre of global political economy from the North Atlantic to the Asia Pacific [see the Asia Pacific Foundation of Canada's report "Building Blocks for a Canada-Asia Strategy" (2016)]. Of at least equal consequence has been the erosion of state-centricity in international relations and emergence of new actors. Power is shifting up (to central agencies and supra-national institutions), out (to multinational corporations, NGOs, private philanthropic foundations), and down (to sub-national players such as states, provinces, cities, and even to celebrated individuals such and Bill Gates and Bono).

Globalization, shifting power, the emergence of a heteropolar world order, the profusion of new actors, and the emergence of complex, transnational issues have radically altered the diplomatic playing field.[30] The preconditions to improved performance will require more than symbolic gestures and gratifying media coverage.[31] Traditional diplomatic methods and tools need to be supplemented by less conventional, more innovative approaches to statecraft.[32] Clearly, major adjustments to reduce hierarchy, encourage imaginative thinking, and sharpen effectiveness will be needed if Canada's global presence is to become more than spectral. Shortcomings need to be addressed, institutions renewed, and international policy made more supple and responsive. Even at that, elemental structural and process reforms, the leveraging of social media, and otherwise substituting technology for labour, while indispensible, will not in themselves be adequate to address the challenges facing Canada's government.[33]

How, then, to begin to compensate for ongoing resource scarcity, compounded by a decade of international policy darkness? The diplomatic business model requires a comprehensive overhaul and strategic reconstruction from the ground up. If Canada is to regain its stature as a creative, engaged, and valuable player on the world stage, and thereby burnish its tarnished brand, the performance of the foreign ministry will have to improve. Drastically, action will be necessary at multiple levels. For starters, a thorough-going public sector *leadership transition remains high on the order paper.* The Harper government placed a premium on controlling communications and stifling dissent. In the ideologically charged atmosphere which prevailed, senior managers were rewarded for keeping the lid on. Pushing back, defending public service values, and speaking truth to power were discouraged, while sycophants prospered. With the sea change in political tone and direction, members of GAC's leadership cadre should have been screened to ensure the presence of competencies and aptitudes essential to the provision of fearless advice in support the current government's initially progressive, participatory, and inclusive vision. Had that occurred, a transfusion of new blood would almost certainly have been judged essential.[34]

MAKING DIPLOMACY JOB ONE

While the deterioration of Canada's global image and reputation was undoubtedly accelerated by the Harper government's inept handling of international relations, the hard reality is that this country's global power and influence have been locked into a pattern of relative, yet inexorable decline since the late 1940s. Canada's international role and place were artificially exaggerated in the wake of World War II; as Europe rebuilt and Asia re-emerged, downsizing and accommodation have become inevitable. Today, in the ultra-competitive, globalizing, and increasingly *heteropolitan* environment which prevails, Canada's vulnerabilities must be managed, its strengths leveraged, and its soft power maximized. Each of those imperatives is predicated upon the existence of a lithe, agile, and high functioning foreign ministry and the resumption of diplomatic initiative.[35] Bureaucratic self-service, sclerotic systems, and ossified structures won't do.

The continuing evolution away from state-centricity requires that diplomacy become more public, inclusive, and participatory. Responding to that imperative, and recognizing that the foreign ministry is not a cathedral, the foreign service is not a priesthood, and diplomacy is not liturgy, collectively represent the *sine qua non* for bringing Canada back. By privileging diplomacy, embracing innovation, and re-profiling representation abroad, Canada could both advance its interests and make a significant contribution to global peace and prosperity.

Might a commitment to burnishing the *diplomatic* brand represent the best strategy for a government still finding its way forward? Perhaps, especially given Canada's strong internationalist traditions. Showcasing diplomacy per se as the contemporary international policy instrument of choice seems ideally suited as a means to bridge from a noble, yet increasingly distant "Pearsonian" past to a still undefined, but quite possibly inspiring future.[36]

Diplomacy's greatest comparative advantage over other international policy tools resides in its proven ability—through effective interpersonal communication and the existence of well-operating feedback loops integrated into the policy development and decision-making apparatus—to alter behaviour on both ends of conversation. For diplomats, this means not only standing up for your country abroad, but also, when necessary, to your country at home.

Success at developing a new narrative for diplomacy as a smarter, faster, more effective, and above all, non-violent approach to the management of international relations could prove not only relevant, but transformative. The free flow of ideas, including contending and dissenting views, represents the lifeblood of diplomacy. In the context of a country as dynamic, diverse, and multicultural as Canada, and if combined with the right mix of methods, institutions, and resources, the infusion of a commitment to new diplomatic thinking could make a real difference.

Still, much has been lost. Poor advice, dulled reflexes, a deficit of expertise, and a large dollop of simple incompetence might help explain the fiasco of Trudeau's "Mr. Dress-Up" family visit to India in February

2018.[37] A former senior official remarked to me recently that if Canadian diplomats are to undertake the heavy lifting necessary to deliver professionally on the government's agenda, they will have to relearn how to use muscles that have been atrophying for years. It is difficult to expect a patient who has been on life support and in a near catatonic state for ten years to suddenly get up off the gurney and run a marathon.

What, then, to do?

A Seven-Point Plan

In keeping with the name change and need to engineer a higher-functioning foreign ministry, I would propose the implementation of a comprehensive suite of seven deep and, in some cases, difficult reforms:

Articulation of a New Mandate and Mission

The locus of departmental activity at GAC could be usefully elevated by several levels of analysis to create a central agency for the management of globalization.[38] This would mean allowing specialized line departments to lead on issues within their remit, while concentrating on cross-cutting issues and serving as a catalyst for whole-of-government international policy development and integration, which is no one else's job. That sort of reorientation would allow the ministry to get out of the weeds and end costly turf wars with other departments. The new focus would be on knowledge-based problem-solving, the provision of intelligence, analysis and advice, and the delivery of high value-added programmes and projects, such as good governance, sound public administration, democratic development, human rights promotion, the rule of law, and so forth.

Identification of Strategic Priorities and Interests

Since the last over-arching international policy review in 2005, the global landscape has become almost unrecognizable. The implications for Canada of power shifts from the North Atlantic to the Asia Pacific, the explosive growth of social and digital media, and the emergence of artificial intelligence, quantum computing, and Big Data have not been thought through. Add to that the outstanding questions about Canada's military involvement in Iraq (such as Operation IMPACT) and the Baltic states and the challenge of managing a growing number of transnational, science and technology-based threats, ranging from climate change and environmental collapse to urbanization, public health, and pandemic disease, and it becomes evident that a full and fresh assessment of grand strategy is overdue.[39]

Cultural Transformation

Foreign ministries most everywhere are known for their authoritarian social relations, conservatism, and change resistance. After almost 10 years of battening down the hatches in the face of the Tory onslaught, greater openness and transparency has not come easily.[40] Some of the clever courtiers who thrived on managing upwards have doubtless found it difficult to make the transition from risk aversion to risk management and from following orders to rewarding experimentation and learning from failure. Nonetheless, the days of ambitious careerists getting ahead at the expense of those they supervise, while specializing in making the boss look good, must end. Ditto for blessing the received wisdom, judging ideas by their provenance rather than their quality, and, often under the guise of team playing, running with the herd. Continuous learning—including from failure—an openness to experimentation and the cranking up of training and professional development opportunities represent a more promising way forward. How best to shed those whose specialty is apple polishing and winnow the cadre of chronic under-performers? Ensure that as a precondition for assignment abroad as Head of Mission or promotion to the Executive level, all eligible candidates must demonstrate the ability to serve effectively, and for a minimum of two years, in a secondment or exchange position *outside* of the foreign ministry.

Organizational Flattening

In an era of lateral partnerships, connectivity, and networks, GAC's hallmarks remain its rigid hierarchy, insularity, and jealously guarded fiefdoms. In 2018, the department had as many layers between desk officers and the minister's office—at minimum seven—as it did when I joined the foreign service in 1981. This costly and inefficient model slows bureaucratic process and disempowers those at the working level who are closest to the issues and actually know the files. The foreign ministry would benefit from fewer stovepipes and silos, and the addition of multiple laterally linked docking points. For the Head of Mission, this may mean new fashioning a role as country or regional brand manager, as a network node rather than top dog in a hierarchy. Foreign ministries will never become Silicone Valley-style idea incubators or "skunk works", but absent movement away from the basilica in the direction of the bazaar along with progress in building a more modern and supportive workplace will be impossible.[41]

Tapping New Networks

Connect directly with members of burgeoning and diverse multicultural communities and harness the potential of this largely untapped resource for political, commercial, and scientific purposes.[42] Ventilate the foreign service by turning the inside out and bringing the outside in.[43] Initiate the targeted recruitment of first- and second-generation Canadians and assign political officers to major Canadian cities with a mandate to forge productive and mutually beneficial relationships based on cooperation with and respect for diaspora groups. Engage civil society by renewing long-neglected partnerships with universities, think tanks, and NGOs at home and abroad. Restore cultural programs and reinstate sponsored visits by foreign opinion leaders and rebuild international education programs to dramatically increase the numbers of both foreign students in Canada and Canadians studying abroad.[44]

Flexible Overseas Representation

The connection to and knowledge of place are vital in diplomacy; rebalancing and reinvestment are needed. But the days of cookie-cutter chancelleries and fixed models governing the establishment and operation of missions abroad are long past. Contemporary circumstances demand the design of smarter, lighter, and sometimes more fleeting diplomatic footprints. World cities and major capitals may warrant high visibility and a distinctive physical presence, but in other cases, portability, adaptability, and the avoidance of lingering legal and administrative overheads will be crucial. As bricks give way to clicks, Canada will need at least as many brass plaques on hotel room doors as it does permanent diplomatic premises. Manuals, regulations, and standard operating procedures need to make space for virtuality, creativity, and imagination.

Enlightened Diplomatic Practice

In conflict zones and elsewhere, there will always be a place for traditional diplomacy, with designated envoys transacting the business of governments among themselves, often in confidence. However, in the twenty-first century, as engagement, advocacy, and lobbying have become increasingly determinant in securing desired outcomes, it is public diplomacy (PD), abetted by burgeoning use of the social and digital media, that has become mainstream.[45] Science diplomacy, a specialized sub-set of public diplomacy and vector of soft power that is especially attuned to addressing grand challenges such as management of the global commons and the control of weapons of mass destruction, is particularly relevant.[46] Elevate science diplomacy, which remains almost invisible within the current mix of available tools, to top priority status, and reallocate resources accordingly.[47] Without the robust pursuit of knowledge-based, technologically enabled solutions to the vexing array of *wicked*, S&T-rooted issues which together constitute the new threat set, Canada will be unable to achieve its promise as an evidence-driven problem solver. Canada was once a leader in these areas, but now trails the pack.[48] That must change, with GAC, in close association with science-based departments and agencies, equipped to lead the way forward.

Unlike traditional interstate discourse, in which designated envoys communicate with each other, public diplomacy features the triangulation of influence: diplomats in receiving states communicate directly with foreign publics and leave it to them to move their governments in the desired direction. Closely related to branding and political marketing, with PD there is less of a reliance upon communicating one-to-one, and more upon one to many.[49] Networks and connectivity rule. The emphasis, again, is on soft power, which is earned rather than wielded. Meaningful exchange, genuine dialogue, and active listening, supported by PR tools such as relationship building, reputation management, and image projection, are used to generate persuasion and influence, shape outcomes, engineer a positive pre-disposition and the burnish the national brand. There is less reliance upon convention—or Conventions (e.g. the numerous Vienna Conventions)—and standard operating procedures, more upon improvisation and experimentation, not just in the management of bi- and multilateral relations, but also in the pursuit of commercial and economic objectives, such the promotion of as trade and investment, as well.

Portrait of a public diplomat? The new diplomacy, whether practised in a storefront office, souk, barrio, "banlieue", or conflict zone, requires alternative skill sets, competencies, and criteria not typically associated with Ivy league pedigree or a refined disposition.[50] In the roiling precincts of the twenty-first century, life skills—empathy, resilience, self-reliance, problem-solving, cross-cultural communication, survival—are as important as book learning and knowledge. Today's ideal recruit, perhaps as a result of prior world travel, is less an international policy bureaucrat than a renaissance polymath, a street-smart, tech savvy, policy entrepreneur with natural curiosity, a sense of adventure and a keen interest in both people and places. Part activist, part analyst, part alchemist, she or he is instinctively able to swim with comfort and ease in the sea of the people and will never be seen flopping around like a fish out of water when beyond the embassy walls. Unlike all too many serving envoys, this candidate is emotionally intelligent and self-aware, comfortable with grass roots and ground level experience. Neither introverted nor haughty, the public diplomat prefers mixing with the population to mingling with like-minded colleagues, making contacts and generating intelligence to exchanging hearsay with those who look, talk, and dress alike. Rather than speculate about what might be going on outside the bubble, the public diplomat gets out and investigates.

Would a rebuilding project of this order, if ever undertaken, be enough to bring Canada "back"? Not necessarily. Without it, however, prospects will further recede.

New Day or False Dawn?

Re-engaging with the media and opinion leaders, re-connecting with foreign publics, and substituting of smiles for scowls is only the beginning. Trudeau's election, in combination with the implications of accelerated decline associated with the Trump ascendancy, has created an opening to position Canada as an agile advocate of dialogue, negotiation, and compromise, a champion of diplomatic alternatives to the continuing militarization of international policy and a practitioner of creative, alternative diplomacy. Some key opportunities have been squandered. How better to have commemorated the 150th anniversary of Confederation in 2017 than to have championed the idea that security is not a martial art, but a function of equitable, sustainable, long term, and human-centred development? A more far-reaching set of objectives might have added some meat to the bones to Canada's 2018 G-7 Presidency, and perhaps even softened the impact of the implosion of the Charlevoix Summit.[51]

A fundamental change in direction—not to mention winning a seat on the UN Security Council in 2021—will require all of Justin Trudeau's skill at public diplomacy, supported by an action plan with clear goals and incorporating the full range of reforms set out above.[52]

Still, much more will be needed.

NEW POLICY DIRECTIONS?

What about a concerted effort to embrace science, virtuality, and networks by experimenting with collaborative intelligence generation[53] and open-source policy development[54] to lower overheads and improve results? This must be done across the board, bilaterally and multilaterally, and at both a reconstructed headquarters operation in Ottawa and a more diverse variety of missions abroad.

Why not propose the negotiation of an international convention on the management and stewardship of freshwater resources?[55] Water security is a key issue among the UN's Sustainable Development Goals (SDGs); why not lead on that? Canada is the globe's freshwater reservoir, and such an initiative could do for Trudeau and Freeland what the Land Mine Ban treaty did for Chretien and Axworthy. In a world which appears to be descending into a period of protracted instability—if not coming completely unstuck—this might be just the sort of common objective which would attract action in concert.[56] Shared interest, after all, is the mother of the best cooperation.

A resumption of international peacekeeping training and an intensification of efforts to reach out beyond China to the countries of the Asia Pacific, possibly including a return to Track II activities related to the South China Sea dispute under ASEAN auspices, would compliment these first steps.[57] The Asia Pacific Foundation of Canada has produced some useful new thinking on future Canadian strategy, and Trudeau's visit to China and decision to join the Asian Infrastructure Investment Bank (AIIB) and Trans-Pacific Partnership (TPP) could help to anchor a larger reset in this crucial region.[58] And the list goes on. Based on re-distributive policies allegedly implemented at home, Canada could formulate and promote a list of practical measures intended to reverse growing global inequality.[59] It could champion environmental responsibility in the Arctic, or promote the need to better monitor and protect the health of the world's oceans. But there is no evidence to suggest that any of this is in the offing and time is running out.

To recap. On matters of style, tone, symbolism, and approach—such as the public welcome of arriving Syrian refugees, or the inclusion of opposition politicians in official international delegations—Canadian foreign policy is sporting a new look. In terms of substance, there have also been some real achievements. With key files such as multilateralism, climate change, energy, and environmental protection, directions have been changed and progress made. So, too, the return to peacekeeping operations, albeit in the form of flying blind into a high-risk mission in Mali.[60]

The dismal days of wedge politics and hyper-partisanship in international policy, where most every move was calculated in terms of its domestic impact, have receded somewhat. Nonetheless, not all signs are positive. Export regulations governing arms sales have been diluted, and concerns raised concerning Canada's commitment to human rights, disarmament, and nuclear non-proliferation.[61] The controversial decision to proceed with the $15 billion Saudi arms deal for light armoured vehicles was badly mishandled, as was the flip flop on ISIL's genocidal practices.[62] After handily avoiding participation in the 2004 invasion, it is far from certain that the intensification of the military training and support mission in Iraq will end well. The matter of Canadian treatment of Afghan detainees and the possible commission of war crimes and violation of international humanitarian law remain unfinished business of the first order.[63] The stonewalling continues, but this festering sore on the body politic won't go away.[64] The deployment of a battle group, frigate, and fighter jets to the Baltics under NATO auspices, and a possible defence cooperation agreement with Ukraine, both have a distinctly retro, Cold War feel.[65] Like NATO's relentless eastward expansion, the current military build-up along Russia's frontier is bound to be viewed as provocative.[66]

Deterrence, containment, trip wires... Again? Really? I am reminded of British journalist Robert Fisk's famous observation that "the only thing we ever learn is that we never learn". Iraq, Afghanistan, Libya... failed Western military interventions are legion, and the blowback has been devastating.[67] Armed force is both too sharp and too dull an instrument with which to address the complex problems of globalization—growing inequality, polarization, and the tendency to socialize costs while privatizing benefits. Generals and admirals need not apply. In the rising *heteropolis*, security and development will ultimately be a function of diplomacy rather than defence.

Getting There

PM Trudeau has clearly raised expectations. But on some files—tar sands and pipeline construction, the carbon economy, Middle East peace, conventional European security, arms control—the new boss looks disturbingly like the old.[68] Think "Harper-lite". If he is to avoid the risk of plunging into the perilous "say-do gap", deliberate action will be required.[69] While addressing the UN General Assembly is certainly preferable to opting for a photo-op at Tim Horton's, the earnest (if ineptly chosen) declaration that "Canada is here to help" has yet to be convincingly demonstrated.[70] Calling upon the UN General Assembly to discuss the conflict in Syria may make headlines, but it is not likely to bring peace. Without more concrete evidence—diplomacy of the deed rather than declaration—Trudeau's once hot global brand may continue to cool.[71]

The translation of the PM's considerable celebrity and charisma into actual international influence, and the ability to achieve specified outcomes, will require priorities and an agenda, a strategy and a plan. Moreover, while defence and development reviews have been completed, all elements of the diplomatic ecosystem—the foreign ministry, foreign service, and diplomatic business model—remain under severe stress. The energetic pursuit of full-spectrum diplomacy—traditional, public, digital, and what I term "guerrilla"[72]—would generate efficiency and effectiveness gains far beyond those which have been realized to date.[73] Yet the government's thinking about the crucial diplomatic dimension, and about international policy, and grand strategy more generally, remains ambiguous, with responsibility for public diplomacy still fragmented and diffuse.

These lacunae must be addressed, ideally prefaced by the assertion that there are no military solutions to the profound science and technology-based threats and challenges which, today imperil human survival.[74] Political violence, terrorism, and religious extremism, however troubling, do not threaten life on the planet.

So, is Canada "back"? Not yet, although there remains some hope, however receding, that that it may yet be *en route*.[75] Many analysts give the Trudeau administration the benefit of the doubt.[76] At the end of the day, however, it is most important to watch what governments do, not what they say, and follow the money. The Trudeau government's record has at best been mixed, with the initial encouraging signs compromised by the hoisting of contradictory red flags and a painful lack of serious international policy reinvestment, not least in public or science diplomacy.[77] This is a strategic moment which calls for hard-headedness, not nostalgia—*looking* back does not translate into *being* back. The opportunities are there in Canada's undervalued statecraft tools. The capacity and willingness, however, are at present notably absent.

NOTES

1. Andrew Cohen, "Canadian Prime Minister Pierre Trudeau, Hoping for a Renewal..." *UPI*, January 25, 1984, https://www.upi.com/Archives/1984/01/25/Canadian-Prime-Minister-Pierre-Trudeau-hoping-for-a-ren ewal/4533443854800/.
2. Marius Grinius, "Canada and Asia: Prosperity and Security," Policy Paper, *Canadian Global Affairs Institute*, 2015, https://www.cgai.ca/canada_and_asia_prosperity_and_security.
3. As defined by Joseph Nye Jr. (1990, 2004), "soft power" is the ability of states and other actors within the political system to exert influence over other actors with appeal and attraction, using co-optive power, and without the use of force.
4. Lloyd Axworthy, "Canada and Human Security: The Need for Leadership," *International Journal* 52, no. 2 (1997): 183–96.
5. Jocelyn, Bourgon, "Program Review: The Government of Canada's Experience Eliminating the Deficit, 1994–1999—A Canadian Case Study," *Centre for International Governance Innovation*, September 10, 2009, https://www.cigionline.org/publications/program-review-gov ernment-canadas-experience-eliminating-deficit-1994-1999-canadian.
6. "Canada in the Balkans," *Veterans Affairs Canada*, February 14, 2019, https://www.veterans.gc.ca/eng/remembrance/history/canadian-armed-forces/balkans.
7. Romeo Dallaire, *Shake Hands with the Devil: The Failure of Humanity in Rwanda* (Toronto: Random House of Canada, 2009); Grant Dawson, *"Here Is Hell": Canada's Engagement in Somalia* (Vancouver: UBC Press, 2011).
8. Justin Trudeau, "Minister of Foreign Affairs Mandate Letter," Justin Trudeau, Prime Minister of Canada, February 1, 2017, https://pm.gc.ca/eng/minister-foreign-affairs-mandate-letter.
9. John Duncan, Bill Graham, May Jeong, Bruce Mabley, Naheed Mustafa, Steve Saideman, and Catherine Stalikis, "Afghanistan in Review: Looking Back at Canada's Longest War," *OpenCanada*, 2016, https://www.ope ncanada.org/indepth/afghanistan-review-looking-back-canadas-longest-war/.

10. Bill Graham, 2003. "A Dialogue on Foreign Policy: A Report to Canadians," *Canadian Department of Foreign Affairs and International Trade*, June 2003, https://www.systemsforpeople.com/projects/www.foreign-policy-dialogue.ca/en/final_report/.
11. "A Role of Pride and Influence in the World—Diplomacy: Canada's International Policy Statement," *Ministry of Foreign Affairs, Government of Canada*, 2005, http://publications.gc.ca/site/eng/272595/publication.html.
12. Daryl Copeland, "PD's Most Formidable Adversary: The Say-Do Gap," *USC Center on Public Diplomacy* (blog), June 16, 2009, https://www.uscpublicdiplomacy.org/blog/pd%E2%80%99s-most-formidable-adversary-say-do-gap.
13. Daryl Copeland, "Pushing Peacekeeping Off the Table," *IPolitics* (blog), October 28, 2013, https://ipolitics.ca/2013/10/28/pushing-peacekeeping-off-the-table/; Gergin, Maria, "Silencing Dissent: The Conservative Record," *Canadian Centre for Policy Alternatives* (blog), April 6, 2011, https://www.policyalternatives.ca/publications/commentary/silencing-dissent-conservative-record; William Marsden, "Prime Minister Stephen Harper's UN Performance Ends on High Note," *Canada.Com*, September 26, 2014, http://o.canada.com/news/prime-minister-stephen-harpers-un-performance-ends-on-high-note; John McLevey and Liam Swiss, "North-South Institute Latest Casualty of Ottawa's War on Evidence," *The Star*, September 23, 2014, https://www.thestar.com/opinion/commentary/2014/09/23/northsouth_institute_latest_casualty_of_ottawas_war_on_evidence.html; CBC News, "Troubled Rights and Democracy Agency to Be Closed," *CBC*, April 3, 2012, https://www.cbc.ca/news/politics/troubled-rights-and-democracy-agency-to-be-closed-1.1185276.
14. Antonia Zerbisias, "Critics Slam Stephen Harper Ahead of Maternal Health Summit," *The Star*, May 27, 2014, https://www.thestar.com/news/gta/2014/05/27/critics_slam_stephen_harper_ahead_of_maternal_health_summit.html.
15. John Bell, "Up in the Air," *Literary Review of Canada* (blog), January–February 2012, http://reviewcanada.ca/magazine/2012/01/up-in-the-air/.
16. CTV.ca News Staff, 2008. "Dion Introduces 'Green Shift' Carbon Tax Plan," *CTVNews*, June 19, 2008, https://www.ctvnews.ca/dion-introduces-green-shift-carbon-tax-plan-1.303506.
17. "United States and Canada Unite to Protect the Arctic," *Ocean Networks Canada*, December 20, 2016, http://www.oceannetworks.ca/united-states-and-canada-unite-protect-arctic.
18. Murray Brewster, "Liberals Unveil New UN Peacekeeping Force with Hundreds of Troops, Police Officers," *CBC News*, August

26, 2016, https://www.cbc.ca/news/politics/canada-peacekeeping-ann ouncement-1.3736593.

19. Marie-Danielle Smith, "Foreign Minister Stéphane Dion Unmuzzles Canadian Diplomats," *Embassy News*, November 10, 2015, http://www.embassynews.ca/news/2015/11/10/foreign-minister-unmuzzles-canadian-diplomats/47852.

20. Kathleen Harris, "Queen's Portrait Replaced by Paintings Taken Down by Conservatives," *CBC*, November 9, 2015, https://www.cbc.ca/news/pol itics/canada-foreign-affairs-art-queen-1.3310633.

21. Ian McKay and Jamie Swift, "Warrior Nation, Canada's New Brand," *The Tyee*, August 11, 2012, http://thetyee.ca/Books/2012/08/11/Warrior-Nation/.

22. Aaron Wherry, "'Know Canadians for Our Resourcefulness,' Trudeau Tells Davos," *CBC*, January 21, 2016, https://www.cbc.ca/news/pol itics/trudeau-davos-future-look-economy-harper-1.3412182.

23. Kyle Duggan, "The Global Fund's Personal and Political Footprint," *IPolitics* (blog), September 15, 2016, https://ipolitics.ca/2016/09/15/the-global-funds-personal-and-political-footprint/.

24. Robert Greenhill and Celine Wadhera, "On Paying Its Global Share, Canada's Not Back—It's Far Bac," *Open Canada*, January 11, 2017, https://www.opencanada.org/features/paying-its-global-share-can adas-not-backits-far-back/.

25. Mike Blanchfield, "NAFTA Talks Face Uphill Battle as Mexico, Canada Carry on after Tariffs," *CTV News*, June 1, 2018, https://www.ctvnews.ca/business/nafta-talks-face-uphill-battle-as-mexico-canada-carry-on-after-tariffs-1.3954788; Leyland Cecco, "'Prepare for the Worst': Souring Canada-US Relations Fuel Worries of Trade War," *The Guardian*, June 11, 2018, http://www.theguardian.com/world/2018/jun/11/trump-canada-latest-trade-war-trudeau-relationship-fears;

26. Phil Calvert, "What's Missing from Freeland's Foreign Policy Speech: Asia," *OpenCanada*, June 9, 2017, https://www.opencanada.org/fea tures/whats-missing-freelands-foreign-policy-speech-asia/; Chrystia Free-land, "Address by Minister Freeland on Canada's Foreign Policy Priorities," (speech, Ottawa, Canada, June 6, 2017), Global Affairs Canada, https://www.canada.ca/en/global-affairs/news/2017/06/add ress_by_ministerfreelandoncanadasforeignpolicypriorities.html.

27. Evan Dyer, "Liberal Cabinet Retreat Hears from 'Deliverology' Guru, Again," *CBC*, April 26, 2016, https://www.cbc.ca/news/politics/delive rology-liberal-cabinet-retreat-1.3553024.

28. Roland Paris, "Time to Make Ourselves Useful," *Literary Review of Canada*, March 2015, http://reviewcanada.ca/magazine/2015/03/time-to-make-ourselves-useful/; Stephen Rodrick, "Justin Trudeau: Is the Canadian Prime Minister the Free World's Best Hope?" *Rolling Stone*,

July 26, 2017, https://www.rollingstone.com/politics/politics-features/justin-trudeau-the-north-star-194313/.

29. Julian Dierkes, "The Way Forward for Canadian Digital Diplocmay," *Embassy News*, November 18, 2015, http://www.embassynews.ca/opinion/2015/11/18/the-way-forward-for-canadian-digital-diplomacy/47886; Mark Henderson, "CSA Appointment Lauded But Debate Swirls Over Scope and Breadth of Advisory Role," *Research Money Inc.* (blog), October 4, 2017, https://researchmoneyinc.com/articles/csa-appointment-lauded-but-debate-swirls-over-scope-and-breadth-of-advisory-role/.

30. Daryl Copeland, "Diplomacy, Globalization and Heteropolarity: The Challenge of Adaptation," *Canadian Global Affairs Institute*, August 2013, https://www.cgai.ca/diplomacy_globalization_and_heteropolarity.

31. Peter Stevenson, "With the Rise of Justin Trudeau, Canada Is Suddenly ... Hip?" *The New York Times*, January 16, 2016, https://www.nytimes.com/interactive/2016/01/15/style/canada-justin-trudeau-cool.html,

32. Daryl Copeland and Colin Robertson. "Rebuilding Canada's International Capacity: Diplomatic Reform in the Age of Globalization," *National Newswatch* (blog), April 24, 2015, https://www.nationalnewswatch.com/2015/04/24/rebuilding-canadas-international-capacity-diplomatic-reform-in-the-age-of-globalization/#.Xm0Ni5NKijQ.

33. Roland Paris, "Foreign Policy for the Future," *Canada 2020* (blog), July 6, 2015, http://canada2020.ca/foreign-policy-for-the-future/.

34. Daryl Copeland, "Can Trudeau Coax a Shell-Shocked Public Service Out of Its Bunker?" *IPolitics* (blog), November 13, 2015, https://ipolitics.ca/2015/11/13/can-trudeau-coax-a-shell-shocked-public-service-out-of-its-bunker/.

35. Daryl Copeland, "Canada Falls Flat on the World Stage," *The Star*, September 25, 2015, https://www.thestar.com/opinion/commentary/2015/09/25/canada-falls-flat-on-the-world-stage.html.

36. Peter McKenna, "Opinion: Trudeau Would Revert to Classic Pearsonian Foreign Policy," *The Herald*, October 8, 2015.

37. Paul Wells, "Opinion: Justin Trudeau in the Real World," *Maclean's*, February 22, 2018, https://www.macleans.ca/politics/ottawa/justin-trudeau-in-the-real-world/.

38. Daryl Copeland and Colin Robertson. "Rebuilding Canada's International Capacity: Diplomatic Reform in the Age of Globalization," *National Newswatch* (blog), April 24, 2015, https://www.nationalnewswatch.com/2015/04/24/rebuilding-canadas-international-capacity-diplomatic-reform-in-the-age-of-globalization/#.Xm0Ni5NKijQ.

39. Daryl Copeland, "Opinion: Science Diplomacy for the Age of Globalization," *International Institute for Applied Systems Analysis (IIASA)* (blog), June 6, 2016, http://www.iiasa.ac.at/web/home/resources/

publications/options/160606-Science-diplomacy-age-globalization.html; Chris Westdal, "Opinion: Now Is the Time for Diplomacy," *Rideau Institute* (blog), July 12, 2016, http://www.rideauinstitute.ca/2016/07/12/chris-westdal-now-is-the-time-for-diplomacy-with-russia/.

40. Daryl Copeland, "Can Trudeau Coax a Shell-Shocked Public Service out of Its Bunker?" *IPolitics* (blog), November 13, 2015, https://ipolitics.ca/2015/11/13/can-trudeau-coax-a-shell-shocked-public-service-out-of-its-bunker/.

41. Daryl Copeland and Colin Robertson, "Rebuilding Canada's International Capacity: Diplomatic Reform in the Age of Globalization," *National Newswatch* (blog), April 24, 2015, https://www.nationalnewswatch.com/2015/04/24/rebuilding-canadas-international-capacity-diplomatic-reform-in-the-age-of-globalization/#.Xm0Ni5NKijQ.

42. Rahim Rezaie and Valerie La Traverse, "Diaspora Scientists: Canada's Untapped Resource of Global Knowledge Networks," *Canadian Science Policy Centre*, November 25, 2015, https://sciencepolicy.ca/diaspora-scientists-canadas-untapped-resource-global-knowledge-networks.

43. Daryl Copeland, "Five Ways to Sharpen the Effectiveness of Canada's Diplomatic Corps," *OpenCanada*, May 24, 2018, https://www.opencanada.org/features/five-ways-sharpen-effectiveness-canadas-diplomatic-corps/.

44. "Real Change: A New Plan for a Strong Middle Class," *Liberal Party of Canada*, 2015, https://www.liberal.ca/wp-content/uploads/2015/10/New-plan-for-a-strong-middle-class.pdf.

45. Shaun Riordan, "Digital Diplomacy 2.0: Beyond the Social Media Obsession," *USC Center on Public Diplomacy* (blog), April 25, 2016, https://www.uscpublicdiplomacy.org/blog/digital-diplomacy-20-beyond-social-media-obsession.

46. Daryl Copeland, "It Won't Come Easy: Seven Obstacles to a Science Diplomacy Renaissance," *Canadian Global Affairs Institute*, April 2017, https://d3n8a8pro7vhmx.cloudfront.net/cdfai/pages/1576/attachments/original/1491523938/It_Wont_Come_Easy_-_Seven_Obstacles_to_a_Science_Diplomacy_Renaissance.pdf?1491523938; Michael Hawes, "Canada's Soft Power and Public Diplomacy," *USC Center on Public Diplomacy* (blog), April 2010, https://www.uscpublicdiplomacy.org/pdin_monitor_article/canada%E2%80%99s-soft-power-and-public-diplomacy.

47. Daryl Copeland, "Science and Diplomacy After Canada's Lost Decade: Counting the Costs, Looking Beyond," *Canadian Global Affairs Institute*, November 2015, https://www.cgai.ca/science_and_diplomacy.

48. Daryl Copeland, "Science and Diplomacy After Canada's Lost Decade: Counting the Costs, Looking Beyond," *Canadian Global Affairs Institute*, November 2015, https://www.cgai.ca/science_and_diplomacy.

49. Daryl Copeland, "Public Diplomacy, Branding, and the Image of Nations, Part IV: Some Practical Implications," *USC Center on Public Diplomacy* (blog), June 5, 2012, https://www.uscpublicdiplomacy.org/blog/pub lic-diplomacy-branding-and-image-nations-part-iv-some-practical-implic ations.

50. Jan Melissen, "[Clingendael Paper No: 3] Beyond the New Public Diplomacy," *Clingendael*, October 17, 2011, https://www.clingendael. org/publication/clingendael-paper-no3-beyond-new-public-diplomacy; George Packer, "The Other France," *The New Yorker*, August 24, 2015, https://www.newyorker.com/magazine/2015/08/31/the-other-france.

51. "G7 Summit: War of Words Erupts Between US and Key Allies," *BBCNews*, June 11, 2018, https://www.bbc.com/news/world-us-can ada-44430000.

52. Marta Canneri, "What Will It Take for Canada to Get a UN Security Council Seat?" *OpenCanada*, July 3, 2018, https://www.opencanada. org/features/what-will-it-take-canada-get-un-security-council-seat/.

53. Within the business sphere, collaborative intelligence is defined by William Isaacs (2008) as the use of networks of people dialoguing in order to create optimal and intelligent outcomes.

54. Also known as "open politics", open-source policy development is the application of open-source philosophies developed by software engineers to democratic models of participation that engage all citizens in the creation of policy (Rushkoff 2003).

55. Daryl Copeland, "Bridging the Chasm: Why Science and Technology Must Become Priorities for Diplomacy and International Policy," *Science & Diplomacy* (blog), July 29, 2015, http://www.sciencediplomacy.org/perspective/2015/bridging-chasm.

56. Mark MacKinnon, "Munich, Nice, Turkey, Brexit, Trump: It's All Connected," *The Globe and Mail*, July 22, 2016, https://www.theglobea ndmail.com/news/world/munich-nice-turkey-brexit-trump-its-all-connec ted/article31084101/.

57. Richard Javad Heydarian, "China's Peripheral Diplomacy Disaster," *Al Jazeera*, July 9, 2016, https://www.aljazeera.com/indepth/opinion/2016/06/china-peripheral-diplomacy-disaster-160627122242539.html; Matthew Pennington, "Picking Sides: South China Sea Represents Diplomatic Dilemma," *CTV News*, July 11, 2016, https://www.ctvnews. ca/world/picking-sides-south-china-sea-represents-diplomatic-dilemma-1.2981395; Daryl Copeland, "Diplomacy, Globalization and Heteropolarity: The Challenge of Adaptation," *Canadian Global Affairs Institute*, August 2013, https://www.cgai.ca/diplomacy_globalization_and_hetero polarity.

58. Asia Pacific Foundation of Canada, "Building Blocks for a Canada-Asia Strategy," *Asia Pacific Foundation of Canada*, January 28, 2016, https://www.asiapacific.ca/research-report/building-blocks-canada-asia-strategy.
59. Luke Savage, "Justin Trudeau Is Waging a Phony War Against Inequality," *The Guardian*, May 4, 2018, https://www.theguardian.com/commentis free/2018/may/03/justin-trudeau-phony-war-against-inequality.
60. Murray Brewster, "Liberals Unveil New UN Peacekeeping Force with Hundreds of Troops, Police Officers," *CBC News*, August 26, 2016, https://www.cbc.ca/news/politics/canada-peacekeeping-ann ouncement-1.3736593; Ken Hansen, "Canada's Peacekeeping Mission to Mali Could Become a New Afghanistan," *Maclean's*, May 31, 2018, https://www.macleans.ca/opinion/canadas-peacekeeping-mission-to-mali-could-become-a-new-afghanistan/.
61. Steven Chase, "Ottawa Rewrites Mandate for Screening Arms Exports," *The Globe and Mail*, July 31, 2016, https://www.theglobeandmail.com/news/politics/ottawa-rewrites-mandate-for-screening-arms-exports/art icle31216740/; Stefan Labbé, "Seven Human Rights Violators Buying Canadian Military Goods," *OpenCanada*, August 18, 2016, https://www.opencanada.org/features/seven-human-rights-violators-buying-can adian-military-goods/; Peggy Mason, "Canada Says No to Historic UN Vote on Nuclear Disarmament," *The Hill Times*, November 2, 2016, https://www.hilltimes.com/2016/11/02/canada-says-no-his toric-un-vote-nuclear-disarmament/86139; Marco Vigliotti, "Trudeau Government's Commitment to Nuclear Disarmament Questioned After UN Vote," *The Hill Times*, August 24, 2016, https://www.hilltimes.com/2016/08/24/trudeau-governments-commitment-to-nuclear-dis armament-questioned-after-un-vote/78187.
62. Michael Den Tandt, "Five Ways the Liberals' Policy on Genocidal ISIL Is a Bungled, Confusing Mess," *National Post*, June 16, 2016, https://nationalpost.com/opinion/michael-den-tandt-five-ways-the-liberals-pol icy-on-genocidal-isil-is-a-bungled-confusing-mess; Kristy Wigglesworth, "The Saudi Arms Deal: What We've Learned So Far, and What Could Happen Next," *The Globe and Mail*, January 14, 2016, https://www.theglobeandmail.com/news/politics/the-saudi-arms-deal-what-weve-lea rned-so-far/article28180299/.
63. Omar Sabry, "Torture of Afghan Detainees: The Need for a Public Inquiry," *Ceasefire.ca* (blog), September 23, 2015, http://www.ceasefire.ca/torture-and-afghan-detainees-the-need-for-a-public-inquiry/.
64. Eileen Olexiuk, Alex Neve, Craig Scott, Chris Alexander, and Peggy Mason, "Is the Afghan Detainee Case Unfinished Business?" *Open-Canada*, June 2012, https://www.opencanada.org/features/afghan-det ainee-case-unfinished-business/. Erna Paris, "Will Canada Finally Deal with Its Afghan War Skeletons?" *The Globe and Mail*, January

5, 2018, https://www.theglobeandmail.com/opinion/will-canada-finally-deal-with-its-afghan-war-skeletons/article37500096/. Peter Zimonjic, "Ethics Watchdog Considers Request to Revisit Probe into Sajjan Over Detainee Abuse Inquiry," *CBC News*, May 3, 2017. https://www.cbc.ca/news/politics/sajjan-detainee-abuse-dawson-veterans-1.4098348.

65. Chris Westdal, "Trudeau in NATO Land," *The Hill Times*, July 8, 2016, https://www.hilltimes.com/2016/07/08/trudeau-in-natoland/73245; Teresa Wright, "Trudeau Says Canada Will Add More Troops and Extend Mission in Latvia," *The Star*, July 9, 2018, https://www.thestar.com/news/canada/2018/07/09/trudeau-visits-nato-troops-in-latvia-ahead-of-summit.html.

66. Chris Westdal, "Opinion: Now Is the Time for Diplomacy," *Rideau Institute* (blog), July 12, 2016, http://www.rideauinstitute.ca/2016/07/12/chris-westdal-now-is-the-time-for-diplomacy-with-russia/.

67. Nick Turse, "Tomgram: Nick Turse, Blowback Central," *TomDispatch.Com* (blog), June 18, 2013, http://www.tomdispatch.com/blog/175714/nick_turse_blowback_central.

68. Ross Belot, "McKenna's Going to COP 22 with Nothing to Brag About," *IPolitics* (blog), November 2, 2016, https://ipolitics.ca/2016/11/01/mckennas-going-to-marrakech-with-nothing-to-brag-about/; Mike Blanchfield, "Liberals Criticized for Inaction on Cluster Bomb Treaty Loophole," *IPolitics* (blog), September 11, 2016, https://ipolitics.ca/2016/09/11/liberals-criticized-for-inaction-on-cluster-bomb-treaty-loophole/; Andrew Mitrovica, "Don't Be Fooled, Justin Trudeau Is an Old-Boy at Heart," *Al Jazeera*, July 18, 2016, https://www.aljazeera.com/indepth/opinion/2016/07/don-fooled-justin-trudeau-boy-heart-canada-160713071303349.html; Adam Scott, "Arctic Drilling Ban Reveals Crucial Difference Between Obama and Trudeau on Climate," *Nation of Change* (blog), December 25, 2016, https://www.nationofchange.org/2016/12/25/arctic-drilling-ban-reveals-crucial-difference-obama-trudeau-climate/.

69. Daryl Copeland, "PD's Most Formidable Adversary: The Say-Do Gap," *USC Center on Public Diplomacy* (blog), June 16, 2009, https://www.uscpublicdiplomacy.org/blog/pd%E2%80%99s-most-formidable-adversary-say-do-gap.

70. John Ivison, "Trudeau Wins Over UN with Strange Speech Full of Liberal Platitudes," *National Post*, September 20, 2016, https://nationalpost.com/opinion/john-ivison-trudeau-wins-over-un-with-strange-speech-full-of-liberal-platitudes; Sean Kilpatrick, "Harper Makes Donut Run," *The Globe and Mail*, September 22, 2009, https://www.theglobeandmail.com/news/politics/ottawa-notebook/harper-makes-donut-run/article4286299/; Matthew Kupfer, "'We're Canadian and We're Here to Help': Trudeau Tells UN General Assembly," *CBC News*, September 20,

2016, https://www.cbc.ca/news/politics/justin-trudeau-un-general-assembly-1.3759656.

71. Antonia Zerbisias, "Justin Trudeau's Global Brand Is a Hot Commodity," *Al Jazeera*, September 25, 2016, https://www.aljazeera.com/indepth/opinion/2016/09/canada-justin-trudeau-global-brand-hot-commodity-160925055812119.html.

72. For a further discussion of guerilla diplomacy, see Copeland (2009).

73. Julian Dierkes, "Five Rules to Guide the Future of Canadian Digital Diplomacy," *OpenCanada*, December 2, 2015, https://www.opencanada.org/features/five-rules-guide-future-canadian-digital-diplomacy/.

74. Daryl Copeland, "Science and Diplomacy after Canada's Lost Decade: Counting the Costs, Looking Beyond," *Canadian Global Affairs Institute*, https://www.cgai.ca/science_and_diplomacy.

75. John W. McArthur, "It's Canada's Moment to Seize," *The Star*, August 3, 2016, https://www.thestar.com/opinion/commentary/2016/08/03/its-canadas-moment-to-seize.html.

76. Catherine Tsalikis, "A Foreign Policy Report Card for Justin Trudeau, One Year On," *OpenCanada*, October 19, 2016, https://www.opencanada.org/features/foreign-policy-report-card-justin-trudeau-one-year/.

77. David Carment, Nabil Bhata, Natalie Lamarche, and William O'Connell, "Opinion: Trudeau's Liberals Are Faltering on Foreign Policy at the Midway Point of Their Mandate," *Ottawa Citizen*, March 9, 2018, https://ottawacitizen.com/opinion/columnists/opinion-trudeaus-liberals-are-faltering-on-foreign-policy-at-the-midway-point-of-their-mandate; Steven Chase, "Ottawa Rewrites Mandate for Screening Arms Exports," *The Globe and Mail*, July 31, 2016, https://www.theglobeandmail.com/news/politics/ottawa-rewrites-mandate-for-screening-arms-exports/article31216740/.

CHAPTER 4

Three Cheers for "Diplomatic Frivolity": Canadian Public Diplomacy Embraces the Digital World

Evan H. Potter

This chapter analyses the how Canada's public diplomacy has evolved in the face of contemporary diplomatic practice.[1] It is fashionable to assert that diplomacy—the management of foreign policy—has been forced to radically "reboot" itself over the last two decades in the face of accelerated globalization characterized by intermesticism and intense economic competition among nations, the advent of the Internet and a transition to a Web 2.0 world of proliferating social media, and an ever-expanding list of actors—sub-state bodies, intergovernmental organizations, and social movements—vying for the right to shape international norms and policy.[2] To be sure, diplomacy is evolving at a much faster rate today than in the first 70 years of the previous century; as a result, diplomats and their foreign ministries have been forced to communicate more with publics

E. H. Potter (✉)
Department of Communication, University of Ottawa, Ottawa, ON, Canada
e-mail: evan.potter@uottawa.ca

© The Author(s) 2021
N. J. Cull and M. K. Hawes (eds.), *Canada's Public Diplomacy*,
Palgrave Macmillan Series in Global Public Diplomacy,
https://doi.org/10.1007/978-3-319-62015-2_4

at home and abroad. At the heart of this reboot, arguably, is a reconsideration of the value of public diplomacy within diplomatic practice. Some observers aver that the growing relative importance of public diplomacy within diplomatic practice is "a metaphor for the democratization of diplomacy, with multiple actors playing a role in what was once an area restricted to a few".[3]

I would argue that, on the other hand, despite the new embrace of public diplomacy and the latest generation of new communication tools in the form of social media, the central organizing principle of diplomacy remains the same: the projection of the national interest abroad. To put it crudely, governments will engage in public diplomacy when it is in their interest to do so, whether to promote or defend policies, engineer consent, or to listen to and engage the public. Greater openness and more "talking" by diplomats in the public sphere do not, in and of themselves, imply that foreign policymaking is becoming more democratic. Diplomacy is either adapting to the reality of a shrinking and more transparent world in which diplomats have to be seen to be heard, or, as Clay Shirky argues, being seen and "on message" everywhere is simply not enough, and foreign policy outcomes can no longer be fashioned in the absence of genuine public engagement.[4]

It is my contention that the tools and management of foreign policy may be changing, but that the underlying motivation of *raison d'état*, while perhaps not as preeminent as in the century of Louis the XIV (the "Sun King"), is nevertheless an enduring force. In the end, governments are not facing a binary choice between, on the one hand, using public diplomacy tools—educational and cultural programmes, outreach to diaspora communities, embassy websites, and Tweeting envoys—for strategic communication or relationship-building, or, on the other, using them to initiate greater openness in foreign policymaking. The tools themselves are value-neutral and will be used for good or ill to maximize what the executive of government perceives to be the national interest.

The first section of this chapter examines public diplomacy as a field of study and concept in the Canadian context. The second section analyses the impact of a number of overarching trends on contemporary diplomatic practice, showing that public diplomacy in a digital world can no longer be considered a peripheral or "third pillar" of Canada's foreign policy as more sub-state and non-state actors flex their influence on the world stage.[5] The third section is devoted to exploring the role that social media, so-called Web 2.0 diplomacy, is playing in reviving debates about the ability of public diplomacy to create a more democratic and open Canadian foreign policy. The final section offers some observations on the future of the digital dimension in Canada's public diplomacy and whether its ascendance in the practice of foreign policy portends a more democratic Canadian foreign policy.

Public Diplomacy: Concept and Practice

The renewed interest in public diplomacy has spurred a remarkable level of multidisciplinary study.[6] Political scientists, such as Joseph S. Nye Jr., are interested in conceptualizing the role of **soft power** in international relations.[7] Public relations scholars note the convergence between the goals of public diplomacy and the goals of public relations, and match symmetrical and asymmetrical forms of public relations to forms of diplomatic communication.[8] Historians, such as Nicholas Cull, offer absorbing histories of the vicissitudes of American public diplomacy.[9] Given that the term public diplomacy has American heritage and was coined in 1965 by Edmund Gullion, dean of the Fletcher School of Law and Diplomacy at Tufts University, American public diplomacy practitioners provide illuminating insights into the machinery and design of public diplomacy programmes.[10] Diplomatic studies scholar Geoffrey Wiseman has developed the term **polylateralism** to denote that the diplomatic landscape is no longer the monopoly of nation states.[11] Simon Anholt has taken public diplomacy and incorporated it into the study of **nation-branding**.[12] Although the field of strategic studies has not embraced public diplomacy, given the ascendance of new types of conflict such as "three-block wars" (combining humanitarian, peacekeeping, and military combat within the same mission) and the counter-insurgency campaigns launched by the United States in Iraq and Afghanistan, where the centre of gravity is the civilian population and incidents can go viral on YouTube within seconds, there is a plethora of articles and books (produced mainly by US military war colleges) on the "doctrine" of strategic communication in zones of conflict.[13] Military doctrines posit that a firewall must exist between Information Operations (military public affairs, psychological operations, deception, and cyber-war) and public diplomacy, with the latter perceived as the exclusive purview of civilian agencies such as foreign ministries.

There are also national differences with respect to public diplomacy approaches. America's public diplomacy, which was professionalized under the institutional auspices of the United States Information Agency and the Voice of America during the Cold War, has been oriented to supporting overarching US foreign policy objectives such as fighting communism or militant Islam. In stark contrast, historically, the UK, through the establishment of the British Council in 1934 and the BBC World Service, has sought to create a more arms-length relationship between its Foreign and Commonwealth Office and these two highly visible platforms that seek to influence global public opinion. In recent years, however, the British Council's mandate has become more closely aligned with cultural diplomacy than with the promotion of international cultural relations.

The French, meanwhile, have a decidedly more holistic view to *la diplomatie ouverte* or *politique d'influence*. Historically, France practised a *mission civilisatrice* in its colonies and French diplomats are often bemused with the Anglo-American world's tendency to spend so much time parsing the concept of public diplomacy when, for them, it is clear that *everything* official French government institutions do and say—whether it is a French government agronomist working to increase crop yields in a developing country or a member of the French Foreign Legion protecting civilians during a riot or a teacher giving a course on French history in a French lycée in Beijing—will have some effect on global public opinion about French people, France's policies, and the quality of its goods and services.

The major powers of Asia, notably India and China, are catching up to the West by using "soft diplomacy" to shape global public opinion and reduce resistance to their respective economic and military expansions. With the success of the 2008 Beijing Olympics as a backdrop, Chinese soft power has been expressed through the slogan of "peaceful development". There are over 500 Confucius Institutes worldwide promoting Chinese culture and language. India, meanwhile, has tapped into the enormous resource of Non-Resident Indians, the millions of expatriate Indians abroad who provide a pool from which to draw "citizen ambassadors".

Canada, for its part, takes an instrumental view to its public diplomacy. From 1970 to 2005 this included an emphasis on cultural diplomacy, scholarship programmes, and academic relations through Canadian Studies programmes worldwide to promote a general understanding of Canada and its people. During the tenure of Prime Minister Stephen Harper (2006–2015), Canadian public diplomacy at the federal level became more narrowly focused on economic imperatives and nation-branding using two main channels: advocacy programmes to promote inward direct investment, a trade liberalization agenda (e.g. free trade agreement with the European Union) and initiatives such as the Keystone XL pipeline, as well as international education marketing aimed at attracting foreign students.[14]

In the light of the inter-disciplinary breadth of the term and the differing approaches to understanding it, it is not surprising that one study refers to 150 definitions of the term, leading some to wonder if there will ever be a consensus.[15] In the interest of concision, a nation's public diplomacy is the sum of the efforts by the official institutions of one nation (or of a sub-national jurisdiction) to influence the elite or mass public opinion of another nation for the purpose of turning the policies or views of that target nation to advantage. Its purpose is to inform, understand, and influence foreign publics in order to achieve foreign policy goals. Public diplomacy becomes the governmental dimension of state/provincial, regional, and national soft power. That is to say, public diplomacy is only one slice (and sometimes a very small one) of the sum total of a nation's or sub-national jurisdiction's ability (through the collective contributions of its official institutions, people, and enterprises) to attract positive attention or voluntary "followership" from a global audience. In short, public diplomacy is the governmental exercise of soft power.

As a further elaboration, public diplomacy functions in three ways: temporally, instrumentally, and within a domestic context. As Fig. 4.1 shows, in practice, public diplomacy reflects short-, medium-, and long-term efforts by governmental bodies to shape public opinion. Typically, media relations is the "sharp end": the most highly controlled, short-horizon, process-driven public diplomacy activity (measured in hours and days) that is designed to inform and influence public perceptions by embedding key government messages (official positions) or corrections in media coverage through official statements and news releases. Advocacy refers to issue-management and lobbying and is often considered the most "strategic" form of public diplomacy because its goal is to achieve specific policy outcomes, such as negotiating trade agreements or blunting negative publicity (e.g. criticism of Canada's seal harvest or oil sands development in its western provinces). It can involve the coordination of multiple players in and out of government. Relationship-building develops mutual understanding and is frequently associated with longer-term educational and cultural exchanges (e.g. Canadian Studies programmes abroad) that may take decades to produce any measurable,

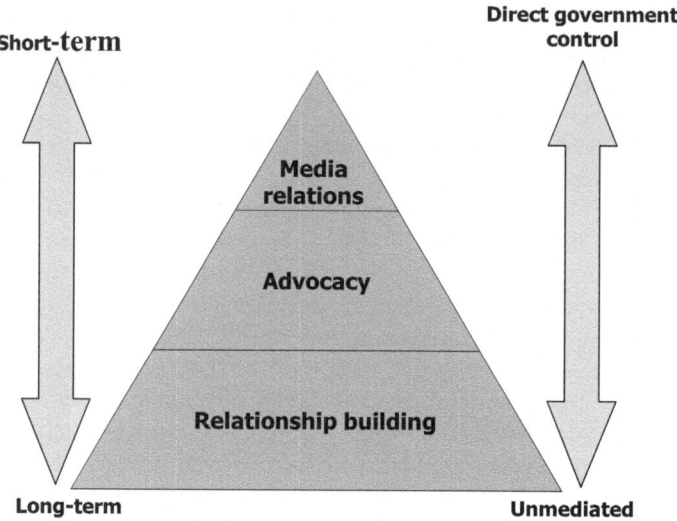

Fig. 4.1   Canada's public diplomacy triangle

positive changes to foreign public opinion. Paradoxically, although they have the greatest credibility because they are the least mediated forms of public diplomacy, programmes that reinforce mutual understanding are under the most budgetary pressure in the United States, Canada, and the UK because it is often difficult to prove a direct return on investment. In Canadian practice, public diplomacy incorporates what Philip Seib refers to as a "slow, incremental process", but it is not defined by it.[16]

The second way of perceiving public diplomacy considers the array of instruments used by a variety of government agencies and departments, running the gamut from international sports (e.g. Olympics, Commonwealth Games, Jeux de la Francophonie), cultural, and academic programmes to international state broadcasting (e.g. *TV-5, France24, BBC World, Deutsche Welle*), government-financed democracy-building, and election monitoring efforts. The third way sees public diplomacy as Janus-faced: looking inward to domestic audiences and looking outward to foreign publics at the same time. Given the transnational nature of issues and growing intermesticism—the cross-fertilization of the domestic and international policy agendas in areas as diverse as fisheries or education—governments need to be attractive not only to foreigners but also to their own citizens, "who will then gladly associate their actions abroad with their state and hence promote its soft power".[17] A foreign ministry's public diplomacy now reaches "inside" to enable its own highly connected citizens—students, artists, journalists—to be more informed about their country's international role since they became de facto "citizen ambassadors" (for good or ill) in their interactions with foreign audiences.

The normative question about whether the ascendance of public diplomacy in Canadian diplomatic practice augurs a greater democratization of Canada's foreign policy arises when the changing contours of the contemporary global environment are investigated. Although it is beyond the scope of this chapter to provide a detailed assessment, more intense competition for global markets, new actors, and novel information technologies are forcing traditional or "classic" state-to-state diplomacy (privileged and secret exchanges of information between governments) to blend with public diplomacy. This blending highlights the question of whether the practice of public diplomacy is forcing the foreign policy process to move out of the black box of government, or whether the evolution of public diplomacy's scope and practice is no more than a refined and sophisticated form of international political advertising or propaganda. In other words, is the relationship-building dimension, which assumes an indirect form of government influence through, for example, the selection of scholarship-eligible countries (e.g. hoping that foreign students who receive scholarships from your government will emerge sympathetic to your country's interests once they reach positions of power in their homelands) merely a longer-term form of strategic communication?

The Changing Context: Trends and Actors

Public diplomacy's goals and many of its tools have not changed radically because nations will always need to communicate information and persuade at the different levels of the public diplomacy "triangle" (see Fig. 4.1). As I have written elsewhere, what has radically changed is the environment in which public diplomacy takes place, as evidenced by more democracy movements, larger diaspora communities, a broadened definition of security to include human security, and a more intrusive global media in the form of international satellite broadcasters (e.g. Al-Jazeera, *RT*).[18] Cutting across these trends is the introduction of the Internet in the early 1990s and the rapid penetration of social media (see below) since the mid-2000s, creating important consequences for the public dimension of diplomatic relations.

The most obvious overarching trend is that, in a globalized world, public opinion matters more than ever and managing it is more crucial (though not necessarily determinant) for achieving specific outcomes with respect to high (political/security) and low (trade and investment) policy. This is because the level of public access to both open and secret information is astonishing (e.g. **Wiki Leaks**) as is the concomitant need for governments to manage perceptions, given that the unabated information flow cannot be permitted to enter an official vacuum. Consider that almost half the world's population (3.9 billion) uses the Internet and more than 5 billion have mobile devices. Five hundred million tweets are sent every day and Facebook has over 3 billion users. A persistent blogger sitting in his or her university dormitory room can, with some free time and persistence, organize a global boycott of a product, company, or even a country. This would have been inconceivable a decade ago.

Coupled with this ubiquity of information is a declining trust in government, making it all the more probable that individuals and groups will mobilize resistance to government policies and actions. As prominent *Wall Street Journal* columnist Peggy Noonan writes: "Here is a fact of the age: people believe nothing. They think everything is spin and lies. The minute a government says 'A' is true, half of the people on earth know that 'A' is a lie".[19] The irony is that more information often begets more distrust (especially when people's biases are confirmed in the nooks and crannies of the Web), which forces governments either to stay silent (allowing the misinformation or disinformation to gain new adherents) or to adopt a counter-attack mode through more "strategic" messaging, a process that is hardly conducive to dispelling the notion that the foreign policy process is opaque. In response to the vulnerabilities inherent in a global infosphere, there is a tendency by public and private institutions alike to rely on closely managed communication—a zero-sum game of framing and counter-framing issues. This deepens levels of public cynicism towards governments and fosters a yearning for increased "authenticity" among citizens who want deeper levels of engagement and movement away from repetitive official talking points that offer no means of compromise or mutual learning. At the level of public diplomacy, social media offers diplomats in foreign ministries—perhaps the most "inauthentic" of public institutions given the need, at times, for "ambassadors to lie for their countries" and, by custom, not to interfere in the domestic affairs of the countries to which they are accredited—an opportunity to step away from behind their masks as official representatives so that they can reach out directly and more informally to individual citizens and social movements. There is ample incentive to do so since the policy challenges of the contemporary world are so multifaceted that they cannot be resolved by governments alone.

To say that nation states are not alone in practising public diplomacy is, in the early twenty-first century, somewhat of an understatement. At the intergovernmental level, institutions as diverse as the World Trade Organization, the European Union, the International Atomic Energy Agency, and the North Atlantic Treaty Organization (NATO) are concerned enough about the dangers of not being present in global public opinion that they have instituted elaborate public diplomacy programmes to remind both elite and mass publics about the important work they do. NATO, a cold war-era organization, in engaged in sophisticated information programmes in out-of-area military theatres (e.g. Afghanistan) as well as within its member and partnership states (notably in Eastern Europe) to ensure that there is continued public understanding (if not support) for its mandate. This meant that Anders Fogh Rasmussen, the NATO Secretary General (2009–2014), had an active Twitter and Facebook account in order to "brand" the organization by humanizing it through him (e.g. providing photographs of his grandchildren) and to project key NATO messages directly to global audiences rather than being beholden to the filter of media outlets. As Melissen observes, intergovernmental organizations are relatively new to the business of public diplomacy and their "activities in this field are usually more about straightforward communication and information efforts than about engaging with people".[20]

Parallel to this state-level of public diplomacy is the burgeoning regional public diplomacy of sub-state actors. There are long-standing economic and cultural relationships among, for example, Flanders in Belgium, Catalonia in Spain, and Quebec in Canada, which serve to promote their distinctive identities and interests on the global stage and can act as domestic nation-building instruments.[21] For example, education is a provincial responsibility in Canada, giving Canadian provinces (particularly Québec) a distinct role in any international educational agreements to foster academic exchanges. With its wide array of official representation abroad in Europe, Asia, the United States, and Latin

America encompassing trade, education, cultural and immigration port-folios, not to mention its alliances through Regional Leaders Summits (Québec, Bavaria, Upper Austria, Sao Paulo, Georgia, Western Cape, and Shandong), Québec is a practitioner *par excellence* of public diplomacy and probably one of the most active sub-state actors in the world. Of course, the overlapping public diplomacies of regions and nations could create an "information fratricide" of competing messages in the eyes of foreign audiences, though, on balance, there appears to be a net benefit to having national and sub-national resources devoted to promoting economic and cultural links.

In comparison with official state-based public diplomacy, which, as Melissen points outs, is "structurally constrained", by risk avoidance and red-tape, the international campaigns of non-governmental organizations such as Greenpeace, Médecins san frontières, Human Rights Watch, and Amnesty International, in addition to the celebrity diplomacy of Bob Geldof, Bono, George Clooney, and Angelina Jolie, have captured the public imagination because they are less constrained by **realpolitik** and oriented towards achieving immediate visible results.[22] A prominent example of how social movements can exert pressure on nation states and achieve foreign political outcomes is the 1990s campaign resulting in the Convention on the Prohibition of the Use, Stockpiling, Production and Transfer of Anti-Personnel Mines and on their Destruction, better known as the Ottawa Landmine Treaty. However, for every Ottawa Treaty there are numerous global grass-roots initiatives that have stalled due to state intransigence and interference. This is not to deny the ability of social movements and celebrities to complement the efforts of the international donor community and to attempt to frame the international agenda on urgent causes in the same way as non-governmental anti-slavery move-ments did in the nineteenth century. That said, global public opinion may coalesce around one issue such as the plight of child soldiers without any significant state action being taken, while another, such as "blood diamonds", receives both high visibility and diplomatic action. As active as the NGO movements are, they will never have the financial and sheer logistical capacity of nation states, making it naïve to believe that the protection of civilians in Darfur or the reconstruction of Haiti will occur because George Clooney or Sean Penn has episodically garnered positive media attention for their respective "diplomatic" causes.

This is not to say that official public diplomacy cannot learn from the techniques employed by the NGO sector and the corporate sector in terms of deepening engagement with target publics and becoming obsessed with the "customer journey" or refining the application of **corporate social responsibility**. Indeed, the pressures of globalization and economic competition have given rise to an increased interest in what some have termed corporate diplomacy and the new field of nation-branding. Corporate diplomacy reflects the need for corporations to be attuned to how governments react to public pressures that may affect their bottom lines. Certainly, oil and mining companies with multi-billion dollar investments in some of the most politically unstable regions of the world are actively engaged in managing local and international perceptions of their operating procedures, which invariably brings corporate public relations (social assistance to local communities and lobbying local, private, and public sector powerbrokers) in direct contact (and sometimes conflict) with diplomatic interests. Nation-branding is the process of trying to determine how the sum of the constituent elements of a nation's image (its people, policies, culture, and industry) can be marketed to attract investment, tourism, skilled migrants, and foreign students. Whereas soft power is a concept associated with international politics, nation-branding is focused more clearly on the economic dimension of soft power. Chancelleries, foreign ministries, and trade ministries in countries large and small are preoccupied with how to coordinate government and private sector resources to project a clearer and more attractive brand in the interests of enhancing domestic economic prosperity.

The radical change in the environment for public diplomacy can be summed up in the idea of social power, what van Ham writes is "the capacity to establish norms and rules around which actors' actions converge".[23] In short, diplomacy is being societized, giving its public forms more prominence. While there is no doubt that there are more points of access by non-governmental organizations, citizens, and corporations to the establishment of international rules and norms, the actual distribution of power between state and non-state actors will vary on an issue-by-issue basis. As with state-based public diplomacy, NGO and corporate forms of "diplomacy" are not altruistic. They are interest-based. Greenpeace's values and means of expressing them are not universally shared; it probably has as many detractors as it has supporters. Finally, some may quibble with characterizing the international efforts of social movements, celebrities, and global corporations as public diplomacy, a practice that has been associated with the external communication of sovereign entities acting on behalf of national or sub-national populations. In other words, the Canadian government's diplomacy is on behalf of all Canadians and everyone is a shareholder in the government's action because they are citizens (the government is an expression of the citizens' sovereignty); Greenpeace Canada, on the other hand, acts on behalf of its members and does not act on the behalf of all Canadians. It may be more accurate to conclude that these non-governmental actors are engaging in international public relations and lobbying, making the environment for public diplomacy more interconnected and contributing to a thicker form of **network diplomacy** for foreign ministries and their diplomats to navigate.

WEB 2.0 DIPLOMACY: A NEW PUBLIC DIPLOMACY FOR THE TWENTY-FIRST CENTURY?

The digital diplomacy context has changed dramatically over the last two decades with transition from Web 1.0 to Web 2.0 diplomacy.[24] Foreign ministries must, once again, fundamentally rethink how they manage information to ensure that they provide their governments with an "information edge".[25] Digital media channels (a foreign ministry's network of online platforms, such as embassy homepages and social media sites) have the advantage of scale: they allow diplomats to have more conversations with more people across more spectrums, especially if they cannot physically be in a location. The Internet is no longer "just" a site of information. It is a site of coordination, since all media have converged on to one platform. With social media channels, foreign ministries have an opportunity to engage in information-gathering, message dissemination, monitoring and surveillance, engagement, and evaluation—all in real time.

Although the transition from a broadcast to a network environment has been widely accepted and adopted by foreign policy practitioners, the shift from a "need to know" to a "need-to-share" mindset has been more challenging and raises fundamental questions about the ethos and practice of public diplomacy in the coming years. Is online or digital diplomacy going to be another form of media monitoring—tracking online debates and noting supporters and critics, or, will diplomats insert themselves into online conversations that are open to a global audience? Is the purpose of sharing information online another means of one-way broadcasting of a country's ideals, policy, and brand, or, is it designed to open a dialogue and create communities of interest in which diplomats and citizens collaborate on shared concerns? Another question relates to the perennial public diplomacy conundrum of how to measure public diplomacy's longer-term effects. This is difficult to do under the best of conditions in the offline world and more so in the online world that offers the advantages of anonymity. Together, these questions point to an essential question posed by this chapter and formulated by Charles Causey and Philip Howard as: "Are the efforts of diplomats to increase their online and social media presences genuine efforts to engage in a new form of public diplomacy? Or are these efforts merely traditional statecraft wrapped in a new online packing?"[26] A hint at the answers to the above questions can be found through a brief reflection on implications of the Arab Spring for digital diplomacy and the selection of three cases of Canadian digital diplomacy.

The now somewhat maligned "Arab Spring" (2010–2012) offers a number of lessons for the future of digital diplomacy as a form of public diplomacy. From the digital media perspective, no knowledgeable observers of the unique social and political dynamics in play during these revolutions make the technologically determinist argument that the plentiful supply of mobile phones and the on-the-ground live reporting by Al-Jazeera or Al-Arabiya (outside the direct control of the governments of Tunisia and Egypt) were the catalysts in toppling autocratic regimes. However, there is no question that the information technologies and more transparent media reporting challenged ruling elites, allowed diaspora communities to have real-time information, and weakened state authority. That being said, as the cases of any number of other authoritarian regimes (Syria, Iran, Russia, Belarus, etc.) show, governments can mount sophisticated online counter-revolutions by simply "turning off the power" and launching cyber-surveillance, though not without incurring significant costs in resources and legitimacy. For public diplomacy, these revolutions show that the "slow pulses" of societal change may be discernible in chat rooms online, lying metaphorically beneath the real-world observable reality of diplomatic soirees and state-controlled media or nominally independent, self-censoring media organizations. It will behoove foreign ministries to spend as much time in the online as offline worlds.

Social media sceptic, Evgeny Morozov, on the other hand, argues convincingly that the problem with Web 2.0 diplomacy is that there may be a tendency by governments to generate more "spam" because no one actually wants the "ideas" and "positions" that, for example, are being inserted by State Department's Digital Outreach Team into online conversation threads.[27] In short, there's a demand/supply problem: with vast supply (speeches, statements, news releases, tweets) but perhaps very modest public demand.[28] Like Nike and Apple, governments must first create a demand for their "online product" of "good ideas". Morozov proposes that rather than dumping content that no one wants online, governments should expand supply in the one area where there is almost an infinite demand: education.

THE DIGITAL DIMENSION OF CANADA'S PUBLIC DIPLOMACY

In 2008, while a Fulbright Research Professor in Public Diplomacy at the University of Southern California, I wrote a report for the Foreign and Commonwealth Office (FCO), in which I tried to examine and predict some of the benefits and risks of Web 2.0-enabled public diplomacy.[29] In those "early days" of the "second generation" of digital diplomacy, I noted that the discussion would be speculative, since virtually no foreign ministries had yet attempted to integrate social media platforms, such as Twitter or Facebook, into their official homepages. Yet there was interest in knowing how social networking sites such as Facebook, YouTube, and virtual worlds—for example, the Second House of Sweden in *Second Life*[30]—could reinforce existing diplomatic relationships and build new ones by mobilizing citizens and even lead to the co-creation of policy.

By 2012, a number of Group of Seven countries, notably the United States, the UK, and Canada, had begun to garner some direct experience with social media to strengthen their respective public diplomacies. A central tenet of public relations is that organizations that cede conversation space, whether online or offline, local or global, risk being misunderstood and having their goals distorted. Governments have to be where their audiences are, and, increasingly, they are in an extroverted, overnight geosocial world of billions of mobile devices and trillions of bits of content shared online or texted.

Led by the example of the US State Department, it could be argued that Canada is a legitimate member of the "first tier" of Web 2.0 diplomacy.[31] Perhaps this adoption of new communication channels was unique to the diplomacy of countries in the Anglosphere because the dominant social media channels in the West had been developed in the United States. Canada's embassy in Washington was an early adopter, using Facebook and YouTube in its "Connect to Canada" public affairs outreach programmes to reach a potential audience of some 800,000 Canadians in the United States. In a short period of time, throughout the Canadian diplomatic network, there were "hot spots" where Canadian diplomatic missions were experimenting with the new channels to reach their local audiences. Canada soon had a number of discrete examples of deploying social media channels as part of official public diplomacy strategies.

Three very different types of Canadian digital diplomacy—as practised by Canadian diplomats in Austria and China and as directed by Canada from Ottawa towards Iran and the Iranian diaspora—will illuminate some of the strategies and challenges associated with Web 2.0 Canadian diplomacy. I can draw some tentative conclusions to the questions posed in my 2008 study: How can diplomats make best use of the advantages of scale offered by the ever-expanding array of social networks? How can they work with existing online communities of interest to develop, advocate, deliver, and review policy? In 2008, I assumed that growing global activism would force foreign ministries to move into virtual spaces and inform online debates and engage in corrective blogging to counter misinformation and disinformation (e.g. in 2006 the US Department of States had launched "Digital Outreach" teams to counter ideological support for terrorism). I noted that since Foreign Affairs and International Trade Canada (DFAIT)—now Global Affairs Canada—was the first foreign ministry to experiment with online interactive platforms in the early 2000s to engage citizens directly in the foreign policymaking process, there was potential for what were called "e-consultations" to continue using the new channels that were particularly suited to dialogic or symmetrical forms of communication.[32] I went so far as to speculate that there was potential for "policy mobilization" in the development of internal and external "wikis"—what has become known as internal and external "open policy development". Echoing Morozov, I suggested that, from a strategic communications perspective, foreign ministries should not simply transfer their "static content" from their Web 1.0 platforms to the new channels. I also opined that being an "online diplomat" would have potential pitfalls given the blurring of online boundaries between users and producers, authority and amateurism, and play and work. Finally, foreign ministries would also have very legitimate concerns about privacy and security.[33]

BRANDING A HOCKEY-PLAYING, TWEETING
CANADIAN AMBASSADOR IN AUSTRIA[34]

For a small, German-speaking alpine republic, Austria's adoption of Facebook had been quite remarkable. In 2008, only 8% of Austrians used Facebook; by 2011, it was almost 6 in 10 Austrians. There were already 2.7 million Facebook users in a population of 8 million, with almost 1 million users representing public diplomacy's "sweet spot" in the 20–29 age range.[35] Twitter, by contrast, was far less popular with only 75,000 accounts. With most of the successor generation of Austria using social media, it behooved Canada's diplomatic representatives to ensure that they were connecting with future leaders.

Although Canada's embassy to the United States was the pioneer in the use of social media within Canada's global diplomatic network, having already established a Connect-to-Canada network that made use of Facebook and YouTube, the then-named Department of Foreign Affairs and International Trade (DFAIT) had not yet created a so-called model social media mission.[36] Such a mission would have its social media channels conform to all of the Government of Canada's and DFAIT's policies, including ensuring that all content was available in both official languages (English and French), incorporating a "common look and feel" for the integration of these private corporate social media sites into the official Canadian embassy websites, and adhering to the Canadian government's social media usage policy. The Canadian embassy in Austria was selected as one of two pilot embassies for testing Canada's Web 2.0 diplomacy (Austria.gc.ca) in Europe because the country's smaller size allowed both the benefits and challenges of such diplomacy to be in starker relief. It helped that there was an enthusiastic ambassador who, while not a social media "zealot", at least recognized the importance of testing the utility of these new communication channels to raise Canada's profile.[37] From a risk management standpoint, it was felt that any "kinks" in Canada's emerging Web 2.0 diplomacy could be worked through in this sophisticated, high culture country that offered many opportunities for citizen engagement and with which the Canadian government had no serious policy irritants.

The Canadian embassy launched its Facebook and Twitter channels in September 2011 and achieved a significant head-start over most other foreign embassies in Vienna. A survey by the Austrian social media consultancy, Digital Affairs, showed that only Canada and the United States had both Facebook and Twitter channels, and that, comparatively, few other embassies had yet launched a Web 2.0 presence.[38] Judging by the very incremental steps in which foreign ministries around the world were incorporating social media in their operations at the time, it should not come as a great surprise that the vast majority of foreign embassies in a highly connected country such as Austria would still be wedded to a Web 1.0 presence.

The primary purpose of launching a pilot Web 2.0 project in Austria was to test whether the systematic introduction of social media platforms would increase the capacity of the Canadian embassy to present Canada as innovative and very relevant to the social, economic, political, and diplomatic aspirations of Austria. In other words, the embassy's public diplomacy would attempt to move Canada's image incrementally beyond the standard stereotypes held by most Austrians of Canada as a land of vast geography populated by tough (but nice) hockey players. If this were achieved, it would help to advance Canada's own economic and political interests. In short, the guiding principle was to use social media tools to thicken and deepen Austrians' connection to Canada whether in making educational opportunities in Canada more attractive to Austrian students or promoting Austrian environmental technologies to Canadian firms.

From a branding standpoint, it was decided that the Canadian embassy would seek to differentiate itself from other embassies by connecting the well-worn "land of hockey" stereotype with the sophistication of a hockey-playing ambassador. The "Canadian ambassador as hockey enthusiast" theme was thus positioned as an "Embassy brand" and the requisite photos of the ambassador playing in a charity hockey game and meeting with amateur hockey players were posted on the embassy's Facebook channel. To further personalize the association between the ambassador and the social media channels, the embassy's Twitter account was presented under the ambassador's name. At the same time, the embassy's trade section had the ambassador Tweet messages about greenbuilding and other business-related topics and populated the Facebook page with images (often including the ambassador) highlighting cooperation between Austrian and Canadian firms in areas of advanced technology such as biofuel.

The first phase of this pilot project entailed incorporating the social media channels into the embassy's website, acculturating the staff about how their many daily activities (taking part in conferences, leading trade delegations, welcoming visiting Canadian scholars or artists) could provide unique content on Facebook and Twitter channels, and developing a process for approving and translating messages. Mostly, it was about getting embassy personnel to think strategically about the expanding opportunities to get their key messages out through social media and trying to achieve a balance of cultural, policy, and business content. A singular distinguishing feature of social media is that it offered immediate and unfiltered reaction to Canadian policies and embassy-organized events and initiatives. It also allowed staff to test the risk management system that DFAIT headquarters had developed for social media usage. Embassy staff received ongoing training on how to correct misleading or confusing information posted to the embassy's Facebook and Twitter by the public. They were furthermore reminded that public criticism of Canadian government policy or programmes could not be censored as long as they did not violate official guidelines with regard to appropriate language.

Given that these social media channels have been active for some nine years, it is difficult to draw any definitive conclusions (the following case of *weibo* in China is perhaps more conclusive): Canada's fan base for its Facebook was initially modest (83 in March 2012) and it had 70 Twitter followers in contrast to the US embassy's 1312 followers. When this author rechecked the Facebook page (July 2020), it had over 30,000 "likes" and a modest 2200 Twitter followers.

In its first decade of operation, the Canadian embassy's social media channels have displayed a limited range of content with a mixture of official messages re-tweeted from Ottawa-based accounts (e.g. re-tweeting the prime minister's and foreign and trade ministers' key messages), promotion of trade shows, and highlights of the diverse cultural events happening in Austria with a Canadian dimension. There are rarely personal messages from the Canadian ambassador to Austrians. The content does not appear to be designed to resonate with Austrians at an emotional level or to be shared among peers; there are likely no expectations that the any of the Tweets emanating from the Canadian embassy will make Austrian media headlines. There are undoubtedly still pockets of resistance within foreign ministries to posting what some would consider "frivolous" content on government websites such as the ambassador's chef's favourite recipes or photos of the youth soccer team sponsored by the embassy's employees.

Perhaps the biggest challenge is asking public officials to create content that is more personal and, therefore, authentic. This is not the natural inclination of civil servants who have spent their professional lives in a public service culture that values anonymity and prudence (which is another way of saying caution). Few are the public servants who, while discreetly navigating the corridors of power in foreign lands, are likely to jump at the chance to write what amount to "open letters" about themselves or their families—their favourite vacation spots, regions, or sports teams. This also raises uncomfortable questions about civil servants being seen to endorse products or places. Yet, for the purpose of building followers and fans, this is precisely the type of content that is valued by the target audience. As local Austrian fans and expatriate Canadians residing in Austria are pulled in by the original (if not "frivolous") content on the embassy's social media channels, they become "inadvertent" observers of Canada as they inevitably notice other more policy-oriented messaging either on the homepage or interwoven into the content on the social media platforms.

It may still be too early to draw definitive conclusions on the outcomes of what started as a pilot project to test Canada's digital diplomacy. For instance, there has been no need to date for corrective blogging by Canadian diplomats in Austria and there have been few instances of people trying to post inappropriate content. Indeed, there is virtually no comment from self-identified Austrians on the Facebook page and rare is the public comment denouncing Canada's polices (other than immigrants largely from South Asia lamenting the time it is taking for them to receive official assistance with their files). The embassy's Facebook site is, in fact, a bulletin board that has updated content on Canadians and Canadian economic and cultural interests in Austria. Although this may seem to be anachronistic, it nevertheless complements the programme information on the main embassy homepage. To be sure, Canada did gain some modest recognition by being one of the first embassies to deploy social media channels in Austria.

MAKING CANADIAN WAVES IN CHINA: CANADIAN TWITTER DIPLOMACY ON *WEIBO*

It would be difficult to imagine that the Canadian embassy and its consulates have the capacity to reach even a fraction of the 1.3 billion people in a country of China's size. However, online platforms offer a convenient, cost-effective way for Canada's diplomatic mission to go directly—and over the heads of the government-controlled media—to an audience that (unlike in Austria) is thirsting for news on Canada. This is not surprising. China is one of the most important source countries for immigrants to Canada and, with the Canadian government having acquired the coveted Approved Destination Status, there has been an explosion of Chinese tourism. And, not to be overlooked is the fact that the number of Chinese students in Canada has grown by more than 300% over the last decade, demonstrating that Canada is viewed favourably as an education market.[39]

For the Canadian embassy, in fact, the online market—powerful and versatile—was there for the taking and, in June 2011, Canada soft launched itself on *weibo* (china.gc.ca), the most popular microblog in China with 300 million users. Since Twitter, YouTube, and Facebook were blocked in China, foreign embassies had little choice but to use *weibo*. It did not take Canada long to break the 100,000 barrier of followers and by 4 April 2012, it had 186,863, giving it bragging rights as the third most popular embassy on this site behind the United States (447,146), UK (224,100), and ahead of France (158,546) and Japan (142,012). This allowed significant reach and scale in a country of China's size and diversity where, unlike in Austria, a foreign ambassador cannot just jump into his official car and visit a provincial governor and return to the capital in the matter of half a day's travel.

The benefits are not difficult to discern. The *weibo* platform was used to reach a Chinese audience rather than a Canadian expatriate audience. The potential to reach the hard-to-reach in their own language with "thick communication"—messages on Chinese microblog are 140 characters, which is three to four times as much as English-language content on Twitter—cannot be overstated. Perhaps the most significant dimension to Canada's use of *weibo* as a communication platform was that, unlike in the West, microblogging is popular in China because it is considered trustworthy. It is "real news" in a very controlled media environment and is relatively uncensored. This provided the potential for foreign embassies to actually "break" news online and thus to set the public policy agenda on particular issues.

The embassy posted 20–30 messages a week on *weibo* and, in the words of Mark McDowell, the senior Canadian diplomat who launched Canada's social media presence at the embassy (2011–2012), the watchword was to be "informal, diverse, transparent, interesting". Yet public sector organizations are not usually known for being exciting; they are associated with dry and staid content. The goal of creating an informal feel to an official government online presence in order to attract and retain users is usually anathema to the "serious tone" and "informational" character of most communication emanating from diplomatic missions. There is also a tendency by government officials to steer away from producing content that could be interpreted by the Canadian media as frivolous or too flashy and therefore a waste of taxpayers' money. The challenge, as noted in the case of Canada's digital diplomacy in Austria, is that most middle level public servants' ideas of safe as opposed to thought-provoking usually translates into content that nobody will go out of their way to read.

It has been said that in an online environment awash in information, much of which is suspect, "content is king"; knowing what will appeal to an embassy's target audience of Chinese citizens between the ages of 18 and 30 was thus the key concern of the embassy's staff. Weibo's official Canadian content is all in Chinese and generated by Canada's embassy and its consulates rather than by officials in Ottawa. There were three basic types of content: Canadian events in China (culture and visits); embassy news (the ambassador, open house, activities; and news about Canada [such as festivals, travel, food, and the economy]). It quickly became apparent that the challenge was to get the right balance between serious topics (e.g. Canada's approach to food safety) that could be deemed an indirect criticism of China's policies and lighter and potentially less controversial topics, such profiling a Chinese family's crest showing a panda and a polar bear.

McDowell observed that useful information like visas and exclusive content about the embassy and about life in Canada was much more popular than news about Canadian events in China. De-mystifying the embassy and its people was particularly popular.[40] For instance, the visa and immigration section of the embassy had a weekly column and the economic section offered economic news three times a week; an "Inside the Embassy" online magazine featured stories about the embassy every Thursday with photographs and video (the most popular item is food). Saturday's column is by the chef and Sunday's is about the Francophonie.

When the Canadian ambassador to China, David Mulroney, posted online photographs of his official car, a Toyota Camry hybrid, apparently a modest mode of transportation by official Chinese standards, more than 1100 people responded on the Canadian embassy's weibo site, given that even local Chinese officials were whisked around in chauffeur-driven high-end cars such as Audis and Mercedes Benzes. As the *Globe and Mail's* China correspondent Mark McKinnon wrote, "Even the Global Times, a newspaper closely affiliated with the Communist Party, used the online discussion of the official Camry to raise the sensitive topic of government officials and their cars". He reported that Ambassador Mulroney told the Global Times that he released the photographs because "we get a lot of questions about how we operate at the embassy, what rules govern our work, and how much money we spend".[41] The surprising end to this story was that the Chinese government actually changed its regulations on official vehicle sourcing, though no one can prove any causality with the profile on *weibo* of the Canadian ambassador's Camry.

From a strategic communications perspective, the Canadian embassy found that *weibo* was not a platform for messaging in the traditional sense: being preachy is death. That being said, there was a more implicit way of "selling" Canada as a tourism, education, or business destination. Education was perhaps the most useful barometer of the success of social media platforms on multiple fronts: from a public diplomacy perspective, the platforms reach key demographics of the successor generations, who also happen to be the most significant users of social media tools, and who will value the openness of the medium as a means to build mutual understanding; from an economic perspective, moving Chinese students to consider Canada rather than, say, Australia, the UK, or the United States as their first choice for a foreign education, contributes directly to Canada's economic bottom line. For this reason, the Canadian embassy took a more active approach to education marketing by live-blogging from Chinese education fairs. In the future, there would be student video testimonials from Chinese students already studying in Canada.

There was also room in social media to disseminate serious and sensitive messages that could not necessarily be conveyed through official contacts with Chinese media. The case of Lai Changxing was instructive. He was a fugitive from justice who escaped to Canada. After extradition negotiations with China and with the promise that he would not be executed upon his return, Canadian authorities extradited him to China in 2011. The Canadian embassy posted the court ruling on its website and then directed people to it on *weibo*. It is a matter of diplomatic convention that diplomats do not interfere publicly in domestic politics of their host countries. But this does not mean that they cannot use social media to affect public opinion. For instance, Canada values transparency and prudence in the expenditure of public money (e.g. the ambassador's car) and the Canadian government does not support the use of capital punishment. McDowell noted that while *weibo* was not used to send formal messages directly to the host government, the messages sent by the embassy were designed to resonate with the embassy's local followers and, in this way, the Canadian embassy hoped that the host government could, in turn, become aware that certain topics were eliciting considerable online chatter.

The management of Canada's *weibo* site produced some unofficial rules for how Canada's digital diplomacy could support its public diplomacy by virtue of the careful selection of digital content: lecterns, ribbon cuttings, boardroom tables, lines of men in suits, and "meet-and-greet" photographs—in short, organization-centred content—were to be avoided at all costs in favour of audience-centred communication. The local audience was not interested in what was already in the mainstream media; there had to be an effort to create new content that met the audience's interest or co-created content with the audience through contests and giveaways. For instance, rather than showing the Ambassador shaking hands with a local official, the embassy showed the Canadian ambassador in a restaurant tasting local delicacies. To be sure, the constant pressure to create exclusive, new content creates a burden on resources and staffs, since embassies are not newsrooms. But if the audience of 140,000 followers in the months after Canada's launch on *weibo* could be considered to be the equivalent to the newspaper circulation of a mid-size city in Canada, then such an effort could be justified.

DIRECT DIPLOMACY TOWARDS IRAN THROUGH SOCIAL MEDIA

As noted, while the label of the "Arab Spring" has been discredited, the revolutions in Egypt and Tunisia did create a period of unprecedented political ferment in the Middle East and presented a propitious opportunity for countries such as Canada to encourage the advent of more democratic governments. At the same time, the lessons over the previous decade had shown that democratization cannot be imposed from abroad; rather, outsiders can support the democratic process through, for example, electoral assistance, training local people to lobby for legislative changes, etc. In countries with more repressive regimes where such on-the-ground outreach by Canada and other like-minded countries was very limited, the Arab Spring brought renewed focus on a relatively new tool for attempting political change: social media.

Not that the Internet was new. But by 2011, the exponential pene-tration of the Internet (Web 1.0) and the ubiquity of cellular telephones combined with the reach of satellite television gave the millions of citizens across North Africa and the Middle East greater access to events inside their own countries and appeared to reduce the regimes' monopolies on information. The Internet allowed people to become more politically active even in the face of their governments' attempts to control online networks by infiltrating or cutting access to them.

A central question for Canada and many of its allies was how to harness information freedom to advance their interests in this period of political turmoil. Unlike the Canadian experience of using social media platforms in a low-risk environment, such as Austria, to promote the Canadian brand and experimentation with soft content on Weibo and push the Canadian agenda out to the Chinese people in a non-threatening manner over the heads of the state-controlled media, the use of new communica-tion channels, such as social media in the Middle East, arguably presented more risks for Canada and their local publics of interest, precisely because the agenda was overtly political. That is to say, what would become known as Canada's Direct Diplomacy was defined as "the set of activities by which the Canadian government engages directly with political actors in partner countries to assist them in their efforts to effect positive political change".[42]

The concept was broken down into 5 elements: a strategy for Canada to encourage political change in the direction of greater respect for human rights and democratic principles; sustained engagement with civic and political actors within the partner country through platforms such as Face-book, Twitter, and YouTube, as well as the distribution of customized content such as videos, infographics, and narratives to help promote awareness of Canada's perspectives; targeted support to civic and polit-ical actors to make domestic politics more responsive to citizen demands; engagement of the broader population through social media to reinforce Canada's influence; and, finally, an effort to monitor and evaluate the progress of Canada's programming and communications efforts against Canada's strategy. What made this approach unique was that such direct engagement with domestic political actors in a foreign country in a way that can be perceived as promoting regime change has not always been a priority in Canadian foreign policy since this would be construed as meddling in the internal politics of host governments, a practice that is generally viewed as not playing by the diplomatic rules, since it invites reciprocal meddling from the targeted governments.

The idea of Direct Diplomacy was born of diplomatic necessity when Canada closed its embassies in Syria and Iran in 2012. In the absence of official diplomatic relations, Direct Diplomacy became the only form of Canadian government-led agenda-setting in these countries. In Syria, the goal of Canada's campaign was to contribute to a transition from the Assad regime to a stable, inclusive government more respectful of human rights. Much of the campaign involved giving support to civic opposition and political leaders in other regional capitals and through social media.

However, it is the Direct Diplomacy approach directed at Iran that merits this chapter's attention. The stakes were, quite simply, higher with Iran. The purpose, as in Syria, was to expand political space within Iran in support of greater respect for human rights. In addition, however, the Canadian government sought to support the emergence of different voices within Iran on Iran's approach to nuclear weapons and regional security, in part by engaging the Iranian diaspora as a bridge to those inside Iran. The hope was that the cumulative impact of Direct Diplomacy actions would encourage dissidents to express themselves more freely and weaken public support for the regime's international security posture.

Simply put, Iran was a more important foreign policy target for Canada's Direct Diplomacy approach. It also helped that Iran was the most "plugged-in" country in the Middle East at the time with 42 million Internet users (roughly half the population), 43% of which used online chat as a means of communicating with close friends and 58% of which had a Facebook account. In 2013, this high degree of Internet penetration at the time of the Iranian presidential elections prompted Canada to leverage its experience with social media outreach in Syria and turn its attention to developing an online engagement strategy to influence political and social thinking in Iran. It was a delicate balance: to support the people of Iran while using online tools to isolate the regime in domestic and international public opinion.

Canada was not the only country examining how digital diplomacy in the civilian context of a foreign ministry could reinforce its hard power interests. At the time, the United States and the UK were enthusiastically pursuing digital diplomacy targeting civil society in Iran through their respective social media websites. The State Department had a dedicated Farsi language account with more than 80,000 "likes" and 3000 conversations about its content.

The goals of Canada's Direct Diplomacy campaign in 2013 on Facebook and Twitter were decidedly traditional: communicating Government of Canada policies to the Iranian public in Farsi and developing messages that would highlight to the Iranian public the poor performance of their government, particularly ahead of the upcoming Iranian presidential elections that June. The Canadian narrative focused on using creative (and sometimes humorous) means to show the fragility of the Iranian regime such as highlighting poor public services (notably the length of time the average Iranian needed to secure an Internet connection), the poor economic conditions, and Iran's isolation from the rest of the world.

Perhaps the high point of the Internet-based Direct Diplomacy campaign directed at Iran in 2013 was the organization by the University of Toronto's Munk School (with the support of DFAIT) of a two-day conference, the Global Dialogue on the Future of Iran, on May 10, ahead of the Iranian presidential elections. The conference was live-streamed through YouTube and through Facebook, Twitter and Google+ in the hopes of reaching the 300,000 expatriate Iranians in Canada and the millions of Iranians in Iran. It is hard to imagine that Canadian diplomats resident in Iran (if there were official ties between the two countries) would have been able to deliver the message that the then Conservative foreign minister, John Baird, delivered to this conference in his keynote address. Consistent with Canada's official policy on Iran, the speech was blunt and minced no words where Canada stood. It dispensed with diplomatic niceties and called for regime change.[43] More than 2.9 million unique visitors would eventually access the Global Dialogue website (https://globaldialogue.com).

Canadian media commented that Canada was seeking to "restore relations" with Iran—but not the old-fashioned way. Instead of ambassadors and attaches, DFATD was aiming to connect with Iranians directly, via social media. As reported in the *Globe and Mail*, the Dialogue became a permanent feature of Canada's digital diplomacy towards Iran and the Munk School developed technology to circumvent Iran's online censorship. In addition, the School developed a Rouhani Meter (https://rouhanimeter.com), "which tracks which reform promises have been fulfilled by Iranian President Hassan Rouhani, and the Majlis Monitor, which attempts to measure the performance of Iranian parliamentarians".[44] Janice Stein, professor and former director at the Munk School, was quoted extensively in the article, saying that the next phase would involve the creation of a "digital public square" that would use the tools that had already been developed for the Iran campaign to expand the project's reach into other countries and regions. According to Stein, "It's about making space for multiple narratives, it's about making space for different voices".[45]

The case of Direct Diplomacy using primarily digital platforms raises some important practical considerations and theoretical concerns about the nature of social media platforms as forms of hard and soft power in Canada's public diplomacy. Canadian officials were not so naïve as to misunderstand the risks involved in such digital diplomacy, ranging from raising expectations that could not be met with respect to social media outreach, accounts impersonating those of the Canadian government misrepresenting Canada's positions (black flag operations by foreign intelligence agencies), inadvertent support of organizations that did not align with Canadian priorities, and outside actors hacking into the foreign ministry's IT systems to wreak havoc and hijack social media accounts. In the end, it was deemed that the risks were manageable for this digital diplomacy experiment and mitigation measures were put in place.

The question of whether Direct Diplomacy represents hard or soft power or more open, democratic foreign policy is harder to answer. It represents both. It created a greater followership (domestically and internationally) through the presentation of Canada's desire for greater freedom in Iran, but it was unequivocally a highly mediated (by the Canadian government directly and indirectly through the government's support of the Munk project) and strategic form of persuasive communication that had a specific goal: regime change in Iran.

WHAT DOES DIGITAL DIPLOMACY PORTEND FOR THE FUTURE OF CANADA'S PUBLIC DIPLOMACY?

Is it possible or useful to compare the nascent social media Web 2.0 experiences of Canadian embassies in three such different socio-economic and political environments? Can public diplomacy outcomes be realistically assessed based on the number of "likes", conversational threads, Tweets, or sentiment analysis? Indeed, how much further along are we in understanding Web 2.0 diplomacy since the somewhat speculative tone of my 2008 report? As will be shown below, although we will have to wait a number of years in order to have the longitudinal data through which to evaluate the effects of Web 2.0 Canadian diplomacy, there are nevertheless some early indicators of the immediate benefits and inherent limitations of such channels. What is undeniable is that social media channels across the full spectrum of Canada's public diplomacy (Fig. 4.1) have the advantage of scale: they allow diplomats to have more conversations with more people across more platforms, especially—as the case of Iran shows—if they cannot physically be in a location.[46]

It is worth acknowledging that the Stephen Harper-led Conservative government reduced support for the more unmediated forms of longer-term Canadian public diplomacy. Between 2006 and 2015, it is estimated that some $40 million was cut from Canada's public diplomacy programming (arts and culture promotion abroad, the elimination of Canadian Studies after 35 years, and international exhibitions). This represented about 40% of Canada's overall expenditure on public diplomacy by all federal departments and agencies and would be the equivalent of the US State Department's public diplomacy budget being cut by $400 million. The Conservative government argued that Canada's efforts to promote its image and cultural industries would be better aligned with foreign policy priorities. It called for more accountability and oversight in what remained of public diplomacy programming.

That being said, the one area of Canadian public diplomacy immune from these cuts was Canada's move into digital diplomacy. As one Canadian diplomat observed at a conference of former Canadian practitioners of public diplomacy, "digital is the only area where the [public diplomacy] fires have kept burning".[47] In their 2015 Twidiplomacy Study, the international consultancy Burston-Marsteller ranked Global Affairs Canada as the second-best connected foreign ministry in the world with nearly 200 embassies and consulates and ambassadors active on social media. In 2015, Canada delivered more than 30 international digital campaigns, including various free trade agreements, signature initiatives such a maternal, newborn and child health initiative, religious freedom, and Canada's support for Ukraine. Canada's @Canada Twitter accounts, launched in 2014, and "Canada's voice to the world", had over 200,000 followers.

The rapid rate of expansion of Canada's digital diplomacy tools—especially social media—since 2011 bodes well for the Trudeau government's call for a "revitalized" public diplomacy. In his mandate letter from Prime Minister Trudeau, Foreign Affairs Minister Stephane Dion was asked to "revitalize Canada's public diplomacy, stakeholder engagement, and cooperation with partners in Canada and abroad".[48] The Liberal government's 2016 federal budget will have a salutary effect on Canada's place in the global public diplomacy arena. The Canadian government plans to spend an additional $1.7 billion over the next five years on arts and culture, including reviving one of the programmes to promote Canada's cultural industries abroad (Trade Routes International). As well, Canada's 150th anniversary of Canadian Confederation in 2017 created a propitious and unique public diplomacy platform to showcase Canada to the world.

The Trudeau government appears to be ready to address the chronic under-funding of Canada's public diplomacy. However, through its emphasis on having the government show results (encapsulated in its embrace of a philosophy of "deliverology"), it is clear that the government intends to follow the examples of the American and British governments in forcing a closer alignment between public diplomacy programmes and foreign policy priorities.

As I have written elsewhere, historically, Canada's public diplomacy was fragmented across and between levels of government and our nation-brand architecture was diffuse and confusing with multiple logos, brand identities, colour palates, and different approaches to experiential marketing and advocacy. There was no coherent storyline that strategically built Canada's image abroad (in contrast, for example, to the UK's GREAT Britain multi-year campaign). This has made it more challenging for the Canadian federal government's departments (notably Canadian Heritage and Global Affairs Canada) and agencies (e.g. Telefilm Canada, Canada Council for the Arts, National Film Board of Canada, and Destination Canada) to draw on obvious synergies across the Canadian "public diplomacy triangle" and to increase the impact of their public diplomacy tools.

Canada's renewed role as a digital diplomacy pioneer will certainly provide leverage for the Liberal government's desire to revitalize Canada's public diplomacy, but such leverage may prove to be limited in the absence of a national public diplomacy strategy and a decision on whether such tools will be used primarily to promote Canada's brand or to interact with global audiences (including Canada's diaspora). There are, however, a number of lessons from Canada's experience with digital diplomacy that will augur well for the next generation of Canadian public diplomacy.

Lesson 1: The Mode of Delivery—Moving Away from Broadcast to Collaboration

The introduction of Web 2.0 platforms has created expectations that public diplomacy would continue to move along the continuum from broadcast mode to more symmetrical, two-way forms of interactive communication. This chapter is not suggesting that there were only three case studies available to illustrate Canada's early experimentation with attempts to create greater interactivity through digital platforms. This is far from the case since a small number of other Canadian diplomatic missions (e.g. Tunisia, India, The Hague, and the Consulate General in New York) were also experimenting with new social media tools early in the 2010's. It can be said that considerable time has been devoted since 2011 in learning the lessons of the pilot projects and establishing the policy frameworks for managing digital diplomacy, including a digital strategy for Global Affairs Canada.

Canada's experience with *weibo*, for example, shows that this specific embassy tapped into a new, more interactive and consultative channel of communication that allowed it to reduce its dependence on the official Chinese media and talk directly with local audiences who wanted more information on Canada. It developed a demand that already existed (i.e. Chinese curiosity about Canada as an education and vacation destination). In contrast, the Canadian embassy in Austria was faced with local broadcast and print media outlets that were free to report on whatever they chose, though they rarely felt the need to cover Canada. This created an incentive for the embassy to develop a demand for information on Canada by using its social media channels to create a "buzz". In many ways, the social media challenge for Canada's embassies in advanced, liberal democracies is greater since they have to create a demand for engagement when no such "natural demand" may exist.

The idea of pushing the boundaries beyond broadcasting and consulting (i.e. asking for feedback such as "like" or "dislike" in social media) and developing online collaboration and open policy development (i.e. crowd-sourcing) with foreign audiences continues to be a long-term rather than a medium-term possibility, with the notable exception of the Global Dialogue on the Future of Iran, which exemplifies such consultation. This is not a function of technology, since webinars are easy to set up, but it has more to do with the nature of foreign policy decision-making. It is far easier to crowd-source ideas online, through an internal or external wiki, for improving internal administrative processes (e.g. finding more cost-effective ways to manage embassy real estate holdings) or inviting travellers to send their weather reports or observations on natural disasters to the foreign ministry's homepage, than it is to identify solutions to politically sensitive (for Canada or the host country) diplomatic problems. A comfort zone will eventually be reached to open foreign policy deliberations and it may be that the crowd-sourcing is more appropriate for matters of policy implementation (e.g. "what are the most effective forms of sanctions on a country like Iran?" rather than problem definition "Is Iran a threat to world peace?").

It is for this reason that the default response by some diplomatic actors appears to be to use social media channels to "repurpose" approved content such as official announcements, rather than to create or co-create original online content. That is to say, and as Morozov observed, governments tend to use social media channels as another broadcast channel, reinforcing existing messages being delivered in speeches and news releases (often in the same language—unfortunately). On a more optimistic note, the education sector appears to be the lowest-risk arena for diplomatic consultation and outreach, including co-creation of original content. American embassies are particularly adept at creating online contests aimed at local youth populations and then using their embassy YouTube channels to showcase the winning entries.

Lesson 2: Posting the Right Type of Content

Government communications professionals expend considerable resources to ensure that the "container" and the "contents" of their communications match their target audiences. It is the *sine qua non* of effective public information or social marketing campaigns that such campaigns must be highly audience-centred as opposed to organization-centred. If you want to warn teenagers about the health risks of tobacco, you must know something about their existing attitudes and their preferences for how they receive information. In the same vein, if embassies are trying to talk to communities in foreign countries through social media, they must know their audiences' preferred platforms and what type of communications they engage in on these platforms (i.e. native Brazilians are most certainly on Orkut and not on Facebook, but members of the Canadian expatriate community may be on Facebook).

At first glance, managing content for social media may not appear to be any different than preparing other types of embassy communication in terms of process—determine the audience, select the message, adjust the container accordingly (e.g. speech, newsletter, news release, statement on website). However, it should be noted that while diplomats are accustomed to being on "send" mode and delivering "key messages" to the "power elite" of any given society and are usually given the time and space in academic roundtables, private dinners, editorial boards, and trade conferences to do so, they are less (sometimes much less) comfortable in engaging in a public exchange of views on controversial issues—even if that is what their audiences on social media want or expect. This means that foreign ministries must find out through surveys or contests what their local audiences expect to receive. As borne out by *weibo*, research suggests that Facebook and Twitter users may not be looking for the latest news (available in plentiful supply elsewhere) on official government social media websites.[49] It is more likely that online audiences are looking for original content and "news that they can use".

The experiences in Vienna and Beijing show that local audiences are extremely interested in how the embassy works; expatriates are looking for consular information; tourists and business travellers will want updated travel warnings (especially received via smart telephone apps); immigrants are looking for answers to their questions that may not exist in official government publications; others will be interested in being notified about the range of academic and cultural events (and giving their opinions on them). It is worth reflecting on Morozov's injunction to governments to use Web 2.0 diplomacy to respond to an existing demand (whether ideas, values, or specific policies) rather than to "dump" content online. Through its *weibo* platform, the Canadian embassy determined that the Chinese audience wanted more information on educational opportunities in Canada. This offered the embassy an opportunity to orient its online content strategically to sources on Canadian education, including live-blogging from an education fair. In the case of the Global Dialogue on the Future of Iran in March 2014, this initiative held a series of interactive conference on themes—human rights and civil society, entrepreneurship, media and journalism, and communications technology, among others—of interest to young Iranians (https://theglobaldialogue.ca/topics).

The hierarchy of communication needs for social media channels identified above—a mixture of so-called frivolous messages (*weibo* in China) and strategic messages (Global Dialogue on the Future of Iran) that are conveyed in interesting and non-bureaucratic language and indexed to local demand (e.g. what Iranian youth wants to talk about) to ensure an online response—implies a <u>limited interactivity</u>: embassies will gladly receive (and respond to) public views on how to improve, for example, collaboration on education, science, and technology projects, but it is unlikely that they want to initiate an extended back-and-forth dialogue on contentious issues with negative domestic political repercussions (e.g. Canada's seal harvest or treatment of aboriginal people in Canada). Unless the government is explicitly launching a public dialogue on contentious issues using social media (e.g. Keystone XL Pipeline), most users will understand that governments have developed official policies and there is not much point in trying to engineer a debate with public officials since the officials, while possibly attempting to clarify errors of fact, will ultimately direct them to the official decision in news releases or statements. These "official statements" should be confined to the main embassy homepage. In the end, there will be few extended conversations or debates. However, what has been interesting is that the *weibo* case shows that the Beijing embassy has succeeded in acting as a catalyst for discussions among the Chinese.

Therefore, governments engaged in digital diplomacy should not only be asking themselves "what key policy message do we want to deliver to country X through our social media channels?" Perhaps the more important guiding question for a public diplomacy boosted and amplified by digital platforms is: "How can we show country X that we are useful to them?" This is the difference between public diplomacy as selling a message and public diplomacy as marketing a message.

Lesson 3: The Tribulations of Evaluating Digital Diplomacy

Measuring the effectiveness of social media platforms raises the same conundrums encountered by all public information programming, namely, that you can measure the costs (staff time, programme expenditures) but it is more difficult to establish a direct link with results beyond a tally of outputs. For instance, you can measure the outputs of social media (the number of Tweets and posts) and you can measure the out-takes (i.e. the comprehension of these messages) in the form of "friends", "likes", re-tweets, followers, and, as in the case of *weibo*, local media following up on original embassy social media content. However, it is much more difficult to establish the correlation between the use of social media channels and the achievement of specific outcome objectives such as accepting specific advocacy goals (e.g. the right to have a seal harvest, support for a trade liberalization agreement, and the acceleration of Canada's advocated changes as a function of the Rouhani Meter and the Global Dialogue on the Future of Iran).

Public diplomacy 2.0 adds a whole new dimension of interactivity to government communication. Information gleaned from social media channels should, at the very least, inform policy. The feedback from foreign publics and Canadian expatriates (some 2.8 million Canadians living outside of Canada) can identify overlooked economic sectors, adjust misperceptions, and identify collaborations. The challenges are three-fold: the social media content has to be selected and designed to stimulate a response and thereby meaningful feedback; there must be a provision in the social media strategy to convert online contact to offline engagement (at some point there must be face-to-face contact to work together, which was attempted in Canada's Direct Diplomacy approach to Syria in 2011 and 2012); and the evaluation tools that record quantitative traffic on embassy websites have to be presented in context.

The quantitative measures of social media reach through Parature, HootSuite, Quantcast, and other tools are less useful than deeper qualitative assessments. Many Twitter followers have little utility for the embassies and the response to date to the Facebook posting in Vienna have been scarce, very polite and, one suspects, reflective of fairly shallow ties. The question this raises is whether the ties are by nature shallow or whether embassies have to rethink what type of information they post, whether Facebook channels should be the repository of embassy photo opportunities or whether these channels need to be tied to specific public affairs or advocacy initiatives so that their utilities as interactive channels can be maximized. Otherwise, the social media channels, such as Facebook, risk never graduating beyond online bulletin boards, perhaps more timely than pdf quarterly embassy newsletters, but always looking through the rear-view mirror about what has happened rather than stimulating debate and discussion about what should happen.

Conclusion

Does the evolution of Canada's public diplomacy, as it responds to a radically changed environment and the next generation of digital tools, contribute to more democratic (and better) foreign policymaking? This chapter suggests that we must have modest expectations for the future of public diplomacy. There is a curious paradox at work. The more interconnected a world of billions of smartphones becomes and the more influence is distributed among a wider public, the more centralized political decision-making becomes the norm as governments redouble their efforts to "manage", that is to say, control the impact of this global infosphere. This militates against a more symmetrical—and some would say democratic—form of diplomacy and continues to privilege asymmetrical forms in which the state actors, while paying lip service to collaboration and dialogue, seek to persuade audiences and use all the communication and consultation tools at their disposal—digital and non-digital—to do so. In other words, the second and third level of the public diplomacy triangle will remain paramount for *raison d'état*. On the one hand, everything appears to have changed, yet, on the other, states are still able to adapt to ensure that their interests endure.

NOTES

1. This chapter is an updated version of Evan H. Potter, "Entre démocratie et diplomatie publique: Où se trouve la politique étrangère?" in Charlie Mballa and Nelson Michaud (eds.), *Nouvelle politique étrangère*. Québec: Presses de l'Université du Québec, 2016, pp. 153–175.
2. Evan H. Potter, *Cyberdiplomacy: Managing Foreign Policy in the Twenty-First Century*. McGill-Queen's University Press, 2002.
3. Jan Melissen, "Beyond the New Public Diplomacy." *Clingendael Paper*, 3(2), 2011.
4. Clay Shirky, "The Political Power of Social Media: Technology, the Public Sphere, and Political Change." *Foreign Affairs*, January/February 2011.
5. The "Third Pillar" referred to the cultural component of Canada's foreign policy in the 1995 parliamentary review of Canadian foreign policy. See *Canada in the World*.
6. Eytan Gilboa, "Searching for a Theory of Public Diplomacy." *The ANNALS of the American Academy of Political and Social Science, 616*(1), 2008, 55–77.
7. Joseph S. Nye, *The Future of Power*. New York: Basic Books, 2001.
8. B. H. Signitzer and T. Coombs, "Public Relations and Public Diplomacy: Conceptual Convergence." *Public Relations Review, 18*(2), 1992, 137–147; J. L'Etang, "Public Relations as Diplomacy," in J. L'Etang and M. Pieczka (eds.), *Critical Perspectives in Public Relation*. London: International Thomson Business Press, 1996.

9. Nicholas J. Cull, *The Decline and Fall of the United States Information Agency: American Public Diplomacy, 1989–2001*. New York: Palgrave, 2012.

10. Bruce Gregory, "American Public Diplomacy: Enduring Characteristics, Elusive Transformations." *The Hague Journal of Diplomacy*, 6(3), 2010.

11. Geoffrey R. Wiseman, "Polylateralism: Diplomacy's Third Dimension." *Public Diplomacy Magazine*, 4, 2010, 24–39.

12. Simon Anholt, *Competitive Identity: The New Brand Management for Nations, Cities and Regions*. Basingstoke: Palgrave Macmillan, 2007. See also the journal, *Place Branding and Public Diplomacy*.

13. For a primer on strategic communication from an American perspective. Christopher Paul, *Strategic Communication: Origins, Concepts, and Current Debates*. Santa Barbara, CA: Praeger, 2011.

14. Evan H. Potter, *Branding Canada: Projecting Canada's Soft Power Through Public Diplomacy*. Montreal: McGill-Queen's University Press, 2009.

15. Kathy R. Fitzpatrick, *The Future of U.S. Public Diplomacy: An Uncertain Fate*. Boston: Leiden, 2010.

16. Philip Seib, *The Future of #Diplomacy*. Cambridge: Polity Press, 2016, p. 67.

17. J. Bátora, "Public Diplomacy Between Home and Abroad: Norway and Canada." *The Hague Journal of Diplomacy*, 1(1), 2006, 78–79.

18. Potter, 2009, pp. 39–43.

19. Peggy Noonan, "Show the Proof, Mr. President." *Wall Street Journal*, May 6, 2011.

20. Jan Melissen, "Public Diplomacy," in Pauline Kerr and Geoffrey Wiseman (eds.), *Diplomacy in a Globalizing World*. Oxford: Oxford University Press, 2012, p. 198.

21. Melissen, "Public Diplomacy," p. 198.

22. Melissen, "Public Diplomacy," p. 199.

23. Peter Van Ham, *Social Power in International Politics*. New York: Routledge, 2010, p. 8.

24. Nicholas J. Cull, "Wikileaks, Public Diplomacy 2.0 and the State of Digital Public Diplomacy." *Place Branding and Public Diplomacy*, 7(1), 2011; Evan H. Potter (2008). "Web 2.0 and the New Public Diplomacy: Impact and Opportunities," in *Engagement: Public Diplomacy in a Globalized World*. Foreign and Commonwealth Office, UK.

25. The term "information edge" was coined by Joseph S. Nye Jr. and William A. Owens. "America's Information Edge: The Nature of Power," *Foreign Affairs*, March/April, 1996.

26. Charles Causey and Philip N. Howard, "Delivering Digital Diplomacy: Information Technologies and the Changing Business of Diplomacy," in Amelia Arsenault, Rhonda Zaharna, and Ali Fisher (eds.), *Options for*

Influence in Global Politics. New York, NY: Routledge, 2013, p. 2 of typescript made available to the author.

27. Evgeny Morozov, The Future of "Public Diplomacy 2.0", June 9, 2009. http://neteffect.foreignpolicy.com/posts/2009/06/09/the_fut ure_of_public_diplomacy_20.

28. Apart from their utility for school projects, I have never met anyone who relied on an embassy website to become familiar with the policies of that country.

29. Evan H. Potter, "Web 2.0 and the New Public Diplomacy: Impact and Opportunities," *Engagement: Public Diplomacy in a Globalised World.* London: Foreign & Commonwealth Audience, July 2008, p. 121. See also my earlier work on Web 1.0 diplomacy, Evan H. Potter, *Cyberdiplomacy: Foreign Policy in the 21st Century.* Montreal and Kingston: McGill-Queen's University Press, 2002.

30. The Swedish Institute launched the Second House of Sweden, a virtual recreation of its Washington, DC embassy, into *Second Life* in 2007 to considerable media fanfare. As the first country to create such a virtual embassy, Sweden benefited from being the "first in" and it was calculated that the publicity relating to this presence in a virtual world was worth the equivalent of US$750,000 in advertising space. James Pamment, *Place Branding and Public Diplomacy,* 7(2), 132–133.

31. It was widely reported that, in the light of her interest in how the Obama campaign had used social media during the 2008 presidential campaign, Secretary of State Hilary Clinton mandated the Department of State to use social media in innovative ways, including to engage successor generations in regions of the world where there was concern about the impact of radicalization.

32. In 2003, DFAIT managed a citizens' dialogue on Canada's foreign policy. A major innovation was that this "Dialogue on Foreign Policy" was conducted in town halls as well as on a dedicated online platform.

33. Potter, *Engagement: Public Diplomacy in a Globalised,* pp. 125–128. A particularly delicate issue concerns the fact that diplomats—as civil servants—are using the same social media channels for their personal communication as well as career development within their professional communities of interest, giving rise to potential conflicts of interest if their online conversations stray into areas of government policy.

34. The author introduced social media platforms to the Canadian embassy in Austria as a result of spending part of his sabbatical at the embassy in 2010.

35. See statistics for social media use in Austria at http://socialmediaradar.at/facebook.php.

36. This is not to say that other Canadian missions were not experimenting with social media. The difference was that, in the absence of an official

policy, they were not yet in a position to use their official homepages to promote social media content.

37. Fyfe and Crookall divide Canada's public sector employees into three camps on social media issues: "...zealots, who love social media for the experience and opportunity they offer; the collaborators, who see the tools as helping them do their jobs better; and the resisters, who are concerned about the risks associated with government use." See Toby Fyfe and Paul Crookall, *Social Media and Public Policy Dilemmas*. Institute of Public Administration of Canada, 2010, p. 3.

38. Digital Affairs surveyed the websites of a sample of 15 foreign embassy websites and found that, for example, while the UK, United States, Germany, Dutch, Icelandic, and the Scandinavian embassies all had Facebook pages, the Australian, Belgian, Irish, Mexican, New Zealand, Russian, South African, and Spanish embassies did not. The author was provided with a copy of this report.

39. Citizenship and Immigration Canada, "Canada's Immigration Minister Says Doors Are Open to Chinese to Come to Canada," *News Release*, September 15, 2010.

40. Mark McDowell, Personal communication with the author.

41. Mark McKinnon, "Canada's Ambassador to China Does a Little Drive-by Diplomacy," *The Globe and Mail*, January 31, 2012.

42. This was conveyed to the author by the Canadian official who conceptualized the "direct diplomacy" effort. Personal interview, 2012.

43. If there was any doubt about the tenor of Canada's approach to Iran, it was dispelled by then Foreign Affairs Minister John Baird's speech on May 10, 2013, at the Global Dialogue on the Future of Iran conference. "...And so, I say to the Supreme Leader: rather than waste your precious resources trying to scramble this video feed...or trying to shut down the people's websites...or trying to subject your people to the oppressive veil of tyranny...open up. Listen to the Iranian people. Roll back the apparatus of fear. Allow dissenting voices. Embrace freedom of expression. Expand the pursuit of knowledge. Unshackle the people. End your tyranny. Imagine. Imagine an Iran with a political culture based on inclusiveness and freedom. Imagine an Iran where people are free to advocate a point of view and have the courage to test them against opposing views. Imagine an Iran that affords the strongest protections for freedom of expression, freedom of conscience, freedom of assembly, the rule of law. Imagine an Iran that has rigorous checks and balances against abuse of power and corruption...where the rules are the same for every person. Imagine an Iran where government protects people's lives...where government does not silence, imprison and murder ethnic, religious and cultural minorities for their beliefs."

44. Kim Mackrael, "Looking for a Way to Talk to Iran, Ottawa Backs' Direct Diplomacy," *Globe and Mail*, January 6, 2015.
45. Kim Mackrael, "Looking for a Way to Talk to Iran, Ottawa Backs' Direct Diplomacy," *Globe and Mail*, January 6, 2015.
46. This was demonstrated in 2011 during the crisis in Syria when the United States closed its embassy in Damascus, but the American ambassador, Robert Ford, was able to continue to reach out to Syrians through social media.
47. This observation was made at a seminar on Canada's public diplomacy organized by Global Affairs Canada in April 2016. The author was the rapporteur at the conference.
48. The Trudeau government made all the prime minister's mandate letters to his Cabinet Ministers public.
49. Van Noort, p. 19.

CHAPTER 5

Bridging the 49th Parallel: A Case Study in Art as Cultural Diplomacy

Sarah E. K. Smith

On the evening of 20 March 1981, a new art gallery named 49th Parallel: Centre for Contemporary Canadian Art held its first opening at 420 West Broadway Street, New York. Its inaugural exhibition *Plus Tard and Other Works* comprised sculpture and photography by internationally established Canadian artist Michael Snow. Amongst the most prominent works in the show was *Plus Tard* (1977), a series of twenty-five colour photographs shot in the National Gallery of Canada, featuring paintings by Tom Thomson and the Group of Seven of canonical wilderness images associated with Canadian nationalism.[1] Snow's photographs blurred and distorted the paintings, thus commenting on the passing of time, each a testament to the artist's movements through the gallery.[2]

From the outset, 49th Parallel, which featured innovative and experimental art, including video, installation, and performance, appeared to fit naturally within its lower Manhattan neighbourhood. During this period, SoHo was a key site of the international art scene and home to numerous

S. E. K. Smith (✉)
Communication and Media Studies, Carleton University, Ottawa, ON, Canada
e-mail: sarahek.smith@carleton.ca

© The Author(s) 2021
N. J. Cull and M. K. Hawes (eds.), *Canada's Public Diplomacy*,
Palgrave Macmillan Series in Global Public Diplomacy,
https://doi.org/10.1007/978-3-319-62015-2_5

private galleries and artist-run spaces. The Canadian press identified 420 West Broadway as one of the "most heavily trafficked gallery buildings in the heart of New York's art world."[3] 49th Parallel shared this prestigious address with several large galleries, including renowned tastemakers Sonnabend and Leo Castelli.[4] The presence of Canadian government representatives and New York politicians at 49th Parallel's opening event, however, indicated something unusual in the nature of this institution. Amongst prominent artists, curators, and dealers from Canada and the US, guests included Mark MacGuigan, Canadian secretary of state for External Affairs, Ken Taylor, Canadian consul general in New York, and New York Mayor Ed Koch.[5] While ostensibly a new commercial gallery, 49th Parallel was in fact a special "pilot project" and "experiment" of the Canadian government's Department of External Affairs (now Global Affairs Canada).[6]

The initiative was the result of the government of Canada's significant financial investment in creating a showcase for Canadian visual artists abroad. In part, the aim of 49th Parallel was to teach Americans about Canada. Guy Plamondon, consul for cultural affairs at the Canadian Consulate General in New York, conceived the gallery and argued for the institution as an educational tool and marker of cultural parity. "Americans don't know us as well as we know them," he explained to the press. "It's important to show that we have people who compare easily with what we see here [in the US]."[7] Yet, Canadian government officials who sought to seamlessly integrate 49th Parallel into its surroundings also downplayed the national orientation of the gallery—a defining feature of the institution. 49th Parallel had a long and rich history of solo and group exhibitions during its operations over more than a decade until the institution closed on 30 June 1992. Throughout that time, the gallery occupied an uneasy and, at times, controversial space in the political and arts spheres. In this chapter, I examine 49th Parallel's trajectory, revealing how the gallery offered a new model of cultural exchange.

I begin by contextualizing 49th Parallel within Canadian cultural diplomacy programmes of the period, before examining three specific moments in the gallery's administration: (1) the direction of External Affairs, (2) increased professionalization, and (3) a private-public partnership. 49th Parallel's unique approach and structure, and the reactions it provoked from artists, curators, and politicians, not only reveal the ebbs and flows of Canada-US relations during a significant era of change, but also provide insights into the public discourse surrounding cultural diplomacy in North America in the late twentieth century. These debates centred on the efficacy of contemporary art to promote the state and the models that were employed to do so, pulling the gallery in different directions as it attempted to address various constituencies. In concluding my assessment of the gallery, I speak about the changes currently underway in Canada's public diplomacy and argue that cultural diplomacy has much to offer engaged, global communities as a means of bridging real and perceived borders.

EXHIBITING DIPLOMACY: CANADIAN ART ABROAD

The use of culture to convey values, beliefs, and ideologies on behalf of individuals and communities is not new, and there is a long history of visual art being used to negotiate a variety of relationships. Visual art is well-suited to such a role, given the Western perception of culture as a universal conduit across differences of language, religion, and ethnicity. Thus, control of cultural goods and their circulation, which often lies in the hands of the state, becomes very important as a means to build relationships between communities. "If the artworks are of universal significance, speaking across cultural boundaries," Judith Huggins Balfe argues, "so is their discerning patron or owner."[8] This relationship is predicated on mutually reinforcing assumptions of value—the value of the objects, which are accorded cultural and national importance, and the prestige and power of the institutions and communities associated with the display of the works.

Diplomacy via cultural envoys, known as cultural diplomacy, is conventionally understood as a means of "soft power," a resource marshalled to attract support and obtain acquiescence, in contrast to the "hard power" exerted through military and economic means.[9] Broadly defined, cultural diplomacy is a term that encompasses a range of activities and actors. As Nicholas J. Cull points out, such initiatives are united by their attention to the international environment and by their mobilization of material and immaterial cultural goods. Cultural diplomacy, as Cull defines it, is, "an actor's attempt to manage the international environment through making its cultural resources and achievements known overseas and/or facilitating cultural transmission abroad."[10] Cultural diplomacy functions by providing narratives and images that change perceptions, shift understandings, and convey new information. As Patricia M. Goff explains:

Cultural diplomacy can tell another story about a country (or province or state or regional grouping). This may be a story that differs from what official policy would imply. It may be a story that counters what opponents are recounting. In doing so, cultural diplomacy can offset negative, stereotypical or overly simplistic impressions arising from policy choices or hostile portrayals. It may also fill a void where no stories of any kind exist.[11]

Seeking to create a foothold for Canadian cultural production in New York's competitive market, 49th Parallel told a new story about Canada that emphasized the nation's innovation and cultural parity with the US. The gallery employed contemporary art to this end, directing its efforts at a specific, elite New York cultural audience. Yet, scholarship on cultural diplomacy has largely focused on US and Soviet initiatives that flourished during the Cold War, including specific studies of music, dance, and international exhibitions.[12] This emphasis has not gone unchallenged.[13] Jessica C. E. Gienow-Hecht argues that scholars' focus on US and Soviet cultural diplomacy has led to a lack of studies addressing non-state actors and cultural diplomacy initiatives in other periods.[14] Attention to Cold War dynamics has also significantly overshadowed examinations of more nuanced cultural diplomacy programmes initiated by middle powers such as Canada, including 49th Parallel.[15]

49th Parallel was part of External Affairs' larger cultural diplomacy efforts in the second half of the twentieth century. The department's interest in cultural programming emerged, according to Andrew Fenton Cooper, in response to initiatives by the Quebec government to engage in cultural promotion abroad in the 1960s.[16] External Affairs officially took on the role of arts promoter in 1965, initially focusing on international tours of Canadian performing arts. By the 1980s, the public diplomacy activities of External Affairs were considerably more complex. Writing about the promotion of Canadian visual art abroad in 1985, Joyce Wayne explained:

Today, arts promotion is the title of one of seven divisions – including cultural policy, academic relations, external information, domestic information and the historical and international expositions divisions – that all come under the supervision of Richard Tait, director general of the Cultural and Public Information Bureau, one of three bureaus answering to the assistant deputy minister, Social Affairs and Programs Branch.[17]

Within these public diplomacy activities, 49th Parallel was, in some respects, similar to the cultural centres operated by External Affairs—a model often employed by Canadian government representatives to explain and contextualize the gallery.

In this period, Canadian cultural centres existed only in Europe, specifically Paris, London, and Brussels.[18] These centres were closely connected to Canadian diplomatic outposts in these cities. As such, they were not viewed as part of the local artistic community. They offered comprehensive arts programming, of which visual art was one component. Their offerings in this field represented the broadest possible range of Canadian art through equal attention paid to different styles and geographic regions. Writing about the centres in 1981, Georges Bogardi characterized them as "very much aware of their official character."[19] Canada's art community, however, dismissed visual art programming at these cultural centres as "pedestrian offerings."[20] This was due, in part, to the fact that professionals with expertise in the field did not coordinate the selections.

External Affairs also engaged in visual art through its support of discrete exhibitions staged by partners, including the National Gallery of Canada. In the 1980s, one of the most prominent exhibitions involving contemporary art that External Affairs supported was *OKanada*, presented at the Akademie der Kunste in West Berlin in 1982–1983. The Canada Council, and to a lesser extent, the German government, also contributed to this rich programme of events encompassing historical and contemporary art, architecture, film, and literature. Its scope and presence were clear in its promotion as the "largest exhibition of Canadian culture assembled outside our borders."[21] Despite the ambition of the programme, *OKanada* was deemed unsuccessful due to dismal attendance and a lack of positive response from German art critics.[22]

Within this context, 49th Parallel offered a different way for External Affairs to promote Canada and its cultural accomplishments, while connecting with an internationally recognized art scene. The gallery stood out—then and now—as a significant investment in contemporary art, a field rarely connected to national sentiment and state promotion projects. In the following sections, I trace the evolving administration of the gallery, drawing on materials in the 49th Parallel Fond held by the National Gallery of Canada Archives. This documentation reveals that 49th Parallel was pulled in too many directions and never really gained a clear sense of itself. The gallery also grappled with the difficulties of an arts institution to live up to the kinds of metrics imposed by bureaucracies. These causes of failure must be surmounted if new cultural diplomacy efforts are to succeed in the future. In the face of such obstacles, however, 49th Parallel responded with remarkable flexibility and innovation, adjusting its structure and programming. The history of the gallery demonstrates the gains 49th Parallel made within the arts community of New York, while also revealing the myriad challenges External Affairs grappled with in supporting the gallery.

A New Model to Showcase Canada (1981–1984)

The idea to employ contemporary art to promote Canada abroad came from Guy Plamondon, consul for Cultural Affairs at the Canadian Consulate General in New York.[23] An employee of External Affairs from 1965, Plamondon's background was in law, though he was greatly interested in contemporary art. Early in his career at External Affairs he participated in a range of cultural programmes, notably, the creation of the cultural affairs division in 1966 and the establishment of Canada's cultural centre in Paris, which opened in 1970.[24] In a document produced for the consulate in 1978, Plamondon presented a detailed proposal for an ambitious multi-purpose arts space to be run by External Affairs.[25] He suggested the purchase of an entire building in SoHo to house a Canadian art centre, which would comprise living quarters, artist studios, an auditorium, library, bookstore, professional art gallery, and potentially a second smaller gallery space for young artists. Within the building, he proposed a programme of high-quality Canadian visual art, including resident artists, contemporary art shows, and touring exhibitions from regional museums and private galleries in Canada.

Plamondon's report claimed an initial positive response to this idea, noting "tremendous interest" from cultural communities and other stakeholders in Canada and New York.[26] The undisputed expense of this large cultural project was politically justified, Plamondon argued, because "Canada would have a very visible presence in this very powerful megalopolis," and be "the centre of much of what is happening on the international scene in matters of business, finance, marketing, culture – in summary, in every conceivable field."[27] Plamondon identified Canadian art as the best way to connect with these disparate communities in New York, while also serving to raise Canada's profile abroad.

Of course, business and finance were of particular interest to the Canadian government. Plamondon made clear that since 1974, the US had been a "priority target."[28] He also noted Canadians and Americans' lack of knowledge about each other, citing the fact that Canadians and Canadian products were often mistaken as American and hinting that increased cultural distinction was important.[29] (Here, his comments reflect Canadian fears of US cultural imperialism in the 1980s and 1990s.) Plamondon also emphasized the need for Canadian culture to access larger markets in the US in order to grow. His proposed "Canadian Art Centre," which would inform the mandate of 49th Parallel, would help to educate Americans in a positive manner about Canadian art, and, by proxy, Canada, thus presenting a solution to these various issues.

After Plamondon's championing of the gallery for several years, External Affairs approved the proposal in November 1980, and in February 1981, the secretary of state for External Affairs, Dr Mark MacGuigan, announced a pilot project under the name 49th Parallel: Centre for Contemporary Canadian Art / 49e Parallèle: Centre d'art Canadien contemporain.[30] The goal of the initiative was to create a permanent outpost in the vibrant artistic neighbourhood of SoHo—an experimental, cutting-edge gallery exclusively showcasing contemporary Canadian art. Subsequent announcements by the minister picked up on Plamondon's 1978 proposal, noting that the gallery "reflected the Canadian government's view that New York is clearly the visual arts capital of the world, and is the place where the vitality, range, and proliferation of new and experimental Canadian artistic expression should be showcased."[31] Plamondon was appointed the first director of 49th Parallel, a duty he carried out in addition to his other responsibilities at the consulate.

Analysis of the records of the gallery from 1981 to 1992 reveals that 49th Parallel underwent three distinct administrative periods, coinciding with the tenure of its three directors: Plamondon (1981–1984), France Morin (1984–1989), and Glen Cumming (1989–1992). During the first two periods, the leadership of Plamondon and Morin strongly shaped the direction of the gallery. The same was true to a lesser extent during the third period under Cumming, for the structural reasons detailed below.

The first administrative phase of the gallery witnessed the establishment of 49th Parallel and its direct administration by the Canadian government (under the leadership of then-Prime Minister, Pierre Trudeau). During this period, the gallery was run by employees of the Canadian Consulate

General in New York and funded entirely through External Affairs. Robert Handforth, a cultural affairs officer who had been at the Canadian Consulate General since 1980, assisted Plamondon, and, like him, also continued to work at the consulate while running the gallery. Handforth brought great expertise in Canadian art and theatre. Prior to joining External Affairs, he held positions at the Canada Council and Stratford Festival. He also had significant knowledge of Canada's burgeoning contemporary art scene as a co-founder and publications manager at Art Metropole, a key institution established in 1974 in Toronto by the Canadian art group General Idea. Additionally, Handforth had served as director of A Space, a prominent gallery in Toronto.[32]

Plans for 49th Parallel came together quickly—by 6 February 1981, six weeks before the opening of *Plus Tard and Other Works*, External Affairs had secured a lease to a gallery on the fourth floor of 420 West Broadway.[33] This SoHo location was described in the press as a "competitive" and "critical art forum" that provided access to premier commercial galleries engaged in avant-garde art.[34] Handforth explained that with this location, "we have purchased a great deal of good will and visibility for our artists for a very reasonable amount of money."[35] Living up to its moniker as the "cultural capital of the USA," the SoHo neighbourhood included the aforementioned Leo Castelli and Sonnabend galleries, as well as André Emmerich, John Weber Galleries, Sperone Westwater Fisher Inc., Nancy Hoffman Gallery, Paula Cooper Gallery, Sculpture Now Inc., The Drawing Center, Max Hutchinson, O. K. Harris, Heiner-Friedrich, Inc., and Holly Solomon Gallery.[36]

Plamondon's interest in works that "reflect[ed] the newest, freshest and most contemporary Canadian art forms" was a perfect fit for SoHo. 49th Parallel's programming would include works in media such as installation, video, photography, and performance. A consulate statement reinforced this approach, noting the gallery will present, "contemporary and experimental visual arts and will include aspects of the literary and performing arts, as well as independent film and video, *in all of these stressing the new and experimental.*"[37] Furthermore, "We'll try to show the kind of art that New Yorkers naturally expect to see in Soho," Plamondon explained.[38] The commercial appearance of 49th Parallel was, however, somewhat misleading, because 49th Parallel was legally unable to sell the work it displayed on its premises.[39] 49th Parallel's lease was secured by the consulate, which conferred tax-exempt status on the gallery. Sales of exhibited artworks were prohibited because these trans-actions would jeopardize this arrangement.[40] While the gallery gave the impression of a commercial space, visitors interested in acquiring a work were referred to the appropriate art dealer in Canada. In the case of a sale, 49th Parallel's policy was a suggested 20% donation to the gallery in lieu of the traditional 50% commission taken by commercial galleries.

The gallery's affiliation with the government of Canada was similarly complicated. 49th Parallel was conceived to promote Canada abroad, nevertheless, the gallery "consciously tr(ied) to avoid any kind of 'insti-tutionalized feeling,' both out of respect for their neighbours, and out of sensitivity for the kind of high quality Canadian work they want[ed] to introduce to the New York public."[41] In this statement, Plamondon and Handforth made clear the crux of 49th Parallel's model of cultural diplomacy in which nationalism was a covert, but simultaneously driving force. The art was intended to speak for itself as an exemplar of contem-porary Canadian practice, holding its own in the international art sphere while concurrently promoting the Canadian state. The masked role of the Canadian government is evident in debates over the gallery's name. 49th Parallel / 49ᵉ Parallèle was ultimately selected because this refer-ence to the latitude of a portion of the Canada-US border did not overtly signal "Canada."[42] A memorandum from 1981 notes that the name indicated "low-key identification, memorability and suggestion of metaphor."[43] The gallery's ambiguous approach to national orientation would dog discussions about the efficacy of the gallery's promotion of Canada throughout its tenure.

Despite a proclaimed emphasis on the novel and experimental, 49th Parallel's opening exhibition featured work that did not live up to these aims. The gallery's entrance into the New York scene came via a show by Michael Snow, an artist whose reputation was already very well established both within and outside of Canada. In fact, he was known in New York for having lived there during the 1960s, when he produced some of his most iconic works, including the experimental film *Wavelength* (1966–1967). His reputation was cemented in key exhibitions in the 1970s, including when he showed at the Venice Biennale as the first solo artist to represent Canada. In short, Snow could hardly be considered an edgy choice at the time of 49th Parallel's launch in 1981. Before the show even opened, the director of the National Gallery of Canada (who loaned work to the exhi-bition) chided Plamondon: "While we are supportive of the principle of encouraging the exhibition of works by Canadian artists outside Canada, it has been our understanding that as a centre for contemporary art, the Consulate's Gallery would *primarily be exhibiting current work*. We are concerned that in the future the Gallery's collections not be viewed as a standard source for exhibitions."[44] Artist Leslie Reid raised similar criticisms in the context of a hearing on Canadian culture when she decried 49th Parallel's programming just one month after the gallery opened as "history on display."[45]

Certainly, Snow's work did not entirely support Plamondon's rhetoric.[46] *Plus Tard* (1977) was the most recent work in the exhibition, produced four years prior. The other works in the show were produced during Snow's time in New York, including the photograph *Atlantic* (1967), and sculptures *Scope* (1967) and *Blind* (1968). Given the accelerated timeline of the gallery's opening, Snow's works had to be assembled quickly based on availability. It was significant, however, that, given a quasi-commercial art context that emphasized new production, the works had been exhibited before. Moreover, none of the works were available for sale.[47] While I hesitate to place too much emphasis on the first exhibition, this show was important because it garnered wide attention in Canada and in New York. Subsequent exhibitions, such as that of art collective General Idea later in 1981, came closer to fulfilling the gallery profile Plamondon espoused.

It is important to note that 49th Parallel drew on Canada's network of artist-run centres for its programming (the so-called parallel gallery system), connecting recently established alternative spaces with new audiences. In the absence of a developed commercial system, parallel galleries emerged across Canada in the late 1960s and 1970s. Prominent examples include A Space in Toronto (one of the earliest established parallel galleries) and the Western Front in Vancouver. Supported by the Canada Council, these institutions contributed significantly to the development of the Canadian art scene and provided key support for artists working in emerging media, including video, performance, and conceptual art. 49th Parallel was able to harvest the first decade of the parallel gallery system, and the works it showed in its early years reflected the production of these key nodes in the Canadian cultural landscape.[48]

Thus, the first few years of 49th Parallel's operations brought mixed success. Initially, the gallery achieved press coverage in key US contemporary art magazines, including *Art in America* and *Artforum*. This coverage, however, died down after the gallery's opening, reflecting the absence of ties between 49th Parallel and the New York art scene. In addition, several key elements of the gallery came under criticism from Canadian artists and gallerists, including its lack of commercial viability, despite a mandate to increase sales of contemporary Canadian art in the US. Arts professionals in Canada did not hesitate to voice their concerns. Canadian dealers considered the gallery a disincentive to open branches in New York. Regina artist David Thauberger, whose work was shown at 49th Parallel in its first year, commented that the gallery was "confused," acting simultaneously as "trade exhibit, museum, [and] commercial gallery."[49] Additionally, the gallery's ambiguous relationship with the Canadian government was cause for criticism. Some wondered if the state's use of Canadian artists was appropriate, and others, whether the Canadian origins of the gallery were too concealed. The gallery's nationalistic purpose, its desire to avoid overt branding, and its interest in being seen as a key player in the arts scene, together set up a conflicting mandate and a framework that made touting the "Canadianness" of the gallery and the works it showed difficult.

After two years of operations, Plamondon stepped down from his role as director to take on other duties within External Affairs. At this time, the department implemented several key changes in the gallery's administration, demonstrating flexibility and responsiveness. First was the creation of a seven-member advisory committee, announced in March 1983.[50] The committee, as reported in *artmagazine*, represented the regions of Canada.[51] Second, External Affairs recognized the difficulties inherent in having a director who simultaneously managed a full role at the consulate. The next director would be devoted solely to the gallery.

Ultimately, the first administrative phase of 49th Parallel revealed mixed success. While the gallery fielded some criticism from the Canadian arts community, its innovative approach also generated a great deal of interest from other constituencies, as demonstrated by press coverage of its activities. It appeared that Plamondon's—and by extension the Canadian government's—calculation that contemporary art could best represent Canada as an innovative nation and attract the attention that Canadian cultural centres in other international cities seemed unable to generate, had paid off. A further defining element of this period was the full commitment of External Affairs to the gallery, which would acquire other government and private partners as the institution developed.

BECOMING PROFESSIONAL (1984–1989)

49th Parallel gained a new orientation and outlook with the appointment of France Morin as director in 1984. Morin's tenure was characterized by an increasing professionalization and a deepening of the gallery's ties to the SoHo art scene, as well as to arts communities in Canada. This shift marked a further separation of the gallery from the consulate, though External Affairs continued to oversee the gallery and provide substantial budgetary support. Well versed in contemporary art, Morin was a curator from Quebec (previously affiliated with Vehicule gallery), who, with Chantal Pontbriand, had founded the esteemed arts periodical *Parachute*. Furthermore, Morin's knowledge of French and of Quebec's contemporary art scene allowed 49th Parallel to address criticisms that it did not fully represent Canadian art.[52] The institution was a prominent international post and Morin's appointment could also be considered a means to affirm the gallery's commitment to Quebec and francophone communities.[53]

Morin brought a strong vision to 49th Parallel's programming. Her first exhibition featured photographer Robin Collyer (b. 1949). Another early show, *Canada/New York*, sought to pointedly comment on Canada within a New York context by featuring Canadian artists living in New York.[54] Morin went on to undertake ambitious collaborative projects with other New York commercial galleries, for example, *Icarus: The Vision of Angels*, a 1986 show that addressed flight and contemporary art, which was lauded in *Artforum*. Created with Ronald Feldman of Ronald Feldman Fine Arts, this thematic exhibition brought together Canadian and US artists alongside historical icons associated with flight from Leonardo da Vinci to Alexander Graham Bell—a move away from the national justification that had appeared to underwrite programming during the gallery's first period. Canadian gallerist René Blouin under-scored the shift at 49th Parallel under Morin's direction, identifying her expertise in contemporary art as essential to the gallery's success. "France Morin is not a bureaucrat," he explained, "she doesn't work from nine to five and attend cocktail parties. She takes risks and fights for the artist she exhibits."[55] Morin's appointment provided a clear indication that the mandate of the gallery was now to seriously engage within the sophisticated New York scene and execute innovative programming.[56]

Only one year into her tenure, however, 49th Parallel experienced its most significant setback. In March 1985, a confidential report titled

Canadian Cultural Centres Abroad was leaked to the press. It drew 49th Parallel into the public eye in Canada and cast it in a negative light. The report was commissioned by External Affairs and conducted by the Canadian consulting firm Woods Gordon. Referred to as the Woods Gordon report, this document assessed Canadian cultural centres in Paris, London, Brussels, and New York. In strong language, the report decried 49th Parallel, noting the gallery's lack of impact. It also singled out its covert operation as a weakness of the institution. The report advised the closure of 49th Parallel, as well as the Canadian cultural centre in Brussels.[57] As a debate over the gallery's future played out in the press, supporters countered that the report was superficial, drawing on limited and inappropriate sources. No dealers, museum directors, art consultants, or critics were interviewed, only bureaucrats and two Toronto-based artists. By this point, 49th Parallel had exhibited work by approximately two hundred artists, and under Morin had secured corporate sponsorship from Air Canada and ongoing collaborations with other commercial galleries in New York. Supporters further mentioned that other countries, including Australia and New Zealand, were interested in 49th Parallel as a model for cultural diplomacy.

The debate thus reveals attitudes towards cultural diplomacy in the period, with key figures voicing their support for 49th Parallel. In the New York art scene, several famed American cultural figures backed the gallery, including American painter Leon Golub, New Museum founder and art historian Marcia Tucker, and art historian and critic Donald Kuspit. In Kuspit's words: "[49th Parallel] is an important representative of Canada, diplomatically and intellectually as well as specifically artistically."[58] Tucker went further in her praise, noting that the gallery "fosters a valuable exchange between American and Canadian artists, which results in increased dialogue, joint exhibition and publication projects, and mutual respect."[59] German artist and New Yorker Hans Haake made a clear case for the gallery's achievements, stating: "Canadian art was practically unknown outside of Canada before the establishment of the 49th Parallel."[60] The support of such high-profile individuals provided a significant defence of the gallery and also spoke, to a large degree, to the inroads Morin had made within New York's art scene.

Much of the response, however, was also negative and no consensus about the work of the gallery and its objectives could be reached in the public realm. In the aftermath of the report, it was evident that 49th Parallel enjoyed strong support from arts communities on both sides of the border. It was not, however, clear that the gallery had much backing outside of artists, curators, dealers, and cultural critics. The debate also raised key questions about Canadian cultural diplomacy initiatives: What was worthy of government spending? What could art do to promote the state? And, how exactly could Canadians know if such programmes were working? In this period, the consulate in New York affirmed the gallery's purpose, stating: "any nation that wants to be taken seriously in financial and diplomatic circles must have a certified cultural presence."[61] In the lead up to the 1989 Free Trade Agreement between Canada and the US trade provided the key reason for External Affairs' support of 49th Parallel.[62] The challenge for bureaucrats was how to substantiate the connection between the gallery and increased trade.[63]

Here, it is worth noting that the 1980s were a significant period for Canada's "special relationship" with the US. Under the leadership of Brian Mulroney, elected prime minister in September 1984, the Canadian government pursued free trade agreements to increase the integration of the US and Canadian economies. A particularly notable moment in Canada-US relations was the Shamrock Summit of March 1985, which brought together Mulroney and US President Ronald Reagan. The meeting is noted for the warm relationship between Mulroney and Reagan, exemplified by their televised rendition—with their spouses—of the song "When Irish Eyes Are Smiling."[64] Increased economic integration of Canada and the US, however, raised anxieties among many Canadians, especially in the cultural sphere, about American cultural imperialism. Such concerns were further complicated by the economic recession of the early 1980s. In a political climate charged with cost-cutting, art was seen as a frill.[65]

The Woods Gordon report threw 49th Parallel's future into uncertainty for many months, and ultimately, cast a large shadow over its remaining years of operations. Almost immediately following its release, the gallery needed to renew its lease, which prompted further discussion about External Affairs' ongoing support and 49th Parallel's expense. In the months that followed, 49th Parallel was significantly restructured. It received recognition from the Canada Council and, in 1986, became a non-profit corporation with a board of directors.[66] But discussion of the gallery's direction continued. By the end of this period, it had significantly diversified its funding structure. External Affairs no longer solely funded the gallery, which now also drew programming support from the Canada Council and the federal communications department, while also seeking private backing.

A Private-Public Partnership (1989–1992)

Morin continued to lead the gallery until 1989. When she left, Glen Cumming assumed the directorship (beginning in November).[67] Like Morin, Cumming was well versed in contemporary art having previously served as director of the Art Gallery of Hamilton. This shift in leadership from Morin to Cumming was marked by the gallery's embrace of commercial aims, a change initiated in the mid-1980s under Morin's direction. Cumming's tenure marked the third administrative phase of the gallery, which lasted until its closure in 1992 and witnessed the most radical changes to the mandate and administration of 49th Parallel. Considered in relation to his predecessors, however, Cumming had the least impact on gallery programming due to structural changes that increased the roles of others in deciding what exhibitions were staged.

These structural changes were brought about by the gallery's three-year partnership with the Professional Art Dealers Association of Canada (PADAC). Initiated in 1989, this move placed greater emphasis on the commercial potential of the gallery. PADAC assumed administrative control of the gallery and, as a result, 49th Parallel rededicated itself to promoting commercially viable contemporary Canadian art in New York's competitive market. Nevertheless, the gallery continued to receive significant funding from External Affairs, which gave $400,000 of its $600,000 annual budget. The new administration sought to secure the remaining $200,000 from corporate funders.

The gallery, in effect, had become a private-public partnership to a large degree spearheaded by Olga Korper, a gallery owner in Toronto and President of PADAC in the 1980s. 49th Parallel's new assertive approach was considered a "major assault" on the New York market, and by implication, something that had been missing since its inception.[68] The gallery directed its efforts toward the placement of Canadian art in US exhibitions and collections.[69] In accordance with these goals, Korper noted that 49th Parallel would not borrow works, but instead feature art that in large part was for sale or available for exhibition at other galleries. In a bid to signify this change to visitors, "gallery" replaced "centre" in 49th Parallel's name in November 1989.[70] Addressing the arts community directly, Korper expanded on 49th Parallel's new approach in a letter to *C Magazine* in 1990. In it, she clarified the unique partnership between External Affairs and PADAC during the trial period and explained that dealers could apply for shows and benefit from cost sharing, while public galleries (including parallel galleries) could also provide works for display. Pushing back on criticism that a commercial focus would lead to poor quality exhibitions, she noted:

> The intent of the new priorities of the 49th Parallel is not to become a purely commercial venture which would compromise the quality of the exhibits, but to focus on placing the work in Public Galleries, private galleries, group exhibitions beyond our borders, collections of some significance, and lastly, to make the work overtly available to the general viewing public.[71]

This mandate, according to Korper, was not an extreme departure from 49th Parallel's previous activities. PADAC's role did, however, have a significant impact on the work of the gallery, namely in reducing the autonomy and vision exerted by its director.

Despite the new administration and mandate, within a year and a half, it was clear that the gallery was not financially viable. The poor economic climate that weakened the sales market did not help. The gallery also had difficulty building profiles for the artists it exhibited, artists largely unknown to US audiences. In part, this is because 49th Parallel deviated from the commercial gallery practice of programming a select roster of artists through repeat showings, instead, programming new artists in each exhibition. In 1991, Korper and Cumming publicly acknowledged that 49th Parallel would never be financially self-sustaining and noted difficulties in obtaining corporate support.[72] At this point, the gallery was besieged by rumours of its own demise, which were reported in a Canadian press eager to rehash the debates of the Woods Gordon report. Aware the gallery was in a precarious situation, Cumming told *The Globe and Mail* in April 1991 he was conscious of talk of the gallery's closure and expected, at the least, significant restructuring.

In the end, 49th Parallel did not respond to these challenges as it had in the past through creative changes to its structure and administration. Instead, the gallery ceased operations on the 30th of June 1992, when its lease at 420 Broadway expired.[73] For over a decade, 49th Parallel had successfully faced competing pressures to provide a new model for promoting Canada abroad. Its hybrid character—part cultural centre, part commercial gallery, part envoy for the Canadian government—rendered it unable to fully satisfy the different communities it served, thus drawing criticism from all sides.[74] Its most successful period came in the mid-1980s under the direction of France Morin when the gallery made significant strides toward connecting with arts communities in Canada and New York through quality programming. This goodwill was eroded by a subsequent shift toward the commercial value of art. Once attention focused on the economics of art, the failure of the works on display to sell in the US market was tied to the perceived inability of the centre to "sell" Canada's image abroad. This failure was compounded by structural factors, including the gallery's organization and a prohibition on direct sales, as well as market factors that made it difficult for the gallery to demonstrate its fulfilment of its new aims.

While 49th Parallel is often cast as a failure, the fact that this experiment in cultural diplomacy operated for over a decade is evidence of its success and of the potential of its hybrid structure. I suggest that the gallery should be studied for what it did do, rather than what it did not. That is, 49th Parallel ought to be upheld as proof that cultural diplomacy projects can productively mobilize a diverse range of actors. Moreover, 49th Parallel's work in New York reveals the possibilities for engagement when dominant modes of representation—in this case, of historical Canadian landscape art—are challenged. While the gallery's changing mandate demonstrates its response to criticism, its flexibility also allowed it to explore different approaches to cultural diplomacy. 49th Parallel was a space of possibility, and one that benefitted from its high public profile and desirable location.

The gallery's trajectory, moreover, tracks the ongoing privatization of culture in the late twentieth century, as well as changes to cultural centres more broadly.[75] Responsive to criticism, the institution showed flexibility and creativity in continually restructuring in an attempt to succeed. These changes, however, also meant that the gallery was perhaps not given adequate time to find its footing, or, that the demand to make a clear profit through the sale of artwork was always an impossible goal. The record shows that 49th Parallel was burdened by expectations, many of which could not be easily assessed and some that did not directly link to the work undertaken by gallery staff.[76] Here, Cynthia P. Schneider's comments regarding the efficacy of cultural diplomacy are relevant: "Cultural diplomacy cannot be effectively measured; it makes a qualitative, not quantitative, difference in relations between nations and peoples."[77] The issue of identifying appropriate metrics for success continue to plague many discussions of cultural diplomacy for practitioners and scholars.[78]

49th Parallel demonstrated that new and creative approaches to cultural diplomacy could capture the public's attention, for better or worse. Despite the gallery's closure, its duration attests to its success—initially, an ability to capture attention within New York's competitive art market and, later, an ability to attract the attention of commercial dealers within Canada, who saw the gallery as a foothold in the US market. Through administrative changes, the gallery was able to bridge the divide between diplomats and professional art communities in Canada. Moreover, it evidenced a sensitive approach to cultural diplomacy, a new means of connecting to foreign audiences outside of the traditional purview of Canada's cultural centres.

Implications for Public Diplomacy in Canada

A great deal has changed in the field of Canadian cultural diplomacy since 49th Parallel closed in 1992. While cultural diplomacy flourished under the Liberal leadership of Prime Minister Jean Chrétien (1993–2003), over the last decade, the climate has become less hospitable to cultural diplomacy initiatives. This change was especially marked under the Conservative government led by Prime Minister Stephan Harper (2006–2015), during which time state-sponsored cultural initiatives abroad were a low priority, as was culture writ large. This demotion became most apparent in the 2008 elimination of the government programmes Trade Routes, run by the Department of Canadian Heritage, and PromArt, a programme of the Department of Foreign Affairs and International Trade (DFAIT). With $9 million and $4.7 million budgets respectively, these programmes provided key means for the Canadian state to support the circulation of Canadian culture abroad, and arts groups across Canada loudly protested their elimination.[79] Further disinterest in public diplomacy is evidenced by the government's abolishment of the Understanding Canada programme in 2012.[80] This programme run by DFAIT since 1977 provided key funding for Canadian Studies programmes abroad.[81] Its cancellation was widely decried by academic communities.[82] Summarizing the developments in this period, Cull identified a shift in Canada's international engagement, noting a withdrawal from cultural work and a sole focus on international advocacy—an approach he characterized as a "dangerous strategy."[83]

The change of government in 2015 heralded a chance for a new approach to arts, culture, and Canada's role in the world. Prime Minister

Justin Trudeau's ministerial letters to the (now former) minister of Global Affairs Canada, Stéphane Dion, the minister of International Trade, François-Philippe Champagne, and the minister of Canadian Heritage, Mélanie Joly, reveal the Liberal government's renewed attention to public diplomacy.[84] The letter to Dion makes clear that public diplomacy, culture, and increasing ties across North America are issues of primary importance. Amongst several top priorities, the instructions to Minister Dion included: "Revitalize Canada's public diplomacy, stakeholder engagement, and cooperation with partners in Canada and abroad"; and, "Increase Canada's cultural interaction with the world." The letter specifically identifies PromArt and Trade Routes, noting they will be restored and updated with increased funding.[85] The letter to Champagne specifically tasks him to assist Joly with the restoration of PromArts and Trade Routes.[86] Joly's letter further outlines significant investment in culture and similarly tasks her to "Restore the Promart and Trade Routes International cultural promotion programs, update their design, and increase related funding."[87]

Furthermore, the National Gallery of Canada has once again become a platform for significant diplomatic events, including the North American Leaders' Summit in June 2016, attended by the President of Mexico, Enrique Peña Nieto, and the President of the United States, Barack Obama.[88] More broadly, the current government has signalled a return to global affairs, for instance, campaigning to secure a seat on the United Nations (UN) Security Council in 2021. In an address to the UN General Assembly in September of 2016, Trudeau explained the Canadian government's interest in "re-engaging in global affairs," and his desire to do so through the UN. In his words, "It doesn't serve our interests – or the world's – to pretend we're not deeply affected by what happens beyond our borders."[89]

The issue of how culture is deployed in the service of Canada's foreign affairs has more recently been taken up by the Senate Standing Committee on Foreign Affairs and International Trade. In a study launched in November 2017, the committee is exploring the impact and utilization of Canadian culture and arts in Canadian foreign policy and diplomacy, and other related matters.[90] To date, the committee has heard testimony from key constituencies in Canada and abroad, including scholars and former diplomats, representatives of arts organizations and arts councils, Canadian government stakeholders, and a leading Canadian visual artist.[91] These presentations underscore concern with the withdrawal of Canadian cultural programming during the Harper years, with testimony including calls for increased investment and a cohesive strategic approach to Canadian cultural diplomacy. In opening testimony to the committee, former diplomat and Vice President of the Canadian Global Affairs Institute Colin Robertson sounded a note of caution, warning: "If we continue to treat cultural diplomacy as an afterthought within Canada's international relations, we miss opportunities to use our foreign policy to generate economic, political and security benefits for Canadians."[92]

I am particularly struck by the fact that the Senate study has allowed for the voice of artists to be heard—a constituency rarely brought into discussions of international affairs. Conceptual artist Jana Sterbak spoke to the difficulty of employing contemporary art in the service of foreign policy aims, emphasizing the innovative nature of professional contemporary art production—precisely what 49th Parallel was created to foreground. She argued that the excellence of Canadian art production provides its currency abroad. "If you ask any seasoned art professional," she stated, "they will confirm that the *experimental nature* of Canadian art is precisely what makes it attractive in international circles." Notably, this type of cultural production is not always palatable to the masses. Sterbak underscored this point, counselling the senators: "Please remember that we are not obliged…to like it, but you are obliged to afford the kind of respect to contemporary artists that you would accord to any other specialized professional in their field."[93] Sterbak's testimony made clear that the challenges of employing art in the service of national promotion continue since 49th Parallel, pointing to the complexities of how culture is deployed in cultural diplomacy projects. She also made clear the global nature of the professional art world and the need to uphold professional standards in government engagement with the visual arts.

The Senate study, as well as Trudeau's ministerial letters, signal a strong interest in rethinking Canada's approach and a potential return to a robust public diplomacy programme, including support for cultural diplomacy initiatives. In 2018, it remains to be seen *how* programs like Trade Routes and PromArt will be revitalized and what impact they will have on the perception of Canada in the world. Likewise, the Senate study and its recommendations will provide another point of consideration for the government, and, in fact, will require a response which will give a further indication of how changes might be realized. These responses, as well as any subsequent policies and programs, will take time to implement.

Regardless, I recommend that any new approaches address the issue of metrics, foreground listening as an approach to engagement, and prioritize innovation, in order to maximize gains from a revitalized cultural diplomacy programme.

The case of 49th Parallel makes clear the difficulty of justifying cultural diplomacy programmes, given the limits on assessing soft power. In part, metrics (or lack thereof) led to the gallery's closure. These difficulties have not been resolved in the ensuing years. Instead, it remains paramount that new cultural diplomacy initiatives be evaluated in appropriate terms. In this regard, the 2012 study by the British Council, *Trust Pays*, provides a key piece of evidence in support of culture and trade. This study provides substantial quantitative data for how cultural relations, defined as arts, education, and English-language activities, fuel trust in the UK, which, in turn, drives business and trade.[94] These findings are pivotal to establishing the legitimacy of cultural diplomacy and grounding discussions in quantitative evidence. That said, I also suggest that quantitative and economic metrics can be limited. Often, these measures of assessment fail to fully address the long-term benefits of investment in cultural diplomacy. Culture is both an economic and a social good. As such, there is a pressing need to develop qualitative assessment measures, which can help to address the complex impact of cultural diplomacy.[95]

New approaches to cultural diplomacy must also allow for frank, candid, and respectful engagement with international partners. Addressing best practices for public diplomacy, Cull advocated for listening as a key element of any strategic use of culture in the service of foreign affairs. In his words: "the most important part of the public diplomacy and cultural diplomacy is *listening first*, listening to the foreign public, finding out what the world needs, and then thinking how Canada's interests intersect with this need." He underscored the need for authentic and reciprocal engagement, explaining: "It isn't enough to think who Canada would like to be in the world. You have to tie it to specific needs and present something of genuine interest and genuine value."[96]

Finally, the innovative nature of 49th Parallel stands out in the history of Canadian cultural diplomacy initiatives involving visual art. The gallery was unique in championing contemporary Canadian art abroad and its administrative trajectory reveals institutional flexibility. 49th Parallel was able to capture public interest given the inventive nature of its approach. The gallery was also able to respond to different pressures and challenges

by novel changes to its operating structure, which allowed new adminis-
trators, such as Morin, to enhance the gallery's professionalism, and new
partners, such as PADAC, to engage in its mission. These aspects of the
gallery's history speak to the importance of innovation in any cultural
diplomacy project.

49th Parallel's endurance for over a decade demonstrated the Canadian state's interest in employing culture to change attitudes south of the
border. Moreover, the gallery's programming exemplified the potential of
cultural diplomacy initiatives to bridge differences. Cultural diplomacy, as
Goff notes, "is, by its very nature, contingent and ad hoc ... [It] can be
helpful in bridging difference and in opening new avenues of communication. It cannot change outcomes where policies are entrenched, but
it can soften, clarify, complicate, and provide expanded opportunities
for connection."[97] While 49th Parallel only bridged relations within a
specific, targeted community of the avant-garde, the structure of its
activities point to the challenges and benefits of innovative partnerships
between government, cultural sector actors, and private parties. Looking
ahead at the changing landscape of Canadian cultural diplomacy, new risks
will hopefully be taken, and new partners and communities engaged and
listened to. Through innovative approaches to cultural diplomacy that
take culture's role in international relations seriously, new partnerships
can be established to promote Canada abroad, and more importantly, to
address issues of global concern.

Acknowledgements I thank the participants at the 2016 conference "'Re-
booting Canadian Public Diplomacy': The Current State and Future Prospects
for Public Diplomacy in Canada" for their suggestions, as well as organizers
Nicholas Cull and Michael Hawes. I also thank Cyndie Campbell and Philip
Dombowsky for their guidance in accessing the 49th Parallel / 49ᵉ Parallèle
fonds at the National Gallery of Canada Library and Archives.

NOTES

1. In a 1970 catalogue, art historian Dennis Reid identified the Group of
   Seven's aim to promote "a Canadian art for Canadians." This stance, Reid
   explains, dovetailed with the institutional aims of the National Gallery of
   Canada during the tenure of Eric Brown (1912–1939). Lynda Jessup later
   addressed the gallery's ongoing promotion of the group in an article first
   published in *Fuse Magazine*. D. Reid (2007) "Introduction to the Group
   of Seven," and L. Jessup (2007) "Art for a Nation?" *Beyond Wilderness:*

The Group of Seven, Canadian Identity and Contemporary Art (Montreal: McGill-Queen's University Press).

2. Martha Langford argues against understanding Snow's work as a critical commentary on Canadian nationalism. See M. Langford (2014) *Michael Snow: Life & Work* (Toronto: Art Canada Institute), pp. 29–30.

3. Nancy Tousley (1985) "Government Advised to Close N.Y. Gallery," *Calgary Herald*, 30 March.

4. National Gallery of Canada Archives, 49th Parallel Fonds, Administration Files, Box 36, File 1, "49th Parallel / 49^e Parallele: Centre for Canadian Contemporary Art, Position Paper," 1.

5. "Canada's Art Child Christened," *Globe and Mail* (Toronto), 23 March 1981.

6. The Department of External Affairs was renamed the Department of Foreign Affairs and International Trade (DFAIT) in 1995. In 2013, the name changed again when it merged with Canadian International Development Agency and became the Department of Foreign Affairs, Trade and Development (DFATD). In 2015, the department assumed its current name, Global Affairs Canada. In this chapter, I employ the name appropriate to the period when discussing this department. National Gallery of Canada Archives, 49th Parallel Fonds, Administration Files, Box 36, File 1, "Basic Background," 4.

7. J. S. Hage (1981) "49th Parallel: Canada Opens Showcase Gallery in New York," *The Ottawa Citizen*, 11 April.

8. J. H. Balfe (1987) "Artworks as Symbols in International Politics," *International Journal of Politics, Culture, and Society*, 1, no. 2, The Sociology of Culture, 195, 210, 214–215.

9. J. S. Nye, Jr. (2004) *Soft Power: The Means to Success in World Politics* (New York: Public Affairs), pp. 6–7.

10. N. J. Cull (2009) *Public Diplomacy: Lessons from the Past* (Los Angeles: USC Center on Public Diplomacy/Figueroa Press), p. 19.

11. P. M. Goff (2013) "Cultural Diplomacy," *The Oxford Handbook of Modern Diplomacy*, eds A. F. Cooper, J. Heine, and R. Thakur (Oxford: Oxford University Press), p. 421.

12. For example, see P. M. Von Eschen (2004) *Satchmo Blows Up the World: Jazz Ambassadors Play the Cold War* (Cambridge: Harvard University Press); N. Prevots (1998) *Dance For Export: Culture Diplomacy and the Cold War* (Middletown, CT: Wesleyan University Press); G. Barnhisel (2015) *Cold War Modernists: Art, Literature and American Cultural Diplomacy* (New York: Columbia University Press); and A. J. Wulf (2015) *U.S. International Exhibitions During the Cold War: Winning Hearts and Minds Through Cultural Diplomacy* (Lanham, MD: Rowman & Littlefield).

13. See *Searching for a Cultural Diplomacy* (2010) eds J. C. E. Gienow-Hecht and M. C. Donfried (New York and Oxford: Berghahn Books).

14. J. C. E. Gienow-Hecht (2010) "The Anomaly of The Cold War: Cultural Diplomacy and Civil Society Since 1850," *The United States and Public Diplomacy: New Directions in Cultural and International History*, eds K. A. Osgood and B. C. Etheridge (Leiden: Martinus Nijhoff), p. 31.

15. Only very recently has 49th Parallel been subject to scholarly examination. For instance, E. Diggon (2016) addresses the curatorial dimension of 49th Parallel's programming in "Experimental Diplomacy: Art and International Cultural Relations at 49th Parallel," *Journal of Curatorial Studies*, 5, no. 3, 388–408. Other unpublished research on 49th Parallel includes B. Anderson (2012) "49th Parallel: Centre for Contemporary Canadian Art and Canada-US Relations, 1981–1992," MA Major Research Paper: Queen's University (Kingston); and E. Cunningham (2001) "Taking a Bite Out of "The Big Apple": The 49th Parallel: Centre for Contemporary Canadian Art, 1981–1992," MA Thesis: Carleton University (Ottawa).

16. A. F. Cooper (1985) "Introduction," *Canadian Culture: International Dimensions*, ed. A. F. Cooper (Waterloo, ON: Centre on Foreign Policy and Federalism, University of Waterloo/Wilfrid Laurier University), p. 5. Simon L. Mark explains that Quebec's cultural diplomacy activities can be traced to the Quiet Revolution and the province's desire for recognition of cultural distinctiveness at home and abroad. See Mark (2010) "Rethinking Cultural Diplomacy: The Cultural Diplomacy of New Zealand, the Canadian Federation and Quebec," *Political Science*, 62, no. 1, 62–83.

17. J. Wayne (1985) "Does Canada Have a Cultural Foreign Policy?" *Canadian Art*, 2, no. 2, 35.

18. In the 1980s, Canada directed significant attention to its cultural centres. During this time, Canada House in London underwent renovation. Additionally, plans were announced to expand Canadian cultural offerings in cities including Mexico City, Tokyo, and Washington, DC. See L. B. Bowen, "Canada House Is Home to Art," *Toronto Star*, 20 June 1981.

19. G. Bogardi (1981) "Gallery for Canadian Artists Set for N.Y.," *The Montreal Gazette*, 17 January.

20. Wayne, "Does Canada Have a Cultural Foreign Policy?" 36.

21. Wayne, "Does Canada Have a Cultural Foreign Policy?" 34.

22. Wayne, "Does Canada Have a Cultural Foreign Policy?" 35.

23. The press credited Plamondon with conceiving of the gallery in 1977. See J. B. Mays (1982) "Controversy Flares Around the 49th Parallel," *Globe and Mail*, 20 March.

24. National Gallery of Canada Archives, 49th Parallel Fonds, Administration Files, Box 36, File 1, "Bio of Guy Plamondon & Robert Handforth," 19.

25. National Gallery of Canada Archives, 49th Parallel Fonds, Administration Files, Box 36, File 1, "Consulate General New York Cultural Affairs Programme, Establishment of a Canadian Art Centre," 14 February 1978.
26. The document lists the range of individuals contacted about the project and their city of origin. Notably, it also cites an agreement in principal with US Secretary of State John Roberts, indicating the high-level nature of the conversations. NCGA, "Consulate General New York Cultural Affairs Programme, Establishment of a Canadian Art Centre," 16, 22.
27. NCGA, "Consulate General New York Cultural Affairs Programme, Establishment of a Canadian Art Centre," 23.
28. NCGA, "Consulate General New York Cultural Affairs Programme, Establishment of a Canadian Art Centre," 1.
29. NCGA, "Consulate General New York Cultural Affairs Programme, Establishment of a Canadian Art Centre," 1.
30. National Gallery of Canada Archives, 49th Parallel Fonds, Administration Files, Box 36, File 1, Press release, "New York Show-Case for Canadian Artists," Department of External Affairs, 13 February 1981.
31. National Gallery of Canada Archives, 49th Parallel Fonds, Administration Files, Box 36, File 1, "Canada to Open Unique Soho Art Centre 49th Parallel: Centre for Contemporary Canadian Art, First Canadian Cultural Facility in the United States," Canadian Consulate General, 20 March 1981.
32. NGCA, "Bio of Guy Plamondon & Robert Handforth," 21.
33. L. B. Bowen (1981) "Ottawa Opens Art Gallery in New York," *The Toronto Star*, 22 March.
34. N. Tousley, "Government Advised to Close N.Y. Gallery."
35. The rental cost of the gallery space was widely noted in the press at the time. At $72,000 a month it accounted for 60% of 49th Parallel's total budget in 1981. See "New York's 49th Parallel," *Visual Arts Ontario* (1981), p. 3; and J. S. Hage (1981) "49th Parallel: Canada Opens Showcase Gallery in New York," *The Ottawa Citizen*, 11 April.
36. NGCA, "Consulate General New York Cultural Affairs Programme, Establishment of a Canadian Art Centre," 8, 16.
37. "Canadians Open Gallery in SoHo," *New York Times*, 29 March 1981 [author's emphasis].
38. As cited by Bogardi, "Gallery for Canadian Artists."
39. This inability to sell artwork proved to be an ongoing issue with the gallery's model of operations. C. Anka (1983) "Showcase of Avant Garde Scene Acquires Taste for Canadian art," *The Ottawa Citizen*, 26 March.
40. A 1991 document on the future of 49th Parallel authored by the Undersecretary of State of External Affairs explains the gallery's historic position on sales, stating: "...since the gallery is, for practical and other reasons, a creature of the Canadian consulate, NYC, the regulations of the U.S. State

Department and the federal and New York State tax authorities would not permit the gallery to conduct direct commercial operations while enjoying tax-free status." National Gallery of Canada Archives, 49th Parallel Fonds, Administration Files, Box 37, File 2, "Future of the 49th Parallel Gallery, NYC," 19 December 1991, p. 2.

41. C. Corbeil (1981) "Canada Sets Up Visual Art Gallery in New York," *The Globe and Mail*, 5 February.

42. Other top contenders included "Canada Space / Espace Canada" and "Studio Canada." National Gallery of Canada Archives, 49th Parallel Fonds, Administration Files, Box 36, File 1, "Name for New Cdn Art Facility in NYork," 22 January 1981.

43. NGCA, "Name for New Cdn Art Facility in NYork."

44. Hsiio-Yen Shihto to Guy Plamondon, Correspondence, 24 February 1981. National Gallery of Canada Archives, 49th Parallel Fonds, NGC 4.0, Bbox 1, File 1, Michael Snow Exhibition (21 March–11 April 1981) [author's emphasis].

45. A. M. Ashley (1981) "Hearing Told of Canada's 'Cultural Poverty'," *The Ottawa Citizen*, 16 April.

46. Critical reception was poor. A review in *Arts Canada*, for instance, critiqued the choice of Snow as well as the fact that the exhibition did not attempt to position his oeuvre in a new way. See R. Christ (1981) "Michael Snow," *Arts Canada*.

47. *Blind*, *Plus Tard*, and *Scope*, were loaned by the National Gallery of Canada, *Next* (1980) was loaned by the Anthology Film Archives, New York.

48. R. Skoggard (1981) "The 49th Parallel," *Art in America*, 17.

49. Mays, "Controversy Flares."

50. Six individuals were initially appointed for a two-year term, including Alvin Balkind, Claude Bouchard, Eric Cameron, Thérèse Dion, Chantal Pontbriand, Jeffrey Spalding, and Elke Town. See "Department of External Affairs – Communique," March 1983, NGCA 4.0., Box 37, File 5, "Consulting Committee – General."

51. R. Skoggard (1983) "The 49th Parallel: After Two Years," *artmagazine*, 33.

52. Early in Morin's tenure, however, the gallery faced charges that it was too focused on Montreal and Toronto to the exclusion of Vancouver.

53. Here it is worth noting that since the 1960s and the establishment of the Maison du Québec in Paris, Quebec had been making its own moves to advance state relations with France via culture. Such moves caused a great deal of unease amongst Canadian federal government officials. Referencing this situation, a draft report on "International Cultural Relations" produced by External Affairs and Communications makes this adversarial relationship clear: "The creation of our centre in Paris, for

example, was motivated in part by the need to respond to the challenge posed by Quebec's efforts to promote its cultural presence in France. The Centre was intended as a deliberate assertion of the federal claim to represent the Canadian cultural fact abroad in its entirety, to speak on behalf of all Canada, including French Canada." Cultural and Public Information Bureau, "International Cultural Relations" (first draft, October, 1984), NGCA, 49th Parallel Fond, 4.0, Box 36, File 2, "49th Parallel – Restructuring (1984)," 22.

54. The exhibition received mixed reviews from critics. It featured work by nine artists: Simon Cerigo, David Craven, Stephen Lack, Marcus Leatherdale, John Massey, Dorothea Rockburne, Jana Sterbak, Robert Walker, and Krzysztof Wodiczko.

55. As cited by Wayne, "Does Canada have a Cultural Foreign Policy?" 38–39.

56. Morin also did outreach for the gallery and Canadian art scene. For instance, she and a 49th Parallel staff member manned a Canadian art booth at the Chicago International Art Exposition at Navy Pier in 1986. In a memorandum, she supplied to the undersecretary of state for External Affairs documenting her work, she noted that she amassed "a variety of books, catalogues, journals and brochures [representing Canadian visual art], the majority of which were given away." Morin to Under-Secretary of State for External Affairs (Ottawa), Memorandum, 30 May 1986, NGCA 4.0, Box 40, File 10, "Chicago Art Fair – 1986 (Participation In)."

57. In contrast, the report singled out Canada House in London for praise.

58. L. Black (1985) "Gallery Threatened," *Canadian Press*.

59. Tousley, "Government Advised to Close N.Y. Gallery."

60. Black, "Gallery Threatened."

61. As cited by M. Landsberg (1985) "The Bubbling Presence at Canada's Art Embassy," *The Globe and Mail*, 19 October. An overview of the visual arts promotion strategies of Australia, France, Germany, Great Britain, Italy, Japan, and Sweden is provided in Appendix E of "New York City as the World's Art Capital and Its Relevance for Canadian Art and Artists," 6 January 1988, NGCA, 49th Parallel Fonds, 4.0, Box 36, File 5, "49th Parallel – Restructuring (1987)," 10–12. Summarizing its findings (and in contrast to the work of 49th Parallel), the report noted a lack of integration of these national strategies within the New York art scene, a lack of attention to contemporary artists, lack of commercial sales (due to prohibition of sales in government facilities), lack of promotion, and lack of specialists engaged in these activities.

62. Cooper, who noted External Affairs' increasing interest in marshalling cultural diplomacy initiatives in support of foreign trade at this time, suggested something similar. As cited by Wayne, "Does Canada Have a Cultural Foreign Policy?" 39.

63. The Woods Gordon report was very clear in this regard: "The positive influence of cultural activity in terms of trade has largely to be taken as an act of faith ... Thus, in terms of generating direct, hard benefits, cultural centres generate a nice warm feeling, but not much more." Woods Gordon, "Department of External Affairs Assessment of the Concept of Cultural Centres" (draft report, July 1984), NGCA 49th Parallel Fond, 4.0., Box 36, File 2, "49th Parallel – Restructuring (1984)," 22.

64. This closeness stood in sharp contrast to the Pierre Trudeau government's relationship with Reagan, which was notoriously acrimonious.

65. This perception is evidenced, for instance, in the National Gallery of Canada's 1989 purchase of *Voice of Fire* (1967), a painting by US artist Barnett Newman, which was enormously controversial due to the cost of the work.

66. Summarizing the reorganization of the gallery in 1991, J. Bax explained that the shift to a non-profit corporation with a board of directors was meant, in part, to spur greater private sector funding. Correspondence, Bax (Undersecretary of State for External Affairs) to Glen Cumming, 19 December 1991. NGCA 4.0, Box 38, File 1, "Janet Bax – Correspondence."

67. In a move that attests to her credentials and connections within the New York art scene, Morin subsequently took up a curatorial position at the New Museum, where she worked until 1994.

68. I. Vincent (1989) "Canadian Gallery in New York Launching a Major Assault," *The Globe and Mail*, 9 December.

69. This reorganization also had an impact on the type of artwork that 49th Parallel exhibited. As Cunningham notes, programming in the last three years was largely focused on painting. Cunningham, "Taking a Bite Out of 'The Big Apple'," 91.

70. "49th Parallel Report," 13 March 1990. NGCA 4.0, Box 37, File 1, "49th Parallel – Restructuring (1988–1990)."

71. O. Korper (1990) "Letter to the Editor," *C Magazine*, 24, 71.

72. K. Taylor (1991) "Gallery Official Upbeat Despite Low Sales," *The Globe and Mail*, 8 April.

73. As late as 1 April 1992, ideas were circulating to prevent the closure of the gallery. See Glen Cumming to Janet Bax, fax, 1 April 1992, NGCA 4.0, Box 38, File 1, "Janet Bax – Correspondence."

74. A Task Force appointed by the Honourable Joe Clark, minister of External Affairs, identified this issue in a 1989 report. The report asserted, "many of the problems of the 49th Parallel in the past have stemmed from a confusion of objectives. The primary interest of the Department of External Affairs has been in promoting Canada's image and contracts [sic] abroad. This has not always been consistent with the development of living Canadian artists and their reputations in international art circles."

"Draft Report, Task Force on the Future of the 49th Parallel Gallery," n.d., NGCA, 49th Parallel Fonds, 4.0. Box 36, File 2, "49th Parallel – Restructuring (1984)," 3.

75. Tracing the history of cultural institutions abroad, G. Paschalidis (2009) argues that their roles as centres for cultural diplomacy were apparent between the Second World War and the end of the Cold War. He suggests that in response to nation-branding efforts in the 1990s, cultural centres took on a different role as sites of cultural capitalism. See Paschalidis (2009) "Exporting National Culture: Histories of Cultural Institutes Abroad," *International Journal of Cultural Policy*, 15, no. 3, 275–289.

76. Janet Bax (Consul, Cultural Affairs) made this point about 49th Parallel's partnership with PADAC. Citing the depressed art market, the fact that 49th Parallel did not privilege repeat exhibitions (essential to building an audience for an artist's work), and 49th Parallel's complicated tax-free status which precluded sales, she wrote in 1992 that, upon approaching the end of the trial relationship with PADAC, "it is difficult to fairly assess the success of the three year experiment." Bax to Cumming, 17 December 1991, NGCA 4.0, Box 38, File 1, "Janet Bax – Correspondence."

77. C. P. Schneider (2006) "Cultural Diplomacy: Hard to Define but You'd Know It If You Saw It," *Brown Journal of World Affairs*, 8, no. 1 (Fall/Winter), 196.

78. Global Affairs Canada and the University of Southern California's Center on Public Diplomacy recently organized a workshop titled *Diplometrics*, see http://www.canadainternational.gc.ca/ci-ci/highlights-faits/2016/Int_Advocacy_Dig_Age-Promotion_Int.aspx?lang=eng.

79. For instance, see Canadian Dance Assembly/L'Assemblée canadienne de la dance (2008) "End of Trade Routes and Promart Cultural Funding Programs Threatens End of Canada Abroad," Press release, 13 August, http://www.cda-acd.ca/docs/press-releases/end-of-trade-routes-promart-cultral-funding-programs-threatens.pdf. See also, G. Quill and R. Brennan (2008) "Torys Cut Five More Arts Programs," *The Toronto Star*, 16 August, https://www.thestar.com/news/canada/2008/08/16/tories_cut_five_more_arts_programs.html.

80. Correspondence, Roxanne Dubé to Patrick James, 30 April 2012, http://www.iccs-ciec.ca/administration/ckeditor/ckfinder/userfiles/files/SKMBT_C36012050815260.pdf.

81. M. Blanchfield (2012) "Foreign Affairs Cuts Canadian Studies Abroad Program Despite Millions Generated for Economy," *The Canadian Press*, 16 May, http://www.huffingtonpost.ca/2012/05/16/foreign-studies-program-cut_n_1522632.html.

82. See the response of the Canadian Historical Association. Canadian Historical Association (2012) "The CHA Opposes the Cuts Made to National Archives Development Program and 'Understanding Canada' Program,"

http://www.cha-shc.ca/english/advocacy/the-cha-opposes-the-cuts-made-to-national-archives-development-program-and-understanding-canada-program.html#sthash.iSOAImdc.dpbs. Also, P. Martin (2012) "Canada's Image Abroad: Fade to Black," *University Affairs/Affaires universitaires*, 6 June, http://www.universityaffairs.ca/opinion/in-my-opinion/canadas-image-abroad-fade-to-black.

83. In his Senate testimony, Cull spoke about the potential for significant implications to Canada's global standing as a result of this approach. Nicholas J. Cull, "Standing Committee Foreign Affairs and International Trade, Evidence," 30 May 2018, https://sencanada.ca/en/Content/Sen/Committee/421/AEFA/54119-e.

84. That these letters are publicly available online is itself a marker of the change in government.

85. Justin Trudeau (2015) "Minister of Foreign Affairs Mandate Letter," http://pm.gc.ca/eng/minister-foreign-affairs-mandate-letter.

86. Justine Trudeau (2015) "Minister of International Trade Mandate Letter," http://pm.gc.ca/eng/minister-international-trade-mandate-letter.

87. Justine Trudeau (2015) "Minister of Canadian Heritage Mandate Letter," http://pm.gc.ca/eng/minister-canadian-heritage-mandate-letter.

88. The National Gallery was widely used as the backdrop for events under the Liberal government of Jean Chrétien between 1993 and 2003, a practice that was not favoured under Prime Minister Stephen Harper.

89. "Prime Minister Justin Trudeau's Address to the 71st Session of the United Nations General Assembly," http://pm.gc.ca/eng/news/2016/09/20/prime-minister-justin-trudeaus-address-71st-session-united-nations-general-assembly.

90. At the time of writing, this study was ongoing.

91. For a full list of speakers see "Standing Committee Foreign Affairs and International Trade, Studies and Bills," Senate of Canada website, https://sencanada.ca/en/committees/aefa/studiesandbills/42-1.

92. Robertson argued for the significance of culture in Canada's foreign policy, frankly stating: "Canadian culture and the arts should be a major pillar of Canadian diplomacy and foreign policy." See his testimony, "Proceedings of the Standing Senate Committee on Foreign Affairs and International Trade, Issue No. 34 – Evidence – Meeting of November 30, 2017," Senate of Canada website, https://sencanada.ca/en/Content/Sen/Committee/421/AEFA/34ev-53681-e.

93. Author's emphasis. Jana Sterbak, Senate testimony, 31 May 2018, http://senparlvu.parl.gc.ca/XRender/en/PowerBrowser/PowerBrowserV2?fk=490117&globalStreamId=3&useragent=Mozilla/5.0%20(Macintosh;%20Intel%20Mac%20OS%20X%2010_12_6)%20AppleWebKit/605.1.15%20(KHTML,%20like%20Gecko)%20Version/11.1.1%20Safari/605.1.15

94. British Council, *Trust Pays: How International Cultural Relationships Build Trust in the UK and Underpin the Success of the UK Economy*, London: British Council, 2012.
95. These points were made in my testimony to Senate on 30 November 2017. See "Proceedings of the Standing Senate Committee on Foreign Affairs and International Trade, Issue No. 34 – Evidence – Meeting of November 30, 2017," Senate of Canada website, https://sencanada. ca/en/Content/Sen/Committee/421/AEFA/34ev-53681-e.   Further recommendations for metrics to assess cultural diplomacy initiatives can be found in the North American Cultural Diplomacy Initiative's 2018 report, *Cultural Diplomacy and Trade: Making Connections*, Kingston: North American Cultural Diplomacy Initiative, 2018.
96. Author's emphasis. "Standing Committee Foreign Affairs and International Trade, Evidence," 30 May 2018, https://sencanada.ca/en/Con tent/Sen/Committee/421/AEFA/54119-e.
97. Goff, *The Oxford Handbook*, 419.

CHAPTER 6

Intersections and Cultural Exchange: Archaeology, Culture, International Law and the Legal Travels of the Dead Sea Scrolls

Bernard Duhaime and Camille Labadie

In 2003, the Pointe-à-Callière Museum in Montreal organized a major international exhibition entitled "Archaeology and the Bible—From King

This contribution was presented on 30 September 2016 during the Fulbright Canada Colloquium held at the University of Southern California by Bernard Duhaime who was the Fulbright Canada Research Chair in Public Diplomacy at USC in the Fall of 2011. The authors would like to thank the organizers of this event, in particular Dr. Michael Hawes and Prof. Nick Cull. This text was previously published in French in Vol. 23 (2) of the Canadian Journal *Théologiques* (2015) under the direction of Prof Alain Gignac, to which both authors are also very grateful. The authors are also thankful to those who provided comments on this article, in particular Me François Le Moine, lecturer at the Université de Montréal, and Dr. Sarah E. K. Smith for their time and valuable suggestions.

B. Duhaime (✉) · C. Labadie
Faculty of Law and Political Science, Université Du Québec à Montréal (UQAM), Montreal, QC, Canada
e-mail: duhaime.bernard@uqam.ca

David to the Dead Sea Scrolls," for which Professor Jean Duhaime was the scientific advisor.[1] The exhibition, which displayed several pieces on loan from the Israel Museum in Jerusalem, the Israeli Antiquities Authority, and the Library and Archives of Canada, experienced unprecedented success. Both the general public and experts praised the show.[2] The exhibition marked the first time the Qumran manuscripts, notably, the *Manuscript of the War of the Sons of Light Against the Sons of Darkness* and the *Manuscript of Isaiah B*, were exhibited outside of Israel. Six years later, the Royal Ontario Museum (Canada) experienced similar success with "*Dead Sea Scrolls: Words That Changed the World*,"[3] in collaboration with the Israeli Antiquities Authority. This event did not, however, proceed without incident. Even before the exhibition opened a controversy began over the ownership of the scrolls. The Directorate of Archaeology Department of the Palestinian Ministry of Tourism and Antiquities, among others, alleged that the Israeli Antiquities Authority was not the true owner of the scrolls and that the Museum—and by extension, Canada—had violated several rules of international law by showing them.[4] Similarly, in December of 2009, as the exhibition drew to a close, the Kingdom of Jordan contacted the Chargé d'affaires of the Canadian Embassy in Amman and called upon Canada to return the scrolls; they alleged that they were illegally loaned to the Museum by Israel for the purposes of the exhibition.[5] While the Royal Ontario Museum stated that the Israeli Antiquities Authority was the sole owner of the scrolls,[6] a spokesperson for the Canadian Department of Foreign Affairs said that it would be inappropriate for Ottawa to intervene in the conflict, and that the dispute over the scrolls' ownership should be handled by Israel, Jordan, and the Palestinian Authority.[7] The spokesperson for the Israeli Foreign Ministry stated that the scrolls belong to the cultural and historical heritage of the Jewish people, and have no connection with Jordan or its history.[8] These two incidents are reminiscent of those that surrounded McGill University's acquisition of certain fragments of Qumran scrolls in the 1950s, which resulted in a protest from Jordan and, as we shall see below, the cancellation of the sale.

These tensions illustrate the legal, political, and strategic issues surrounding the question of rightful ownership of ancient cultural properties in a globalized society. In recent years, archaeology has indeed proven to be more and more often at the heart of complex political[9] or territorial claims,[10] to which the law struggles to provide simple answers.[11] These issues complicate attempts to integrate archeological exhibitions into the toolbox of public diplomacy, more especially for a nation like Canada which make soft power claims around its adherence to law the norms of international society. This chapter will explore the legal issues raised by the question of ownership of the Dead Sea Scrolls, specifically regarding international legal standards. First, it will provide a brief chronological overview of the discovery and appropriation of these documents. Then, it will further explore the normative framework of international law related to cultural property, with a particular emphasis on international humanitarian law rules applicable in international armed conflict or in instances of occupation. Finally, it will briefly discuss the dispute settlement procedures concerning these archaeological treasures that have emerged in recent decades.

THE DISCOVERIES OF THE MANUSCRIPTS[12]

During the winter of 1946–1947, a young Bedouin from the Ta'a Mireh tribe named Muhammad Hassan edh-Dhib went in search of a lost goat on the desert slopes of Qumran, on the northwestern shore of the Dead Sea. During this expedition, the young man stumbled upon a cave where he found several jars containing relatively well-preserved rolls wrapped in cloth.[13] Hoping to draw some money from this find, the Bedouin turned to an antique dealer in Bethlehem, one Khalil Iskander Shahin also known as Kando.[14] The antiquarian estimated the market value of the 7 rolls presented to him and promised the Bedouin 2/3 of the money he would get from their sale.[15] Under this agreement, the rolls were sold by Kando who, even if he suspected their importance, ignored the nature of the entries they carried. In 1947, three scrolls were purchased by Professor Eliezer Sukenik of the Hebrew University of Jerusalem, and four were purchased by Father Samuel Athanasios March, Superior of the Syrian monastery of St. Mark in Jerusalem. The work of deciphering the manuscripts began with the help of the British and American Archaeological School of Jerusalem. Soon news of the discovery spread to the ears of Father Roland de Vaux, director of the French Bible School and an active archaeologist of Jerusalem, who then organized new excavations in Qumran.[16] In 1948, as political instability in the region put an end to the excavations, Father Samuel decided to get his four rolls safely to the United States.[17]

The discovery of the first rolls coincided with the end of the British mandate over Palestine.[18] On 29 November 1947, the UN General

Assembly adopted Resolution 181, which sought to partition Palestine into two States: a Jewish State and an Arab State, with Jerusalem under international administration.[19] This project was, however, rejected and on 30 November 1947, a conflict broke out between the Jewish and Arab populations. On 14 May 1948, the State of Israel officially declared independence, turning what was then a civil war into the first Arab-Israeli conflict. On 24 February 1949, after a final cease-fire, an armistice was finally signed between the belligerents. After this first conflict, the geopolitical situation in the region changed considerably: the new Israeli State now occupied 81% of the territory of Palestine and took possession of the western part of the city of Jerusalem, which was now cut in half. The West Bank (where Qumran is located) and east Jerusalem were annexed by Jordan, and were supposed to demarcate the new Arab State. However, these boundaries were designed to be provisional, pending peace talks that never took place, and have thus gone unrecognized by the international community.

With a new *status quo* established, the search for the scrolls resumed. From 1949 to 1956, we witnessed a real "race for the fragments" on the banks of the Dead Sea. As Véronique Chemla summarizes: "This adventure combines scientific and political stakes and features many protagonists: treasure-hunting Bedouins, more or less scrupulous intermediary henchmen, engineering researchers-epigraphists, anonymous buyers, field archaeologists [...] [we translate]."[20] The purchase by McGill University of several hundred fragments illustrated the diversity of actors involved in the search for manuscripts.

During the *Congress of the International Organization for the Study of the Old Testament* in Copenhagen in 1953, Father Roland de Vaux took the opportunity to expose the extremely precarious situation of the fragments discovered in the Cave No. 4: as a result of insufficient funds, these fragments were collecting dust, still waiting to be purchased from the Bedouins who originally found them. To prevent the fragments from ending up on the black market and thus being dispersed across the globe, Roland de Vaux appealed to representatives of universities to help purchase the fragments in question. In the event that an institution provided the missing funds, they would be guaranteed export and property rights of the fragments purchased. However, the fragments were to remain in Palestine until they had been reviewed and published, for an estimated duration of 2 or 3 years, according to the director of the French biblical and archaeological School of Jerusalem.[21]

In the spring of 1954, and again in 1955, McGill University in Montreal took up Father Roland de Vaux's offer. With funding from the John Henry Birks Foundation, and following protracted negotiations with the Department of Antiquities of the Jordanian government, the Faculty of Divinity at McGill University bought some 450 fragments discovered in the Cave No. 4 from the Bedouins, thus making McGill University the owner of the largest collection of Qumran fragments in the world, excluding Jordan, at the time.[22]

By the end of 1956, dozens of nearby caves had been excavated. Eleven of them yielded scrolls in varied states of conservation, along with hundreds of thousands of fragments.[23] While most of them were purchased by the Jordanian government and sent to the Palestine Archaeological Museum in East Jerusalem,[24] the fragments were also scattered throughout the world and preserved in various institutions in Europe, the United States, and the Middle East.[25] In June 1954, the four scrolls purchased by Father Samuel were listed for sale in the *Wall Street Journal*. They were acquired by the State of Israel[26] and, finally, reunited with the first 3 scrolls bought by Sukenik. While a vast part of the documentation and research was in the possession of the Jordanian authorities, the 7 original scrolls discovered in 1946–1947 were in the possession of the Israeli authorities. Only a year had passed before the sale was disputed by the Jordanian government, who challenged the legality of transporting these antiques outside their territory of discovery in 1948.[27]

In 1960, when the excavations fizzled out and the work of deciphering the scrolls took center stage,[28] Roland de Vaux contacted the various institutions that had bought fragments to inform them that they needed to acquire export permits from the Jordanian government. However, on 27 July 1960, in an effort to preserve all its archaeological discoveries, the Jordanian government decided to cancel the current arrangements and reimburse the amounts paid by foreign institutions, including McGill University, to acquire the fragments.[29] One of the reasons given by the Jordanian government to explain this change in policy was that "[…] *these scrolls constitute an undivided share of the history of Jordan and, in particular, of the spiritual legacy of all mankind. This being the case, neither the ancient treasure as a whole nor any portion thereof shall be allowed to be lost through transfer of property rights to any party.*"[30] Representatives from McGill University tried, in vain, to get a long-term loan of the fragments purchased, but, like other buyers, only managed to obtain the reimbursement of the amounts paid to acquire them.[31]

In 1966, in a final effort to preserve the unity of its national archaeological treasures, Jordan proceeded to nationalize the Palestine Archaeological Museum, in which were located most of the manuscripts and fragments discovered since 1949.[32] Finally, in 1967, a new geopolitical upheaval occured: the Six-Day War. Following a lightning war against its Arab neighbors, including Jordan, Israel took control of the entire city of Jerusalem and occupied the West Bank, thus taking possession of the Archaeological Museum of Palestine, where the scrolls and fragments discovered in 1949 were being kept. Because Israel's annexation of Jerusalem and occupation of the West Bank were considered illegal under international law and have been repeatedly condemned by the Security Council and the United Nations General Assembly, Israel is recognized by the international community as an occupying power.[33] Following the capture of East Jerusalem, the stored collections in the Archaeological Museum of Palestine, including the Dead Sea Scrolls, came under the control of the Department of the Israeli Antiquities. The scrolls are now stored and exhibited in the Shrine of the Book in West Jerusalem.

The Dead Sea Scrolls are certainly one of the most important archaeological discoveries of the twentieth century. They contain some 900 manuscripts (well-preserved but mostly in fragments) written between 250 BCE and 70 by Essene scribes, a group of religious Jews who had retreated to the desert around the Dead Sea. These manuscripts contain not only various rules relating to the Jewish community and its practices, but also the oldest known editions of certain books of the Hebrew Bible. On a historical and theological level, this discovery is fundamental. Indeed, "today, we know that the fragments of biblical scrolls discovered are essential to better understand how the text received from the Hebrew Bible was constituted" [our translation].[34]

We will attempt to provide a comprehensive background of the political and religious tensions surrounding the disputed ownership of the manuscripts of the Dead Sea, from 1967 through today.

The Israeli authorities consider the Dead Sea Scrolls an integral part of the cultural, historical, and national heritage of the Jewish people and assert that they should therefore remain in Israel's possession for means of conservation and research.[35] Israel, however, does not claim ownership of the documents; rather, they claim "guardianship" to the extent that they are entitled retain and distribute them.[36] It is as the "guardian" of the scrolls that Israel, since 1967, has contributed to researching, reunifying, and publishing the manuscripts. In addition to granting researchers' access to the manuscripts and conserving them in a dedicated wing of the Israel Museum, the Israeli Department of Antiquities has also, since December 2012, partnered with Google on a joint project to make the Dead Sea Scrolls and their translations available for free on the Internet.[37] More than this, since the late 1960s,[38] and particularly since the 1990s, the Israeli authorities have tracked fragments that occasionally appear on the antiquities market.[39] But their self-appointed "guardianship" is far from undisputed; the nature of Israel's possession of the scrolls is contested both by the Palestinian and Jordanian authorities.

On the Palestinian side, ownership claims regarding the scrolls are closely interwoven with nationalist demands of the population: "for the Palestinians, these manuscripts were stolen from the Palestinian land and its people by the Israeli occupiers" [we translate].[40] Since 1967, the issue of recognition of a Palestinian State in the West Bank and Gaza, with Jerusalem as its capital, has been at the heart of debates within the region. In recent years, the situation seems to have evolved favorably for the Palestinians. In October 2011, Palestine became the 195th Member State of UNESCO[41]; since 2012, it has held the status of "non-member observer State" at the UN.[42] On 7 January 2015, Palestine also officially became the 123rd Member State of the International Criminal Court.[43] Considering its statehood is recognized by the majority of the international community, Palestine now seems entitled to claim its sovereignty over its historical and cultural heritage, including the Dead Sea Scrolls, which were discovered on the West Bank, a region that is now legally considered Palestinian territory.[44]

Jordan, for its part, invokes patrimonial reasons to support its claim over the scrolls. In particular, it stresses that although the first scrolls were found by Bedouins in what is now Israeli-occupied Palestinian territory, all discoveries between 1949 and 1967 occurred in the Jordan-controlled West Bank.[45] In 2009, during the exhibition in Ontario, the Jordanian Minister of Tourism and the Minister of Antiquities stated to be in possession of all legal documents proving that Jordan had purchased the scrolls discovered since 1949, and that Jordan was therefore the rightful owner.[46] In addition, according to Robert David, professor of theology at the University of Montreal, the first Dead Sea Scrolls discovered in 1946–1947 actually do belong to Jordan, because the State of Israel did not yet exist when they were discovered: "The texts actually belong to the historical heritage of Jewishness, but until now, we considered the territory [on which a good was discovered] rather than its content."[47]

In 2009/10 this argument formed the basis of Jordan's effort to regain possession of the scrolls through a complaint to UNSECO.[48]

THE DEVELOPMENT OF THE LAW ON CULTURAL PROPERTY[49]

The issues raised by the movement of cultural property and the return of such property are centuries old but have only been formalized in international law since the twentieth century. Sixteenth-century European thinkers questioned the consequences of the plundering of indigenous treasures in the Spanish Americas; in the seventeenth century, the Treaty of Westphalia addressed the return of properties that had been looted during the Thirty Years' War.[50] In 1861, Victor Hugo condemned the looting of the Summer Palace treasures during shipment to China, famously calling France and England "thugs."[51] Accordingly, the early nineteenth century saw the question of restitution of cultural property appropriated during wartime raised under certain peace agreements. At the Congress of Vienna in 1814–1815, many wondered whether the art objects removed by Napoleon and retained by Dominique Vivant Denon at the Louvre Museum would be returned to their original owners. However, although a large portion of the loot was returned, no formal obligation of restitution or compensation was expressly incorporated into the Treaties.[52] After the First World War, the efforts of victors to repair the illicit transfer of cultural items led to the inclusion of the repayment obligation in various peace treaties signed between belligerents. In addition to crystallizing the notion of limitations for crimes related to cultural heritage, the refunds made as a result of the conflict were carried out in order to return the objects directly to whom they were traditionally attached, rather than the place which they were taken from. For example, the Koran offered by the Ottomans to the Emperor William II was returned to Medina, where it was seized.[53] Though several cases of restitution found themselves on the global stage during this period, it was only after the Second World War that heritage claims truly found their place on the international scene with the emergence of three movements of claims.

The first movement of claims that emerged in 1945 was a continuation of the efforts developed in the wake of the First World War. The restitution of cultural property displaced during the conflict, or compensation when such goods had disappeared, was organized by peace treaties signed between the warring parties. This was the case of the Peace Treaty signed between the Allies and Italy, among others, under which the Italian government had to return cultural properties captured during the Italian campaigns in Ethiopia and Yugoslavia.[54] In particular, cultural items moved, confiscated, or destroyed by the Nazis were the subject of many complaints and restitution procedures, on behalf of nations, cultural institutions, and individuals alike, and are still today presented as attempts to repair the suffering and deprivations of war.

A second movement then emerged in connection with the decolonization process, as colonial occupations had largely favored the displacement of local cultural heritages to the western metropolis.[55] Upon independence, newly sovereign States naturally expressed interest in recovering important elements of their heritage, many of which were, and still are, scattered in museums around the world, or in neighboring countries due to territorial changes.[56] These States implore that similar policies to those enacted after armed conflict must be applied, to the extent that most of these countries considered colonization a form of foreign occupation.[57] Although there is no international obligation on the part of former colonial powers to return objects displaced during colonization,[58] refunds are generally perceived as a moral duty and are integrated into a sense of obligation to repair or compensate for the damages of the past.[59]

Finally, a third protest movement has developed with the recent restitution of Aboriginal heritage. Indeed, indigenous peoples have also emerged as collective subjects of rights[60] and consider that they should receive the same ethical sensitivity as victims of wartime spoilation.[61] Indigenous restitution claims are also based on the need to restore the sacred relationship between population, territory, and cultural heritage, and the development of an expanded notion of self-determination of peoples who seek to preserve, revitalize, and develop their cultural and collective identity.[62] Although the existence of a legal obligation to return *stricto* sensu is contested by several entities,[63] the appropriation of indigenous cultural property today is often considered unworthy *a posteriori*, and the return of property is thus encouraged.[64]

To meet these multiple, overlapping claims, laws concerning the return of cultural property have evolved quickly, both on a domestic and international level.

Since the beginning of the twentieth century, most countries have realized that their cultural property requires specific protection. Strategies to this end include public ownership and classifying cultural property as "national treasures" in dedicated registers. Many States have also opted for protective legislation for these goods, prohibiting their export or requiring special authority to do so even when such goods belong to individuals.[65] In Canada, for example, *The Law on Export and Import of Cultural Property*[66] establishes a list of goods or categories of cultural goods whose export is controlled, and provides, in particular, that any person, company, or institution wishing to export such goods must always obtain permission from the Canadian Border Services Agency, or from the movable cultural property Program of the Department of Canadian Heritage.[67]

In international law, various conventions on cultural heritage have also been gradually adopted to frame heritage practices, regulate the exchange of cultural goods, and prevent and punish illegal practices. This was particularly the case with UNESCOs *Convention on the Means of Prohibiting and Preventing the Illicit Import, Export and Transfer of Ownership of Cultural Property* from 1970,[68] which was ratified by 86 States, including Canada, Jordan, and Palestine (but not Israel). Beyond this, the *UNIDROIT Convention on cultural objects stolen or illegally exported*,[69] adopted in 1995, has been seen as a sort of "application decree" of the 1970 convention in that it attempts to organize the return of stolen property through uniform material regulation and administrative and judicial cooperation between nations.[70] Finally, to these various international conventions must be added numerous provisions adopted by regional bodies, including the European Union,[71] as well as many resolutions and recommendations UN or NGOs, which, however, have a moral value rather than a binding force.[72]

Specifically, regarding the Dead Sea Scrolls, most of Jordan and Palestine's claims are based on the annexation of East Jerusalem by Israel after the Six-Day War in 1967. This annexation and the resulting seizure of the manuscripts by Israel therefore requires assessment of the specific provisions of international humanitarian law (IHL) that apply.

International humanitarian law, otherwise known as the law of war or law of armed conflicts (i.e., to say, the international legal regime adopted by States to regulate the conduct of belligerents, their rights, and obligations in the context of an armed conflict),[73] has gradually developed certain legal standards for the protection of cultural property[74] in time of international or internal armed conflicts.[75]

While peace agreements and management of post-conflict international relations have, on occasion, addressed the prickly issue of the return of cultural properties stolen during war, international humanitarian law, or *jus in bello*, has meanwhile been concerned with the obligations of belligerents *not to carry out attacks against cultural property*, as well as obligations to protect those assets and to not appropriate them illegally.

First, we must first remember that IHL prohibits belligerents[76] from carrying out attacks that do not meet the strict requirements of military necessity.[77] In accordance with the principle of distinction,[78] belligerents are forbidden from conducting attacks against civilian objects, that is, objects which are not military objectives, "which, by their nature, location, purpose, or use make an effective contribution to military action and whose total or partial destruction, capture, or neutralization offers in this case a definite military advantage."[79] The *Rome Statute of the International Criminal Court*, which entered into force in 2002, also identifies as a prosecutable war crime in the "extensive destruction and appropriation of property, not justified by military necessity and carried out a large scale unlawfully and wantonly" as well as "intentionally directing attacks against civilian objects, that is, objects which are not military objectives."[80]

Therefore, it can be inferred that the IHL generally prohibits belligerents from carrying out attacks against cultural property since they are, by nature, civilian property, not military objectives (to the extent that they are not used for military purposes). Recall that IHL provides that, in the case of doubt, "an object which is normally dedicated to civilian purposes, such as a place of worship, a house, or other dwelling or a school, is presumed not to be used in order to make an effective contribution to military action."[81]

IHL has also developed numerous standards that explicitly prohibit all forms of attack against cultural property. In the 1907 Hague convention, a number of States agreed to an international obligation to take, "in sieges and bombardments, all necessary measures [...] to spare as far as possible, buildings dedicated to religion, art, science and charitable purposes, [...] provided they are not used at the time for military purposes."[82] Since then, the modern law of armed conflicts has also introduced and developed similar specific prohibitions. In 1954, States adopted the *Convention for the Protection of Cultural Property in the Event of Armed Conflict*, under which parties undertake in particular to "respect cultural property situated within their own territory or that of others high Contracting Parties by refraining from the use of such property, that their protective devices and their immediate surroundings for purposes which might expose it to destruction or damage in the event of armed conflict, and s refraining from any act of hostility against them."[83] Adopted in 1977, the two *Additional Protocols to the Geneva Conventions*, which relate, respectively, to international and non-international armed conflicts, also prohibit, "committing any act of hostility directed against historic monuments, works of art, or places of worship which constitute the cultural or spiritual heritage of peoples; to use such objects in support of the military effort; to make such objects the object of reprisals."[84] In 2004, the *Second Protocol to the Convention for the Protection of Cultural Property in the Event of Armed Conflict*, which Jordan and Palestine, but not Israel, ratified, provided that "any person who intentionally [...] fulfills one of the following acts: c. destruction or appropriation of a large-scale cultural property protected under the Convention and this Protocol; [...] e. theft, pillage, or misappropriation of cultural property protected under the Convention, and acts of vandalism directed against cultural property protected under the Convention" is committing a serious violation of the Protocol.[85]

It is generally recognized today that the prohibition against attacking cultural property is not only binding on the States that have ratified these treaties, but also on all belligerents, as a norm of customary international law. Indeed, international law recognizes the existence of legal rules resulting from a constant and repeated practice by most States, which act in a given way because they feel bound by an international standard, even though that standard may be unwritten. Over time, a majority of States have thus avoided attacking cultural goods, because they considered that international law forbids them to do so.[86] The violation of this customary rule also constitutes a crime under international criminal law that can engage the individual criminal responsibility of the belligerents involved, as was the case during the destruction of cultural property in the recent conflict in the former Yugoslavia.[87]

Secondly, we must remember that beyond the mere prohibition of attacks on cultural property during armed conflict, IHL also requires belligerents to adopt measures to *protect* these assets. These obligations are primarily contained in the *Convention for the Protection of Cultural Property in the Event of Armed Conflict* of 1954, which outlines various standards encouraging States to identify their cultural property by a distinctive mark and to get their cultural property to safety, away from military objectives that may be the subject of attacks.[88]

This obligation to protect cultural property also applies in the context of the occupation of enemy territory by a belligerent party. Indeed, under the 1954 Convention, the warring parties must "as far as possible, support the efforts of national authorities of the occupied territory in order to ensure the safeguarding and preservation of its cultural property."[89] Similarly, "[i]f an urgent intervention is required for the conservation of cultural property situated in occupied territory and damaged by military operations, and should the competent national authorities be unable to intervene, [the occupier must], as much as possible, undertake the most necessary precautionary measures in close co-operation with the authorities."[90]

For the purposes of this discussion, remember that, at least since 1907, IHL prohibits "seizure of, destruction, or willful damage" of "common property, that of institutions dedicated to religion, charity and education, the arts and sciences," as well as "historic monuments, works of art and science."[91] The 1954 Convention (ratified by Israel and Jordan) extends the scope of this standard, forcing the warring parties to prohibit, prevent and, if necessary, stop any form of theft, pillage, or misappropriation of cultural property, practiced in any form whatsoever, including any acts of vandalism against such property. Moreover, these parties cannot "requisition movable cultural property situated in the territory of another [part]."[92]

Again, there seems to be no doubt that these bans are now a norm of customary international humanitarian law[93] binding all belligerent parties to an armed conflict, with the power to engage the international criminal responsibility of those who violate those standards.[94] It was the case of several war criminals convicted at the Nuremberg trials, as well as by French and US military courts for having seized or destroyed cultural property during the Second World War.[95] Much more recently, it was the case of Ahmad Al-Faqi Al-Mahdi who, following the destruction of the Mausoleums of Timbuktu in Mali, was convicted of war crimes and sentenced to nine years in prison by the International Criminal Court.[96]

Finally, remember that IHL provides that the occupying powers have a duty to prevent the illegal export of cultural property from occupied territory and to return any exported cultural goods to the occupied authorities. Indeed, the *First Protocol for the Protection of Cultural Property in the Event of Armed Conflict*, adopted in 1954, a treaty to which Israel, Jordan, and Palestine acceded, provides that "each High Contracting Party undertakes to prevent the export of cultural property from a territory occupied by it during an armed conflict [...]."[97] The protocol also requires parties to "take into its custody cultural property imported into its territory and directly or indirectly from any occupied territory."[98] Again, the content of this standard is now a norm of customary international humanitarian law,[99] which seems to be recognized not only by the UN Security Council,[100] but also by the authorities of Israel and its neighbors.[101]

As we can see, international humanitarian law has developed over the years into a series of very precise standards that not only prohibit the attack on cultural property during international or internal armed conflicts, but which also require belligerents to protect these assets, through prohibition of their requisition, seizure, pillaging, theft, vandalism, or destruction, and even exportation, in the case of occupation.

The Dispute Settlement Procedures Related to Cultural Property

Disputes concerning cultural property are generally complicated by the diversity of goods and legal entities concerned.[102] Indeed, there is a very wide variety of situations that depend not only on the nature of the property claimed, but also on whether the claims are directed from State to State, from State to individuals, from individuals to State, to a community, or to another individual. Individuals or communities may also claim a good located within their own State, or seek restitution from another State, community, institution, or individual. Therefore, given the complexity and diversity of situations regarding cultural heritage restitution, several dispute resolution methods have been developed.[103]

The restitution claims submitted to court often require a blending of the study of public and private law, and/or international law and domestic law. Indeed, when a court is faced with a claim for restitution, several issues must be resolved, particularly where the dispute has an international dimension. First, and to support any application for restitution, the party claiming ownership of a cultural item must be able to prove the existence of his or her right of ownership of this property. To establish their property rights and the sense of belonging that they have with their heritage, some States claims are based on the national protective legislation that they have adopted. However, if the country of origin or provenance of a property is defined in international documents as the one that registers it and distinguishes it as belonging to its cultural heritage, States do not always formally identify the cultural property to which they or their citizens give importance. Moreover, the criteria that determine the membership of a good in a national heritage are vast and, sometimes, the definition of "belonging" isn't recognized from a formal point of view, but rather, in terms of real connection established between a community and an item. According to V. Lyndel Prott, the possession and preservation of a cultural good for an extended period of time can indeed create an "adoption link" or "privileged cultural ties." Thus, some cultural goods can be considered part of the heritage of a State without having a direct link with the culture of that State (e.g., the Mona Lisa, although it has no legitimate link to French culture, is now fully assimilated to the Louvre and the French heritage).[104] Finally, membership and legitimacy conflicts may occur when two States claim an interest over the same property.

When a dispute is international in nature, the court must also determine the applicable law. On this point, it is usually the "law of the location of the object" (*lex rei sitae*) which establishes precedent. In the case of a dispute between foreign jurisdictions, the applicable law is the one of the country where the property is located.[105] In some cases, however, solutions of "special connection" are proposed to reconcile the parties. These solutions aim to identify the jurisdiction having the closest connection with the property in dispute and sometimes recognize the law of the place of theft of cultural property as the most appropriate to resolve a dispute. In some cases, the principle of States' immunity in public international law[106] and in the domestic law[107] of each country, under which a State is protected against prosecution in a foreign court, also comes into play and is often used to slow or even prevent this type of claim.

After these major procedural obstacles, the claims brought before the courts still face many difficulties. They are often complicated by traditional rules of law, such as the principle of limitation, protection of *bona fide* purchasers, or standard rules relating to contract law, which vary considerably from one national jurisdiction to another. They can also be complicated by the determination of unlawful dispossession itself[108] or by material difficulties relating to the traceability of cultural goods.[109]

Considered by many to be lengthy, complex, and expensive proceedings, it was estimated in 2006 that only a few cases of restitution were the direct result of a court order.[110] In 1982, for example, in the case of *Republic of Ecuador v Danusso*, the claim by Ecuador before the court of Turin was successful. The property claimed by Ecuador came from archaeological excavations on the territory of Ecuador and had been purchased by Danusso on-site and illicitly exported to Italy. A property right was granted *ex lege* to Ecuador, that is to say, that this right flowed directly from its internal protective legislation on these goods. Despite the absence of such a law in the Italian legal system, the Italian court had to recognize the title of Ecuadorian property, established in the State.[111] In another case that illustrates the complexity of the course of many cultural assets, a US court ruled that the Greek Orthodox Church was entitled to retrieve icons from a Cypriot church because the US-based merchant who had purchased the icons in Switzerland from a Turkish seller had not exercised due diligence to ensure their provenance.[112]

The legal process is often found inadequate to address complex issues combining law, ethics, history, and morals and to consider other important factors in claims against cultural property, which explains why it has frequently given way to alternative mechanisms and compromises that avoid recourse to the courts.[113]

Although it is a rarity, some States, institutions, and individuals are choosing to make donations or "voluntary" renditions. For example, in 2000, Italy agreed to return the Venus of Cyrene, carried away during the colonial period and claimed by Libya,[114] in a unilateral and unconditional decision. A similar process was also used in 2011 by France to return to New Zealand a Maori heads kept in a Rouen City Museum since 1875.[115] However, the majority of heritage disputes are now regulated through mediation or arbitration processes between the parties. These offer several advantages: they differ from the strict application of law and appeal to norms and values that are not purely legal; they are more oriented toward satisfaction of the parties and the reconciliation of their interests, and, finally, they make possible the direct intervention of various relevant actors, such as museums.[116] As a result, the solutions developed at the end of these processes are extremely varied.

Restitution can, for example, be subject to conditions, or be conducted as part of an exchange. In 2007, the British Museum of Natural History returned the remains of 13 Aborigines to a Tasmanian community in exchange for the preservation of DNA samples taken from the remains for scientific purposes.[117] Along the same vein, a 2006 agreement between the Italian authorities and the Metropolitan Museum of Art in New York provided that in exchange for the return of the Euphronios crater, the museum would lend other goods of equal beauty, historical, and cultural significance.[118] The agreements reached during mediation may also provide formal recognition of the importance of the objects to the cultural identity of one of the parties. For example, the terms of the February 2002 agreement between France and Nigeria provided that

France recognized the Nigerian ownership of Nok and Sokoto artworks in exchange for a free and renewable 25 years' loan of these artworks to the Quai Branly Museum.[119] Extrajudicial processes also allow lawyers to make unprecedented legal arrangements. For example, in 1984, following the failure of a judicial procedure, a joint ownership agreement was established between the Fine Arts Museum of San Francisco and the National Institute of Anthropology and History of Mexico on Aztec murals of Teotihuacán.[120] This agreement provided for a sharing of the frescoes between the two institutions, and the sharing of the costs related to their exhibition and preservation.[121] In some cases, the museums in possession of the property in question can also accept them to be used by the community from which they come from for ritual purposes,[122] or may agree to display copies of the original goods. Finally, other solutions such as the official acquisition of property by a State already in possession of the property, the development of cultural cooperation programs, or the payment of compensation, may be adopted by the parties.

In the hope of emphasizing mediation, the UNESCO has established the *Intergovernmental Committee for Promoting the Return of Cultural Property to Its Countries of Origin or Its Restitution in Case of Illicit Appropriation*,[123] to which Jordan[124] and the Palestinian Authority[125] have chosen to turn with the case of the Dead Sea Scrolls. Established in 1978, this Committee aims to facilitate bilateral negotiations for the restitution of cultural property, particularly when the dispute falls outside the scope of existing international conventions. Composed of 22 UNESCO Member States, the committee has a purely advisory role and provides a framework for discussion and negotiation for States, without seeking to settle their quarrels by making a binding decision. Since its establishment, the UNESCO Committee has served as a forum for the resolution of some disputes over the return of cultural heritage objects. For example, in 1983, it was under the auspices of the Committee and after more than 7 years of negotiations that Italy returned over 12,000 pre-Columbian objects to Ecuador. The moral support of the Committee was then recognized by the Ecuadorian authorities as a significant factor in the success of their cause. However, most disputes now appear to be resolved outside the framework of the Intergovernmental Committee.[126]

While mediation offers routes and promising solutions, many important disputes remain unresolved, including the return of the treasures of the Summer Palace, the Parthenon marbles, and, of course, the contested ownership of the Dead Sea Scrolls. In fact, many return and restitution claims have specific characteristics, making it extremely difficult to formulate legal rules or principles of regulation of general application. The diversity of cultural goods and the variable ways in which they have been lost and acquired make the very idea of generalized solutions highly questionable.[127]

Final Remarks and Points for Reflection

Despite having ratified the 1970 UNESCO Convention, under which the Canadian government has an obligation to seize cultural property illicitly imported or exported on its territory,[128] as well as the *Convention for the Protection of Cultural Property in the Event of Conflict Armed* of 1954, this brief overview of the legal issues and normative frameworks for the protection of cultural property illustrates quite well the complexity of the issues raised by the controversy surrounding ownership of the Dead Sea Scrolls, and explains—at least in part—the reluctance of Canada, and that of other host countries of the exhibition,[129] to take a formal position in the dispute.[130]

First, it should be recalled that the controversy is rooted in a historically complex geopolitical situation. Indeed, it is clear that neither Israel nor Palestine existed, strictly speaking, at the time of the discovery of the first seven manuscripts in 1947, as the region was under the British mandate. From 1948, the region was then reorganized around a series of de facto situations on the ground without recognition of the international community. Whether it is the temporary annexation of the West Bank and East Jerusalem by Jordan from 1948 to 1967, or the occupation of Palestinian territories and East Jerusalem by Israel since 1967, in question, these territorial changes have never been officially sanctioned by the international community.

Added to this particularly difficult geopolitical situation is a complex and tangled legal situation, combining rules of international humanitarian law, public and private international law, and domestic law. However, none of these legal regimes seem able to provide a definitive answer or to address the legal issues raised. We even find that some of the rules from one legal regime may contradict other legal systems. The fragmentation of international law[131] and the lack of prioritization among competing regulatory systems constitute, in this case, a stumbling block that limits the identification of a single, simple legal solution.

Indeed, at the general public international law and IHL level, if the policies adopted to date establish rules and try to provide solutions to the most recent disputes, they suffer from significant limitations, particularly because of their non-retroactive status and their inapplicability to non-party States: if the situation in the dispute predates their adoption, or does not correspond to theft or illicit export, or if the countries concerned are not parties to these texts, the property may not be the subject of an action for recovery on the basis of these agreements. Concerning the purchase of manuscripts by McGill University in 1954 and 1955, for example, Jason Kalman and Jacqueline S. du Toit indicate that, although the fragments never left the Jordanian territory and were the result of "illegitimate" excavations, the purchase did and does not constitute in itself an offence under international law related to cultural goods, since they were purchased legally from the Jordanian government. For the authors, it is indeed important to note that the 1970 UNESCO Convention did not yet exist and has no retroactive force. On the other hand, according to the two authors, although the circumstances of discovery of the fragments in the 1950s (shortly after the first Arab-Israeli conflict) were "volatile," the context of discovery and sale was not one of an armed conflict, strictly speaking. Thus, according to them, the provisions of the 1954 *Convention for the Protection of Cultural Property in the Event of Armed Conflict* should not apply either.[132]

Moreover, if Israel and Jordan were indeed bound by the *Convention for the Protection of Cultural Property in the Event of Armed Conflict* and its first Protocol during the Six-Day War in 1967, and therefore Israel had the obligation not to take ownership of cultural property in occupied territories, several legal issues continue to be controversial. For example, some might call into question the qualification of the legal regime in the West Bank since 1967, arguing that this is not technically an occupation.[133] Others might argue that Jordan itself was occupying the West Bank between 1948 and 1967 and therefore could not appropriate the cultural property in that territory at the time, or claim ownership since 1967. Finally, Palestine, whose international recognition progresses to the full enjoyment of legal personality, will also make its own claims on appropriated cultural property by both Israel and Jordan.

Similarly, at the private international law and domestic law level, the multiplicity of specific legal rules in each State for the protection of their national heritage, as well as the multiplicity of legal principles (principle of limitation, protection of *bona fide* purchasers, contract law, etc.), can be difficult to reconcile. Thus, Israel's ownership of the 7 original manuscripts (purchased, respectively, in 1947 by Sukenik, and at the auction of 1954), and the purchase by Jordan of the manuscripts discovered between 1948 and 1956, raises new questions and disputes combining several competing legal regimes.

Finally, a third level of complexity emerges to the extent that the membership criteria of cultural property to a State or a community are not subject to international consensus and are not legally defined. Thus, the Palestinian Authority and Jordan base their claims on territorial aspects (places of discovery of the scrolls), humanitarian (illegal deprivation following the occupation of East Jerusalem by Israel) and legal (they claim to have proof of purchase of several scrolls) while, for its part, Israel's claims are primarily based in religious notions, invoking the sacred history of the Jewish people and recalling that the scrolls discovered in Qumran are, for the majority, the oldest known copies of biblical texts and are therefore of fundamental importance for the historical and religious heritage of Judaism.

To date, it is clear that the doctrine fails to provide a definitive answer to the question of primacy between a territorial sense of belonging and actual links established between a good and a community, nor a definite answer to the question of primacy between claims based on legal norms and those based on moral, ethical, or religious aspects.[134] It will be interesting to see if, and how, UNESCO will address these issues in the context of the possible investigation of the complaint Jordan filled about the possession of the scrolls by Israel.

Remember, finally, that this debate is part of a current geopolitical situation still tense between the Israeli State and its neighbors, whose conflict for the Dead Sea Scrolls property is one of many events.[135] As highlighted by Gil Desmoulins, the issue of heritage cultural property often has a highly political and diplomatic dimension because of the States' involvement in the protection of cultural property, or the claim of the existence of a national heritage, and the notion of territory it involves.[136] In this case, the question of the Dead Sea Scrolls fits perfectly into this issue and undeniably transcends States boundaries in an extremely complex geopolitical situation.

Hopefully the limits of law, illustrated in this paper, will push the parties concerned to find a negotiated diplomatic solution and a better understanding of the treasures revealed by these scrolls that would benefit all humanity. From this perspective, in the years to come, Canada will have the opportunity to show leadership by finding innovative solutions to address these types of issues. Let's recall to this effect the Canada's 150th anniversary celebrations in 2017, which included, among other things, a theme of nation-to-nation reconciliation with Aboriginal peoples,[137] as well as measures adopted by both provincial and federal governments to promote the restitution of indigenous heritages scattered at home and abroad.[138]

Notes

1. See in this regard Daniel Baril, 'Les manuscrits de la mer Morte revivent à Montréal' (2003) online: iForum, http://www.iforum.umontreal.ca/Forum/ArchivesForum/2003-2004/030915/article2648.htm.
2. Bernard Lamarche, 'Exposition—Musée Pointe-à-Callière: Record d'assistance pour la Bible' (9 September 2003) online: *Le Devoir*, http://www.ledevoir.com/culture/arts-visuels/35670/exposition-musee-pointe-a-calliere-record-d-assistance-pour-la-bible.
3. Royal Ontario Museum, 'Dead Sea Scrolls: Words That Changed the World Opens at the ROM on June 27, 2009' (18 February 2009) online: ROM, http://www.rom.on.ca/en/about-us/newsroom/press-releases/dead-sea-scrolls-words-that-changed-the-world-opens-at-the-rom-on.
4. Ross Oakland, 'Dead Sea Scrolls Stir Storm at ROM' (9 April 2009) online: *The Star*, https://www.thestar.com/business/tech_news/2009/04/09/dead_sea_scrolls_stir_storm_at_rom.html [Oakland].
5. Michael Valpy, 'Dead Sea Scrolls Exhibit Closes Amid Controversy' (3 January 2010) online: *Globe and Mail*, http://www.theglobeandmail.com/news/toronto/dead-sea-scrolls-exhibit-closes-amid-controversy/article4187053.
6. Claudine Douillet, 'Unesco: plainte jordanienne sur la propriété des manuscrits de la mer Morte' (12 January 2010) online: *Alliance*, http://www1.alliancefr.com/uncategorized/unesco-plainte-jordanienne-sur-la-propriete-des-manuscrits-de-la-mer-morte-509388 [Douillet]; 'Les manuscrits de la controverse'(5 January 2010) online: Radio Canada, http://www.radio-canada.ca/regions/ontario/2010/01/04/009-manuscrits-mer-morte.shtml.
7. Douillet, ibid.
8. Ibid.
9. See, e.g., Robin Coningham and Nick Lewer, 'The Vijayan Colonization and the Archaeology of Identity in Sri Lanka' (2000) 74 *Antiquity* 707, pp. 707–712.

10. See, e.g., Michael Asch and Catherine Bell, 'Definition and Interpretation of Fact in Canadian Aboriginal Title Litigation: An Analysis of Delgamuukw' (1993) 19 *Queen's L J* 503.

11. In Canada, for instance, the search for the remains of the Franklin Expedition had not only scientific objectives, but were also aimed at reaffirming Canada's sovereignty over the Northwest Passage into the Arctic Ocean. See, e.g., Stephen J. Harper, 'Franklin Discovery Strengthens Canada's Arctic Sovereignty' (12 September 2014) online: *The Globe and Mail*, http://www.theglobeandmail.com/news/politics/franklin-discovery-strengthens-canadas-arctic-sovereignty/article20590 280/. See also Steve Rennie, 'Franklin Find as Much About Sovereignty as Solving a Mystery' (11 September 2014) *The Canadian Press*, http://www.cbc.ca/news/canada/north/franklin-find-as-much-about-sovereignty-as-solving-a-mystery-1.2763117.

12. See Jean Duhaime and Thierry Legrand, *Les Rouleaux de la mer Morte*, Cahiers Évangile Supplément No. 152, Editions du Cerf, Paris, 2010 [Duhaime and Legrand]. See also Lawrence H. Schiffman, *Les Manuscrits de la Mer Morte et le Judaïsme*, translated and cited by Jean Duhaime, Fides, Anjou, 2003, p. 3 et seq.

13. Although the story of the events varies from one document to another, the most widespread and accepted version is based on the notes of John C. Trevor (1915–2006), one of the first academics to examine and photograph the Dead Sea Scrolls. James C. VanderKam, *The Dead Sea Scrolls Today*, 2nd edition, Cambridge, William B. Eerdmans Publishing Company, 2010 at 2 [VanderKam]. See also Aimé Fuchs, 'Les Manuscrits de la Mer Morte' (18 February 2000), online: IRMA, http://www-irma.u-strasbg.fr/~foata/fuchs/mer.pdf, at 2 [Fuchs].

14. VanderKam, ibid., at 4.

15. Ibid.

16. Fuchs, *supra* note 13 at 3.

17. VanderKam, *supra* note 13 at 12.

18. The *Treaty of Versailles* provided indeed that, at the end of the First World War, the colonies and possessions of the defeated powers would be withdrawn from them, and would be place under warrant pending their accession to independence. Thus, in the aftermath of the conflict, Britain was given a mandate over Palestine and Mesopotamia (modern Iraq and Jordan) which belonged to the defeated Ottoman Empire. Société des Nations, *Traité de Versailles*, 1919 online: Hérodote, http://www.herodote.net/Textes/tVersailles1919.pdf, at art 22.

19. *Resolution Adopted on the Report of the* Ad Hoc *Committee on the Palestinian Question*, Res GA 181(III), Doc off UN GA, 2nd sess, Doc UN A/RES/181/III (1947).

20. Véronique Chemla, 'Qumrân, le secret des manuscrits de la mer Morte' (9 February 2015) online: http://www.veroniquechemla.info/2010/07/qumran-le-secret-des-manuscrits-de-la.html [Chemla].
21. Jason Kalman and Jacqueline S. du Toit, 'Robert Balgarnie Young Scott, Premier spécialiste canadien des Manuscrits de la Mer morte' dans Jean Duhaime and Peter W. Flint, dir. *Célébrer les Manuscrits de la mer Morte: Une perspective canadienne*, Québec, Médias Paul, 2014 at 24.
22. Ibid., at 25. Other Universities and Institutions also proceeded to more modest purchases (Vatican, MA, Heidelberg, Oxford etc.).
23. VanderKam, *supra* note 13 at 17–18.
24. Fuchs, *supra* note 13 at 4.
25. VanderKam, *supra* note 13 at 16. For example, from 1949, the excavations are mostly organized between the Department of Antiquities of Jordan and the French Biblical and Archaeological School of Jerusalem. In 1953, the sharing rule allowed Father Roland de Vaux father to sell, to the National Library of France, some 377 fragments in order to continue financing the excavations he's then leading. Sophie Flouquet, 'Patrimoine biblique; Des manuscrits très politiques' (14 May 2010) online: *Le Journal des Arts*, http://www.lejournaldesarts.fr/jda/archives/docs_article/75658/des-manuscrits-tres-politiques.php. See also Daniel Estrin, 'Dead Sea Scroll Fragments to Hit the Auction Block' (25 May 2013) online: *The Times of Israel*, http://www.timesofisrael.com/dead-sea-scroll-fragments-to-hit-the-auction-block/ [Estrin].
26. Fuchs, *supra* note 13 at 3.
27. VanderKam, *supra* note 13 at 12.
28. Until the late 1980s, the slow pace of the Manuscripts related publications was such that some authors have termed it the "academic scandal of the 20th century." It is usually considered that the work has been significantly slowed by interpretation or translation quarrels, and by the fact that the teams of accredited researchers were extremely limited and, until 1987, excluded the Jewish researchers. The Vatican was also suspected of hindering the search. Fuchs, *supra* note 13 at 5.
29. Schiffman, *supra* note 12 at 17.
30. Jason Kalman and Jacqueline S. du Toit, *Canada's Big Biblical Bargain; How McGill University Bought the Dead Sea Scrolls*, Montréal, McGill-Queen's Press, 2010 at 118 [Kalman et Du Toit. *Canada's Big Biblical Bargain*].
31. Ibid., at 119–120.
32. Ibid. at 123. See also Schiffman, *supra* note 12 at 17.
33. See in particular Resolutions 252 (1968), 476 (1980), 478 (1980). 'La question de la Palestine; Le statut de Jérusalem' online: UN, http://www.un.org/french/Depts/palestine/issues_jerusalem.shtml.
34. Duhaime and Legrand, *supra* note 12 at 162.

35. Estrin, *supra* note 25. Jean-Philippe Nadeau, 'Les manuscrits de la controverse' (5 January 2010) online: Radio Canada, http://www.radio-canada.ca/regions/ontario/2010/01/04/009-manuscrits-mer-morte.shtml [Nadeau].

36. Oakland, *supra* note 4.

37. Chemla, *supra* note 20. See also 'Israël et Google mettent en ligne 5000 images des manuscrits de la mer morte' (4 January 2013) online: Club Innovation & Culture France, http://www.club-innovation-cul ture.fr/israel-et-google-mettent-en-ligne-5-000-images-des-manuscrits-de-la-mer-morte/.

38. In 1967, in particular, the Israeli authorities have obtained the *Temple Scroll* which was still in possession of Kando. Arrested and briefly jailed by the Israeli army under the command of Yadin (son of Professor Sukenik), Kando would have revealed concealing this Manuscript and eventually sold it to the Israeli government for $125,000. Estrin, *supra* note 25.

39. Since 1993, following the death of antiquarian Kando, his heirs have been found to be in possession of dozens of fragments preserved in Switzerland since the 1960s. Numerous fragments have since been sold to private collectors for several million dollars every time. The Israeli authorities consider such transactions illegal and threaten vendors and buyers of prosecution. Estrin, ibid.

40. Jean Ansar, 'Unesco: c'est la guerre archéologique en Palestine, à commencer par la bataille des manuscrits de la mer Morte' (4 November 2011) online: http://archives.metamag.fr/imprimer-met amag-489-Unesco-c%E2%80%99est-la-guerre-archeologique-en-Palest ine-A-commencer-par-la-bataille-des-manuscrits-de-la-mer-Morte-.html. See also Michael Valpy, 'Dead Sea Scrolls Exhibit Closes amid Controversy' (23 August 2012) online: *The Globe and Mail*, http://www.the globeandmail.com/news/toronto/dead-sea-scrolls-exhibit-closes-amid-controversy/article4187053/.

41. 'La Palestine devient membre à part entière de l'Unesco' (1 November 2011) online: *Le Monde*, http://www.lemonde.fr/proche-orient/art icle/2011/10/31/l-unesco-se-prononce-sur-la-demande-d-adhesion-de-l-autorite-palestinienne_1596258_3218.html.

42. *Status of Palestine in the United Nations*, Res GA 67/19, Doc off UN GA, 67th sess, Doc UN A/RES/67/19 (2012).

43. '*La Palestine*' online: Cour pénale internationale, https://www.icc-cpi. int/fr_menus/icc/structure%20of%20the%20court/office%20of%20the% 20prosecutor/comm%20and%20ref/peongoing/palestine/Pages/palest ine.aspx.

44. Estrin, *supra* note 25.

45. Ibid.

46. Nadeau, *supra* note 35. Douillet, *supra* note 6.
47. Nadeau, ibid.
48. 'Unesco: plainte jordanienne sur la propriété des manuscrits de la mer Morte' (11 January 2010) online: http://www.rtl.be/info/monde/int ernational/unesco-plainte-jordanienne-sur-la-propriete-des-manuscrits-de-la-mer-morte-146781.aspx.
49. Although there are several definitions of the concept of cultural property, we propose to retain the broad definition in Article 1 of the *Convention for the Protection of Cultural Property in the Event of Armed Conflict*. Under this definition, the term cultural property covers "(a) movable or immovable property of great importance to the cultural heritage of every people, such as monuments of architecture, art or history, whether religious or secular; archaeological sites; groups of buildings which, as a whole, are of historical or artistic interest; works of art; manuscripts, books and other objects of artistic, historical or archaeological interest; as well as scientific collections and important collections of books or archives or of reproductions of the property defined above; (b) buildings whose main and effective purpose is to preserve or exhibit the movable cultural property defined in sub-paragraph (a) such as museums, large libraries and depositories of archives, and refuges intended to shelter, in the event of armed conflict, the movable cultural property defined in sub-paragraph (a); (c) centers containing a large amount of cultural property as defined in sub-paragraphs (a) and (b), to be known as 'centers containing monuments'." *Convention for the Protection of Cultural Property in the Event of Armed Conflict with Regulations for the Execution of the Convention*, 14 May 1954 (entered into force on 7 August 1956), 249 UNTS 216 at art 1 [*Convention for the Protection of cultural property in the event of armed conflict*].
50. Lyndel V. Prott, dir. *Témoins de l'histoire: Recueil de textes et documents relatifs au retour des objets culturels*, UNESCO, 2011 at 2 [Prott].
51. Victor Hugo, 'Lettre au Capitaine Butler' (25 November 1861) online: *Le Monde Diplomatique*, https://www.monde-diplomatique.fr/2004/10/HUGO/11563.
52. Gil Desmoulins, 'La restitution internationale des biens culturels' (5 October 2012) *Carnet du séminaire carrières publiques de l'IEP de Rennes* at 13 [Desmoulins].
53. Ibid.
54. *Treaty of Peace Between the Allied and Associated Powers and Italy*, 61 Stat. 1245 and Treaties and Other International Acts Series 1648 at art 12 and 37. See also Jean-Marie Henckaerts and Louise Doswald-Beck, *Customary International Humanitarian Law; Volume 1: Rules*, Genève, Bruxelles, CICR, Bruylant, 2006, at rule 41 [Henckaerts and Doswald-Beck, *Customary IHL, Volume 1*].

55. Prott, *supra* note 50 at 207.
56. Ibid., at 195.
57. Ibid., at 12.
58. Numerous resolutions and recommendations of the UN and UNESCO go in this direction, but no binding international instrument exists. Desmoulins, *supra* note 52 at 14.
59. Ibid., at 17–18.
60. See, e.g., *Convention 169 Concerning Indigenous and Tribal Peoples in Independent Countries*, 27 June 1989 (entry into force 5 September 1991) 72 Official Bull. 59 (1989) of the International Labour Organization and the *United Nations Declaration on the Rights of Indigenous Peoples*, Res GA 61/295, Doc off UN GA, 61st sess, Doc UN A/61/L.67 (2006) [*UN Declaration on the Rights of Indigenous Peoples*].
61. Prott, *supra* note 50 at 43.
62. Ibid., at 208.
63. The *United Nations Declaration on the Rights of Indigenous Peoples* recognizes their authority to control the use of their cultural property and encourages States to "provide redress through effective mechanisms, which may include restitution, developed in conjunction with indigenous peoples, with respect to their cultural, intellectual, religious and spiritual property taken without their free, prior and informed consent or in violation of their laws, traditions and customs." *UN Declaration on Rights of Indigenous Peoples*, *supra* note 60 at art 11, 12 and 13. This statement, however, has no binding force.
64. Desmoulins, *supra* note 52 at 20.
65. Ibid., at 4 and 15.
66. *Cultural Property Export and Import Act*, R.S.C. (1985) (c. C-51) online: http://laws-lois.justice.gc.ca/eng/acts/C-51//.
67. On this subject, see the Web site of the Canadian government at: https://www.canada.ca/en/canadian-heritage.html.
68. *Convention on the Means of Prohibiting and Preventing the Illicit Import, Export and Transfer of Ownership of Cultural Property*, 14 November 1970 (entry into force 24 April 1972) 823 UNTS 254 [*Convention on the Means of Prohibiting and Preventing the Illicit Import, Export and Transfer of Ownership of Cultural Property*].
69. *Unidroit Convention on Stolen or Illegally Exported Cultural Objects*, 24 June 1995 (entry into force 1 July 1998) 2421 UNTS 457.
70. Other conventions related to the cultural heritage can also be mentioned, such as the *Convention on the Protection of the Underwater Cultural Heritage*, 2 November 2001 (entry into force 2 January 2009) 2562 UNTS 3, and the *Convention for the Safeguarding of the Intangible*

Cultural Heritage, 17 October 2003 (entry into force 20 April 2006) 2368 UNTS 3.

71. See, e.g., le *Règlement (CEE) n° 3911/92 du Conseil du 9 décembre 1992 concernant l'exportation de biens culturels vers des pays tiers*, et la *Directive (CEE) n° 93/7 du Conseil du 15 mars 1993, relative à la restitution de biens culturels ayant quitté illicitement le territoire d'un État membre.*

72. It may be mentioned, for example, the *UNESCO Recommendation Concerning the International Exchange of Cultural Property* (1976), the *UNESCO Recommendation for the Protection of Movable Cultural Property* (1978), the numerous resolutions of the UN General Assembly and the Security Council, or the various opinions or codes of conduct developed by NGOs such as the ICOM (*International Council of Museums*), the International Council on Archives, the International Council on Monuments and Sites or the International Federation of Library Associations and Institutions.

73. The international humanitarian law is a set of rules that seek to limit the effects of armed conflict. It especially protects people who do not or who no longer participate in the hostilities, and restricts the means and methods of warfare that belligerents can use. See International Committee of the Red Cross, 'What is international humanitarian law?', Advisory Service (December 2014) online: ICRC, https://www.icrc.org/en/document/what-international-humanitarian-law. See also Marco Sassoli and Antoine A. Bouvier, *How Does Law Protect in War?*, 2e éd., CICR, Genève, 2012, 3 vol, online: ICRC, https://www.icrc.org/en/document/how-does-law-protect-war-0, at 131–139 [Sassoli and Bouvier, *How Does Law Protect in War?*].

74. See, e.g., Sassoli and Bouvier, *How Does Law Protect in War?*, ibid., Chapter 9 at 24 and following. François Bugnion, 'La genèse de la protection juridique des biens culturels en cas de conflit armé' (2004) 86:854 RICR 313. Thomas Desch, 'The Second Protocol to the 1954 Hague Convention for the Protection of Cultural Property in the Event of Armed Conflict' (1999) 2 YIHL 63. Jean-Marie Henckaerts, 'New Rules for the Protection of Cultural Property in Armed Conflict: The Significance of the Second Protocol to the 1954 Hague Convention for the Protection of Cultural Property in the Event of Armed Conflict' (1999) 12:3 Humanitäres Völkerrecht 147. Jan Hladik, 'Protection of Cultural Property: The Legal Aspects', in Richard B. Jacques, dir. 'Issues in International Law and Military Operations' (2006) 80 International Law Studies 319. Jean A. Konopka, dir. *La protection des biens culturels en temps de guerre et de paix d'après les conventions internationales (multilatérales)*, Genève, Imprimerie de Versoix, 1997. Vittorio Mainetti, 'De nouvelles perspectives pour la protection des

biens culturels en cas de conflit armé: l'entrée en vigueur du Deuxième Protocole relatif à la Convention de La Haye de 1954' (2004) 86:854 RICR 337. Roger O'keefe, *The Protection of Cultural Property in Armed Conflict*, Cambridge, Cambridge University Press, 2006. Emmanuelle Stavraki, *La Convention pour la protection des biens culturels en cas de conflit armé*, Athènes, Éditions Ant. N. Sakkoulas, 1996. Gerard J. Tanja, 'Recent Developments Concerning the Law for the Protection of Cultural Property in the Event of Armed Conflict' (1994) Leiden Journal of International Law 115. Erika J. Techera, 'Protection of Cultural Heritage in Times of Armed Conflict: The International Legal Framework Revisited' (2007) 4:1 Macquarie Journal of International and Comparative Environmental Law 1. Jiri Toman, *The Protection of Cultural Property in the Event of Armed Conflict*, Aldershot/Paris, Dartmouth Publishing Company/UNESCO Publishing, 1996. 'Special Issue: Protection of Cultural Property in Armed Conflict' (2004) 854 RICR 311. Nout Van Woudenberg and Liesbeth Lijnzaad, dir. *Protecting Cultural Property in Armed Conflict: an Insight into the 1999s Protocol to the Hague Convention of 1954 for the Protection of Cultural Property in the Event of Armed Conflict*, Leiden, Boston, M. Nijhoff, 2010.

75. IHL distinguishes between international armed conflicts and non-international armed conflicts. The first essentially oppose the armed forces of two separate States. See Article 2 common to the four Geneva Conventions: *Geneva Convention for the Amelioration of the Wounded and Sick in Armed Forces in the Field*, 12 August 1949, 75 UNTS 31; *Geneva Convention for the Amelioration of the Condition of Wounded, Sick and Shipwrecked Members of Armed Forces at Sea*, 12 August 1949, 75 UNTS 85; *Geneva Convention Relative to the Treatment of Prisoners of War*, 12 August 1949, 75 UNTS 135; *Geneva Convention Relative to the Protection of Civilian Persons in Time of War* of 12 August 1949, 75 UNTS 287. Since 1977, it is generally recognized that these conflicts also include wars of national liberation against colonial and racist regimes. See Article 1 of *Protocol I Additional to the Geneva Conventions of 12 August 1949 relating to the Protection of Victims of International Armed Conflicts*, 8 June 1977, 1125 UNTS 3 [PA I]. Non-international armed conflicts, or internal conflicts, sometimes also called civil wars, usually oppose the State's armed forces and organized armed groups, or these groups between them. See generally, article 3 common to the four Geneva Conventions. See also *Protocol Additional to the Geneva Conventions of 12 August 1949 on the Protection of Victims of Non-international Armed Conflicts*, 8 June 1977, 1125 UNTS 609 [PA II].

76. IHL designates as belligerents the members of the armies of States parties to an international or internal armed conflict forces, and those

who participate directly in the hostilities in the context of an internal conflict.

77. See Judith Gardham, *Necessity, Proportionality and the Use of Force by States*, Cambridge, Cambridge University Press, 2004, p. 259. Michael N. Schmitt, 'Military Necessity and Humanity in International Humanitarian Law: Preserving the Delicate Balance' (2010) 50:4 *Virginia Journal of International Law* 795.

78. Sassoli and Bouvier, *How Does Law Protect in War?*, *supra* note 73 Chapter 4 at 12 and following.

79. See, e.g., PA I, *supra* note 75 at art 52 para 2.

80. *Rome Statute of the International Criminal Court*, 17 July 1998 (entry into force 1 July 2002) 2187 UNTS 3 at art 8 [*Rome Statute*].

81. PA I, *supra* note 75 at art 52 para 3.

82. *Convention (IV) Respecting the Laws and Customs of War on Land and Its Annex: Regulations Concerning the Laws and Customs of War on Land*, 18 October 1907 at art 27 [*Convention (IV) and Its Annex*].

83. *Convention for the Protection of Cultural Property in the Event of Armed Conflict*, *supra* note 49 at art 4.

84. It is prohibited "(a) to commit any acts of hostility directed against the historic monuments, works of art or places of worship which constitute the cultural or spiritual heritage of peoples; (b) to use such objects in support of the military effort [and] (c) to make such objects the object of reprisals". PA I, *supra* note 75 at art 53, applicable in times of international armed conflict. See also PA II, *supra* note 75 at art 16, applicable in times of non-international armed conflict.

85. *Second Protocol to the Hague Convention of 1954 for the Protection of Cultural Property in the Event of Armed Conflict*, 26 March 1999 (entry into force 9 March 2004) 2253 UNTS 172 at art 15.

86. In 2006, the ICRC has published a study on the content of the standards of customary international humanitarian law, which include among others in times of international armed conflict or non-international "[e] ach party to the conflict must respect cultural property: A. special care must be taken in military operations to avoid damage to buildings dedicated to religion, art, science, education or charitable purposes, and as historical monuments, provided they are not military objectives. B. Property of great importance to the cultural heritage of peoples must not be the object of attack, except in cases of imperative military necessity". Furthermore "[t]he use of property of great importance to the cultural heritage of peoples for purposes likely to expose it to destruction or damage is prohibited, except in case of imperative military necessity." See Henckaerts and Doswald-Beck, *Customary IHL, Volume 1*, *supra* note 54 at rules 38 and 39.

87. *The Procuror c. Pavle Strugar*, IT-01-42-T, Judgement (31 January 2005) (International Criminal Tribunal for the former Yugoslavia, Trial Chamber), Part. B at paras 229–233 and 298–329, online: ICTY, http://www.icty.org/x/cases/strugar/tjug/fr/050131.pdf. See also *Rome Statute, supra* note 80 at art 8.
88. *Convention for the Protection of Cultural Property in the Event of Armed Conflict, supra* note 49 at art 6, 10 and 16.
89. Ibid., at art 5 para 1.
90. Ibid., at art 5 para 2.
91. *Convention (IV) and Its Annex, supra* note 82 at art 56.
92. *Convention pour la protection des biens culturels en cas de conflit armé, supra* note 49 at art 4 para 3.
93. Henckaerts and Doswald-Beck, *Customary IHL, Volume 1, supra* note 54 at rule 40: 'Each party to the conflict must protect cultural property: A. All seizure of or destruction or wilful damage done to institutions dedicated to religion, charity, education, the arts and sciences, historic monuments and works of art and science is prohibited. B. Any form of theft, pillage or misappropriation of, and any acts of vandalism directed against, property of great importance to the cultural heritage of every people is prohibited'.
94. Ibid. See also ICTY, *Tadić case*, 'Decision on the Defence Motion for Interlocutory Appeal on Jurisdiction', The Prosecutor v. Dusko *Tadić*, Case No: IT-94-1-AR72, Appeals Chamber, 2 October 1995. Voir *Rome Statute, supra* note 80 at art 8.
95. Ibid. See also France, Permanent Military Tribunal at Metz, *Lingenfelder case* dans The United Nations War Crimes Commission "Law reports of trials of war criminals", Volume IX, 1949, à la p 67; United States, Military Tribunal at Nuremberg, *Von Leeb (The High Command Trial) case, et* T *Weizsaecker case* dans Trials of War Criminals Before the Nuernberg Military Tribunals Under Control Council Law No 10, October 1946–April 1949, Washington, DC: U.S. Government Printing Office, 194.
96. *Le Procureur c. Ahmad Al Faqi Al Mahdi*, ICC-01/12-01/15, Judgment (27 September 2016) (International Criminal Court). See also Stéphanie Maupas, ' Destruction de mausolées à Tombouctou: un djihadiste condamné à neuf ans de prison' (27 September 2016) en ligne: *Le Monde*, http://www.lemonde.fr/afrique/article/2016/09/27/un-djihadiste-malien-juge-coupable-par-la-cpi-de-la-destruction-de-mausolees-a-tombouctou_5004139_3212.html.
97. *Protocol to the Convention for the Protection of Cultural Property in the Event of Armed Conflict*, 14 May 1954 (entry into force 7 August 1956) 249 UNTS 217 at art 1.
98. Ibid., at art 2.

99. Henckaerts and Doswald-Beck, *Customary IHL, Volume 1, supra* note 54 at rule 41: 'The occupying power must prevent the illicit export of cultural property from occupied territory and must return illicitly exported property to the competent authorities of the occupied territory'.

100. Ibid. See also Security Council, Res. 686, 2 March 1991, at para 2 (d); Res. 1284, 17 December 1999, at para 14 and Res. 1483 (22 May 2003) online: CICR, https://www.icrc.org/customary-ihl/eng/docs/v2_rul_rule41, at para 7.

101. See, e.g., Mahmed Abdallah, *Awad Rawidi & Zeev Matches v. The Israeli Defense Forces*, 283/69, 24:2 PADI 419 (HJC 1970), tel que mentionné dans Shoshana Berman, 'Antiquities in Israel in a Maze of Controversy', Case in 19 *Case W. Res. J. Int'l L.* 343 1987, 356–360 and referring to Islamic Summit Conference, Ninth Session (12–13 November 2000) Res. 25/8-C (IS), online: CICR, https://www.icrc.org/customary-ihl/eng/docs/v2_rul_rule41.

102. Desmoulins, *supra* note 52 at 3.

103. The Artemis platform, online since 2010 by the University of Geneva, includes a rich database (in French and English) containing the presentation of numerous decisions related to art law and cultural property made by alternative methods of dispute resolution or by litigation. Artemis is available at the following address: https://plone.unige.ch/art-adr.

104. Prott, *supra* note 50 at 353.

105. Desmoulins, *supra* note 52 at 6–7. However, this is often seen as "unfair" to the extent that it would tend to favor the "*law shopping.*" In addition, before being acquired by a purchaser in good faith protected under national law, an item may have been stolen or exported illegally.

106. See, e.g., *United Nations Convention on Jurisdictional Immunities of States and Their Property*, 2 December 2004 (shall enter into force on the thirtieth day following the date of deposit of the thirtieth instrument of ratification, acceptance, approval or accession), N/D, GA Res A/59/38 (2 December 2004).

107. In Canada, see *State Immunity Act*, R.S.C. (1985) (c. S-18) online: http://laws-lois.justice.gc.ca/eng/acts/S-18/.

108. Indeed, despite the inalienable character of the crimes related to cultural heritage, a wrongful dispossession can sometimes lose its importance. Regarding the oldest cases for example, it may be considered that the time has purged the vices of the dispossession or, under the law applicable at the time, it is estimated that the dispossession wasn't unlawful.

109. Prott, *supra* note 50 at 325; ArThemis, *supra* note 103.

110. Prott, ibid., at 384.

111. Desmoulins, *supra* note 52 at 6.

112. Prott, *supra* note 50 at 412.
113. However, it is common for arbitration or mediation processes to be adopted by the Parties on decision or recommendation of a court seized of the matter. See in particular Marie Cornu et Marc-André Renold, 'Le renouveau des restitutions de biens culturels: les modes alternatifs de règlement des litiges' (2009) online: Art Law, http://www.art-law.org/centre/publications/jdiCornu-Renold.pdf [Cornu et Renold].
114. Desmoulins, *supra* note 52 at 18.
115. ArThemis, *supra* note 103.
116. Museums can sometimes enjoy certain freedoms in the management of their collections and thus possess a discretionary power to return or exchange cultural items.
117. This mediation was made on the recommendation of the Londoner High Court which had originally been seized of the matter. ArThemis, *supra* note 103. See also Prott, *supra* note 50 at 436–429.
118. Cornu et Renold, *supra* note 113 at 518.
119. Ibid., at 520.
120. Several reasons have been cited by the Fine Arts Museums of San Francisco to begin the negotiation process: '*Personnel at the Museum cited several reasons for the decision to negotiate. First, they felt that the ethical aspects at stake exceeded the complicated legal dispute. Second, they felt that they had a moral duty to find an acceptable compromise to ensure the best preservation of the murals. Third, the Museum accepted the Mexican claim that the murals were of cultural significance to Mexico. Fourth, the Museum was not specialized in Mexican or Pre-Columbian art, so the Mexicans could provide the Museum with important assistance in the conservation of the mural fragments*'. ArThemis, *supra* note 103.
121. Ibid.
122. Desmoulins, *supra* note 52 at 21.
123. *Intergovernmental Committee for Promoting the Return of Cultural Property to Its Countries of Origin or Its Restitution in case of Illicit Appropriation*, UNESCO, online: UNESCO, http://portal.unesco.org/culture/en/ev.php-url_id=35283&url_do=do_topic&url_section=201.html.
124. Douillet, *supra* note 6.
125. Tovah Lazaroff, 'Palestinians Make a Play for Dead Sea Scrolls at UNESCO' (6 November 2016) online: *Jerusalem Post*, http://www.jpost.com/Arab-Israeli-Conflict/Palestinians-make-a-play-for-Dead-Sea-Scrolls-at-UNESCO-471781.
126. Ibid.
127. Prott, *supra* note 50 at 161.
128. The 1970 UNESCO Convention urges States 'to take the necessary measures, consistent with national legislation, to prevent museums and

similar institutions within their territories from acquiring cultural property originating in another State Party which has been illegally exported after entry into force of this Convention, in the States concerned. Whenever possible, to inform a State of origin Party to this Convention of an offer of such cultural property illegally removed from that State after the entry into force of this Convention in both States'. *Convention on the Means of Prohibiting and Preventing the Illicit Import, Export and Transfer of Ownership of Cultural Property, supra* note 68 at art 7a.

129. Since the late 1990s, several countries such as the United States, France, Brazil, the UK, Australia, Germany, and the Vatican have also organized exhibitions of the Dead Sea Scrolls. Although these countries are also parties to at least one of the Conventions mentioned, none has taken measures to seize the manuscripts.

130. "States usually protect themselves against such thorny claims by adopting decrees of unseizability of the works of arts admitted on their territory. Quebec's museums have constantly resorted to this legal strategy, which has been amplified by the claims of the heirs of the Jews and other Europeans despoiled in Germany and then in Europe under Nazi rule. However, it was impossible to know whether Ottawa had used the legal procedure in the case of manuscripts" [our translation]. Stéphane Baillargeon, 'Ottawa refuse de saisir les manuscrits de la mer Morte' (6 January 2010) online: *Le Devoir*, http://www.ledevoir.com/culture/liv res/280532/ottawa-refuse-de-saisir-les-manuscrits-de-la-mer-morte.

131. Mireille Delmas-Marty, *Les Forces imaginantes du droit – Le relatif et l'universel*, Paris, Seuil, 2004.

132. Kalman et Du Toit, *Canada's Big Biblical Bargain, supra* note 30 at 129–130.

133. *Legal Consequences of the Construction of a Wall in the Occupied Palestinian Territory*, advisory opinion (2004) online: ICJ, http://www. icj-cij.org/docket/index.php?p1=3&p2=4&case=131&p3=4, at 136 and 174. Israel stated that the territories occupied after the Six-Day War in 1967 did not fall under the Jordanian sovereignty. Note, however, that this argument was not accepted by the International Court of Justice in connection with this case.

134. Desmoulins, *supra* note 52 at 17.

135. The dispute over the ownership of the Dead Sea Scrolls is reminiscent of the dilemma surrounding the restitution of the Jewish archives of Baghdad. In 2003, American forces deployed on Iraqi soil were led to save a large amount of archives, books, and other documents relating to one of the oldest Jewish communities in the world. Sent to the United States for restoration, these documents have since been the subject of a dispute between the Jewish communities and the Jewish diaspora in Iraq on the one hand, and the Iraqi government on the

other, claiming ownership over the documents. Here, the controversy centers on whether these documents should be returned to the territory from which they originated and therefore to the Iraqi government, or their culture of origin, that is to say to the Jewish communities. See Bruce P. Montgomery, 'Rescue or Return: The Fate of the Iraqi Jewish Archive' (2013) 20 *International Journal of Cultural Property* 175–200.

136. Desmoulins, *supra* note 52 at 3.
137. Office of the Premier, 'Province and Royal BC Museum Join Aboriginal Peoples to Bring Cultural Belongings Home' (21 June 2016) online: BC Gov News, https://news.gov.bc.ca/releases/2016PREM0070-001105.
138. Indeed since 2003, the Government of British Columbia has contributed to the restitution of various Aboriginal artifacts to the communities from which they originated and that were located in museums in the United States, Sweden, and the UK. Ibid.; See also 'G'psgolox pole Returns Home After 77 Years, First Totem Ever to Be Repatriated from Overseas' (26 April 2006) online: *Ecotrust*, http://ecotrust.ca/gps golox-pole-returns-home-after-77-years-first-totem-ever-be-repatriated-oversea/. Several Canadian provinces have also introduced legislation to facilitate such restitutions, like the *Alberta's First Nations Sacred Ceremonial Objects Repatriation Act* (2000) or the *British Columbia the Museum Act* (2003). Voir Florence Dupré, Frédéric Laugrand et Pierre Maranda, dir. *La restitution du patrimoine matériel et immatériel: Regards croisés Canada /Mélanésie*, Québec, Les Cahiers du CIÉRA, No. 2, 2008.

CHAPTER 7

Should Canada Have an International Broadcaster?

Ira Wagman

In taking up the question posed by my title, I start with the spoiler alert that I am leaning in the direction of a "no" answer. For the purposes of this brief chapter, I view taking this stance as decidedly more productive than offering the conventional "yes" position. This is because arguing against the need for a national broadcaster allows us to take a more comprehensive understanding of two themes of public diplomacy that are of interest to me, both as a general area of practice and more specifically as it applies to the contemporary Canadian case. The first considers the place of broadcasting within Canadian life, a status that has frequently seen its lofty promise to bind the country together offset by more sobering realities. The second entails a thorough consideration of the overlap between diplomatic work and media technologies. To be more specific, I want to reflect briefly on the ways our treatment of that overlap carries with it a series of lay assumptions about the capabilities of media technologies and what constitutes effective and ineffective communication. These

I. Wagman (✉)
Carleton University, Ottawa, ON, Canada
e-mail: IraWagman@carleton.ca

© The Author(s) 2021   161
N. J. Cull and M. K. Hawes (eds.), *Canada's Public Diplomacy*,
Palgrave Macmillan Series in Global Public Diplomacy,
https://doi.org/10.1007/978-3-319-62015-2_7

two related themes coalesce around the broader idea, best expressed by Jönsson and Hall, that diplomacy is a *communicative* enterprise—one that dreams of messages reaching their intended destination in the hope of persuading publics to think or behave in a certain way and which uses media technologies as instruments to facilitate what they call "an international society".[1]

In the pages that follow, I want to argue that Canada does not need an international broadcaster for effective and persuasive public diplomacy because, to a large extent, its experience with developing a national broadcasting system has been highly fraught and beset by internal contradictions. The narratives associated with the country's success on the diplomatic stage—those that trumpet its "middle-power" status, its "Team Canada" brand, or its "quiet diplomacy" run parallel to a prominent discourse—particularly in English-speaking Canada—have long seen broadcasting as a medium that routinely fails to achieve its various objectives. Indeed, with the exception of the odd hockey game or Tragically Hip concert that "bring people together", the history of broadcasting in Canada is one of precariousness, hand-wringing, and relentless internal tinkering. One of the features of contemporary diplomatic practices that employ digital technologies, applications, and platforms, is that they may render a discussion about the need for an international broadcaster anachronistic, a hammer at a time when a wrench will do the trick. In Canada, that sense may be even more poignant; as media forms, digital technologies are effectively free of the baggage that broadcasting has carried for many decades.

The main reason why the subject is up for debate is due to the slow diminution of Canada's place within the world of international broadcasting. In operation since 1945 as the "Voice of Canada" broadcasting in German, English, and French, the international service of the Canadian Broadcasting Corporation (now known as Radio Canada International) has been put to use for a variety of purposes: shortwave service during wartime, as a tool for propaganda, and for the distribution of programming specific for international audiences interested in Canada's peoples and cultures. The service expanded from there, with regular transmissions in Czech and Dutch, then Swedish, Danish, Norwegian, Spanish, and Portuguese, among other languages. It provided transmissions of daily UN broadcasts through its Sackville transmitter during the 1950s. Throughout the 1960s, 1970s, and 1980s, the service expanded its range to Africa, Latin and South America, and Australia and New Zealand in an effort to reach new audiences and serve as a tool in Canada's Cold War information efforts.[2] The better part of the recent history of the CBC's overseas service since the 1990s is one of diminution, as a process of staff reductions, budget cuts, and the removal of different linguistic services, occasionally offset by last-minute reprieves and temporary lifelines.

In 2012, Radio Canada International was taken off the air. When a 10% budget cut was imposed upon the CBC by the Conservative government, the international service bore a considerable brunt of the carnage, going from a budget of just over $12 million to slightly over $2 million.[3] What remains from two-and-a-half decades of operational precariousness is a skimpy website that offers visitors a few headlines, some magazine-style stories, a weekly podcast, a smattering of columns, some educational materials about Aboriginal Canadians and the Arctic, and an introduction to Canadian geography in five different languages. This effort is undertaken by a skeleton crew of what remains of RCI's staff operating out of their Montreal office. As Evan Potter puts it mildly in his book, *Branding Canada*, "The history of RCI in promoting what would come to be called public diplomacy is highly chequered".[4]

The nature of that highly chequered history is particularly relevant in the light of the expansion of international broadcasting that occured in tandem with RCI's period of contraction. Pan-Arab broadcasters like Al-Jazeera, traditional broadcasters like the BBC World Service, and newer players like France 24, Russia's RT network, China's CCTV, and the United States's Voice of America and Al-Hurra service are some of the most representative examples. All of these services combine the traditions of multilingual news and information dissemination with the new and expanded connectivity of digital and networked technologies, streaming content live on websites and through the various social media platforms 24 hours a day.[5] The presence of these new modes of service delivery was trotted out as the rationale for the reduction of CBC's service, including cuts to both its linguistic offerings and shortwave service.

Given this apparent disconnect between the decline of RCI and the international expansion of other national broadcasting services, and alongside the more outward-facing stance of the current government, it would stand to reason that a reinvigorated RCI with a prominent place on the digital landscape would be the prudent course of action. The reasons for this are obvious: the CBC's reputation for high-quality journalism and Canada's reputation for tolerance, fairness, and difference seems like a good brand for an information dissemination service operating in the face of an environment characterized by chaos and misinformation. One might argue that in an era of "fake news" and amidst the recent calls that some of these services constitute propaganda arms for foreign governments,[6] a Canadian international broadcasting system might emerge as it does in the global diplomatic sphere, as a "middle" media power.

Such a position would piggyback on Canada's reputation for its contribution to journalism education, including its scholarly involvement in the preparation of model curricula for emerging societies prepared by UNESCO.[7] The argument used by other countries engaged in international broadcasting—especially France and Qatar—that the dominance of American-centric news calls for counter-flows offering different perspectives and talking back to powerful or hegemonic voices should be familiar territory for Canadians, as their own broadcasting and cultural policy apparatus is effectively aimed to ensure the presence of Canadian perspectives amidst the cultural dominance of its neighbour to the south. Some might even note that a revived RCI could play a role in assisting in the distribution and display of Canadian cultural works, making it a tool in a broader cultural diplomacy toolkit that was mothballed by the previous government but which now appears to be back on Trudeau's foreign affairs agenda.[8]

These claims are easily countered by the assertion that the belief in the power of an international broadcaster is reminiscent of a media age defined by a small number of powerful national media organizations, spectrum scarcity, and mass audiences. In a digital world characterized by abundance and fragmentation, access to a variety of cultures and perspectives has never been easier. Given that people can already access the CBC's main website, a dedicated international service might be superfluous or a waste of resources. Indeed, some might argue that silence in this area has hardly damaged our international reputation. Some of the best perspectives about Canada are coming from international broadcasters and legacy media themselves, as recent stories posted on the websites of *The Wall Street Journal* and the expanded Canada section of the *BBC News* service will attest.[9] This is to say nothing about the ways the fawning coverage of our Prime Minister's affairs—shirtless and otherwise—are emblematic of a new (or re-emerging) Canadian brand: a bastion of tolerance and effectively functioning liberal democracy bravely sailing along against powerful currents of neo-populist movements in the United States and across Europe. From this, we can argue that there are simply different—and better—tools for the job than what an international broadcaster can provide.

As persuasive as those two views may be, there are also more subtle angles to the story, ones that tip the balance further towards the "no" side. As I mentioned earlier, part of the problem with the notion of a strong international broadcaster is that Canada has had problems with broadcasting at the national level from its inception. In part, this is due to the law of unintended consequences; what was supposed to be a system to encourage coast-to-coast togetherness simultaneously created flows moving from south to north that were rarely reciprocal in nature. The pressures placed upon the system from various outside forces—powerful US broadcasters airing materials in the same language as much of the country, or English-language programming in Quebec—and its use as a political pawn by both Liberal and Conservative governments have produced a series of highly defensive and bureaucratic measures that have shaped how Canadians experience television and radio. Such measures are well known to observers of the Canadian situation but they warrant a mention here: in return, for the creation of a "mixed" system of public and privately funded broadcasting, came elaborate content quotas that assigned numeric values to cultural texts based on the citizenship of its production team. Such policies helped to establish a system that aimed to be attentive to the needs of different populations within Canada, most notably it's English and French-speaking populations. Those policies also stimulated the development of Canada's independent production sector and contributed to establihing a workforce and infrastructure which would, in turn, facilitate the development of the locations industry that atttracts productions from elsewhere.

At the same time, however, such developments often produced an effect of politicizing cultural consumption in Canada by turning questions about artistic creativity into questions about the extent to which one's artistic vision was expressive of certain inherently "Canadian" values. In return for having strong broadcasters in a position to carry that content, Canada developed a series of foreign ownership restrictions that facilitated heavy media consolidation, one that now runs across various media platforms.[10] In return for occupying that dominant position in the marketplace, those same broadcasters have had to traditionally donate a percentage of their revenues to funds that are channelled back into Canada's independent production sector. As a means of encouraging industrial development, various institutions have been set up at both the federal and provincial level to fund media production, assist in its distribution, and to provide training and marketing to developing talent—but the budgets for those initiatives have rarely been in step with their creative or industrial needs. To defend national licensing rights and as a sop to national and local advertising interests, broadcasters have been allowed to air programs on American networks and replace the commercials with Canadian ones, a situation most notable during the Super Bowl.

We might say then that the primary characteristic of Canadian broadcasting exemplifies what Will Straw has characterized as the compensatory component of Canadian culture: an attempt to make up for the various systemic lacks by offering a range of policy measures intended either to fill specific generic gaps (like children's programming), cushion the blows of the ebbs and flows of media industry shifts, or to develop media production sectors that might not have existed if media production were left to the free market.[11] These are not insignificant developments, given the tremendous economic benefits and professional development opportunities that flowed from various initiatives undertaken at the federal, provincial, and municipal levels. These are reasonable and modest measures for a country positioned so close to the United States and with a population sparsely distributed across a large landmass. However, and perhaps because of those measures, the system has been historically unsuccessful when it comes to attracting audiences for much of its domestically produced programming, which has either been produced with policy initiatives, rather than consumer preferences, in mind, or been treated by broadcasters as a necessary evil for doing business rather than as a marketable asset.[12] Other measures—such as protecting and policing particular genres of programming against competition or rules which have created costly cable packages and unruly contracts—have created levels of consumer frustration that bubble up to the surface during public hearings and now, in the digital age, on social networking platforms.

The tensions between the policy objectives of the public institutions and the consumerist objectives of Canadian audiences have been exacerbated in an age of digital technologies. The speed at which Canadians terminated their cable service and enthusiastically took up new services, such as Netflix, is reflective of the high cost of cable services in Canada as well as broader international trends in the media industries. However, in Canada, such developments are also a specific response to the choice of consuming media largely outside of a heavily regulated environment.

To put it a different way, such developments represent the first time that a collective broadcasting experience oriented around individualistic media consumption could legally take place in Canada, on a mass scale, outside of the elaborate policy and regulatory framework that has largely positioned radio listening and television watching as an extension of national citizenship industrial development, rather than as a tool for entertainment. If international broadcasting is about "the behavior of states in various markets for loyalties", in Price, Haas, and Margolin's formulation,[13] it is clear that Canadians have a loyalty to broadcasting as a form, even if the state's behaviour has historically made it something difficult for Canadian consumers to love.

Against the backdrop of this broad characterization of the history and state of Canadian broadcasting, we could argue that a system that has been understood so powerfully through an internally driven compensatory lens may well be difficult to marshal for external purposes. From this, it is unclear whether that particular Canadian view of the world as expressed through the medium of broadcasting would make for an attractive form of broadcasting address for global audiences. It may be a flippant thing to say, but perhaps the diplomatic brands of Canadian foreign policy work—quiet, modest, conciliatory, careful, and tactful—are not easily converted into compelling television programming. We might say that the most prominent players in the current international broadcasting scene—the United States, Qatar, France, Russia, and China—are countries that either possess considerable technical and industrial production and distribution infrastructure or who have exercised powerful and often repressive traditions of media control, censorship, and manipulation. Since Canada largely lacks these traditions—as do many other countries—it may explain why thinking of international broadcasting against this kind of backdrop is problematic.

The issues surrounding broadcasting may reflect the long-standing ambivalence about Canada's potential to become a global player, like the UK or France; its fate may well lie with countries like New Zealand or Norway, countries which are respected in the global diplomatic landscape, even if they may not be major players in the global international broadcasting landscape. It is telling, then, that sitting at the bottom of the current iteration of Radio Canada International's website is a list of its "strategic partners", featuring the international broadcasting services of places like Poland, Switzerland, and the Czech Republic. The gap between ambition and reality—between what diplomats want and how

RCI sees itself—is something that would need to be resolved if a new, more robust service were to be implemented; a Canadian international broadcasting service, if rejuvenated, would have to consider whether it would want to be playing in the same sandbox with the Americans or with the Swiss.

It is notable to point out that digital platforms like Twitter and Facebook have become of particular interest to public diplomacy practitioners. In a general sense, such platforms offer a range of communicative options that run outside the highly managed discourses of regulated broadcasting. They also offer the extensive reach and flexibility for a range of efforts that were previously unheard of. In the Canadian context, such platforms provide the potential for forms of communicative exchange that transcend the more compensatory stance that has characterized national broadcasting. Some of the biggest beneficiaries of these new platforms have been diplomats themselves, who make use of services like Twitter to engage in public discussion, to relay important information, and to counter misinformation circulating in cyberspace. The efforts of people like Sweden's Carl Bildt or former US Ambassador to Russia, Michael McFaul, are excellent examples of individual officials performing some of the informational work once undertaken by media institutions.

What is striking about the emergence of Facebook and Twitter as diplomatic platforms is the apparent disregard for the fact that such platforms are owned and controlled by American companies, and that so many of us are incredibly naïve about how that data is being used and manipulated. The recent scandal involving Cambridge Analytica has also drawn attention to the ways parties work closely with Facebook to use personal data for political advantage. From the perspective of Canada's historical approach to media technologies, this development shows that a turning away from the *nationalism* that once characterized Canada's cultural policies in many previous media forms has given way to a *promotional* agenda, one that appears unconcerned with these matters and considers diplomatic work through the lens of nation branding.[14] Whereas many argued that Canada must have its own radio and television frequencies, broadcasters, and programming, such sentiments seemed to run out of steam during the jump online, as many seemed happy to scour the Internet with Canadian editions of Google and to practice social networking with Canadian ads running along the side. Perhaps, this is because so many of the objectives of public diplomacy—sharing, monitoring, disseminating, and listening—are so highly compatible with the capabilities and surveillance logics of those same new media companies.

Might it be necessary to move away from discussions of Canada's place in international broadcasting, as it appears that the CBC has done in the case of RCI? For reasons outlined in this paper, the answer here is, "yes". With the argument in this chapter, I am advocating for a theory of public diplomacy that embodies a richer sense of media awareness. This particular view of public diplomacy is far more concerned with the history and characteristics of media forms in different contexts than it is preoccupied with analyses of the effectiveness of specific campaigns. To a degree, an orientation with effects is tied inextricably to the study of communication in university settings, as the field itself achieved disciplinary status in the post-war context through its primary an interest in studying propaganda.[15] However, a shift away from these concerns and towards this different approach draws attention to the fact that diplomatic work and media technologies are so closely interlinked.

There is the face-to-face work where dialogue and dispute are carried out and where the handshake, the backslap, or the wink are the media of expression. Or, as we know, there are the reams and reams of paperwork in which diplomacy takes place, the files on different countries and their leaders, the portfolios that ministers must assume, and the role played by passports, telexes, cables, and phones, and now, of course, e-mails.[16] Such facts of diplomatic life reveal themselves in the most unfortunate of cases, with WikiLeaks serving as a powerful example. In Mark Kristmanson's paper from this volume, we can see the importance of gifts as media of exchange between countries or among cities. In each of these cases, we might paraphrase Marshall McLuhan's famous maxim that these mediums play some role in determining the nature of the messages being communicated and channelled through them. At the same time, however, thinking of diplomatic initiatives with an attention to media forms should serve as a reminder that discourses of effectiveness and failure are pervasive in the literature on public diplomacy. These motifs—rarely defined—feature in large because part of its address to both scholars and practitioners who are preoccupied with operationalizing its findings for its various readership and stakeholders. As laudable as that initiative may be, there is something to be said about taking a more critical look at the communicative vocabulary being deployed in assessing various public diplomacy initiatives. Moreover, new expectations that diplomatic work will be undertaken both internally, through these more discreet communicative channels, and externally, through social media, calls for an appreciation not only of the effectiveness of the messages, but also of how these developments—what some media theorists refer to as "mediatization"—change the very nature of diplomatic work.[17]

If states and the media have always been in tension, it is interesting to note that the turn towards digital diplomacy means that diplomats and their offices now behave in manners which are similar in some ways to media institutions, with access to some of the same tools for information distribution that were once largely limited to those legacy institutions. As a result, that newfound power must also be balanced with a greater sense of responisbility for what it means to undertake diplomatic affairs on largely unaccountable platforms such as Facebook and Twitter. Against this backdrop, it would be best to leave a discussion of international broadcasting largely behind or, at the very least, to address it in a broader conversation about what this means for the ways states now communicate with the public, both at home and abroad through powerful platforms. Here, Canada's future decisions on how best to communicate its foreign affairs will make it a compelling case study for theorists and practitioners of public diplomacy.

Notes

1. Christer Jönsson and Martin Hall, "Communication: An Essential Aspect of Diplomacy", *International Studies Perspectives* 4:2 (2003), p. 195.
2. For excellent accounts of the history of Radio Canada International, see Arthur Siegel, *Radio Canada International.* Oakville: Mosaic Press, 1996 and Elzbieta Olechowska, *The Age of International Radio: Radio Canada International 1945–2007.* Oakville: Mosaic Press, 2007.
3. See Angelini Irinci, "Radio Canada Goes Off-Air, Moving Online-Only After 67 Years of Shortwave Service", *J-Source.ca.* https://j-source.ca/art icle/radio-canada-international-goes-off-air-moving-online-only-after-67-years-of-shortwave-service/. Accessed 15 July 2020.
4. Evan Potter, *Branding Canada: Projecting Canada's Soft Power Through Public Diplomacy.* Montreal: McGill-Queen's University Press, 2009, p. 82.
5. Among the recent studies documenting these developments include Philip Seib, *The Al-Jazeera Effect: How Global Media Are Reshaping World Politics.* Lincoln: University of Nebraska Press, 2008; Hugh Miles, *Al-Jazeera: How Arab TV News Changed the World.* Grove Press, 2005; Raymond Kuhn, "France 24: Too Little, Too Late, Too French", in

Stephen Cushion and Justin Lewis, eds., *The Rise of 24-Hour Television: Global Perspectives*. New York: Peter Lang, 2010, pp. 265–280; Anne Genets, *The Global News Challenge: Market Strategies of International Broadcasting Organizations in Developing Countries*. London: Routledge, 2013; and Tine Ustad Figenschou, *Al-Jazeera and the Global Media Landscape: The South Is Talking Back*. London: Routledge, 2014.

6. Consider the recent characterization of RT as being engaged in "deceitful propaganda" by newly elected French President Emmanuel Macron. See James MacAuley, "French President Macron Blasts State-Owned Media as 'Propaganda'", *Washington Post*, May 29, 2017. https://www.washingto npost.com/world/europe/french-president-macron-blasts-russian-state-run-media-as-propaganda/2017/05/29/4e758308-4479-11e7-8de1-cec59a9bf4b1_story.html?utm_term=.86847271743b. Accessed 6 June 2017.

7. UNESCO, *Model Curricula for Journalism Education*. Paris: UNESCO, 2007.

8. Julian Dierkes, "Five Rules to Guide the Future of Canadian Digital Diplomacy", *OpenCanada.ca* December 2, 2015. https://www.openca nada.org/features/five-rules-guide-future-canadian-digital-diplomacy/.

9. See Gavin Hewitt, "Canada: The Different Voice", *BBC News*, September 19, 2016. http://www.bbc.com/news/world-us-canada-37406857. Accessed 19 September 2016. See also Allison Kite, "America Divided by Politics, United by Love of Canada: WSJ/NBC News Poll", *Wall Street Journal*, September 21, 2016. http://blogs.wsj.com/washwire/2016/09/21/america-divided-by-politics-united-by-love-for-canada-wsj nbc-news-poll/. Accessed 21 September 2016.

10. This argument is a feature in Maurice Charland's article, "Technological Nationalism", *Canadian Journal of Political and Social Theory* 10:1 (1986), pp. 196–220.

11. Will Straw, "Dilemmas of Definition", in Joan Nicks and Jeanette Sloniowski, eds., *Slippery Pastimes: Reading the Popular in Canadian Culture*. Waterloo Wilfrid Laurier Press, pp. 105–106.

12. See Paul Attallah, "A Usable History for the Study of Television", *Canadian Review of American Studies* 37:3 (2007), pp. 325–349.

13. Monroe Price, Susan Haas, and Drew Margolin, "New Technologies and International Broadcasting: Reflections on Adaptations and Transformations", *Annenberg School of Communication Departmental Papers 1-1 (2008)*.

14. This topic is discussed in detail by Mellissa Aronczyk. See *Branding the Nation: The Global Business of National Identity*. Oxford: Oxford University Press, 2013.

15. See Jefferson Pooley and David Park, eds., *The History of Media and Communication Research: Contested Memories*. New York: Peter Lang, 2008.
16. One example is Craig Robertson, *The Passport in America: The History of a Document*. Oxford: Oxford University Press, 2010.
17. For an articulation of this argument, see Andreas Hepp, *Cultures of Mediatization*. London: Polity Press, 2012.

CHAPTER 8

Dualistic Images of Canada in the World: Instrumental Commonalities/Symbolic Divides

Andrew F. Cooper

The traditional narrative regarding Canada's image in the world is one of internal consensus, in which a common messaging occurs, whatever the government in power. The dominance of this narrative goes hand in hand with the pursuit of a bipartisan foreign policy. This view holds that even if there has not been a complete conceptual agreement about Canada's positioning in the world, there is a considerable level of agreement that Canada has been obsessed with its status in the international order and its ranking in the international system, amid a mix of liberal internationalism and small 'c' conservative constraint or 'limitationalism.'[1]

The distant exceptions to this narrative are viewed as legacy issues or as the particular obsessions of specific prime ministers. The clash over the Suez Crisis between the peacekeeping-oriented Pearson Liberals and the

A. F. Cooper (✉)
Balsillie School of International Affairs, University of Waterloo, Waterloo, Canada
e-mail: Andrew.cooper@sympatico.ca

© The Author(s) 2021
N. J. Cull and M. K. Hawes (eds.), *Canada's Public Diplomacy*,
Palgrave Macmillan Series in Global Public Diplomacy,
https://doi.org/10.1007/978-3-319-62015-2_8

173

Anglo-sphere Diefenbaker Conservatives is commonly put into this category. Yet, it should be highlighted that the Diefenbaker government also set the bar high for future governments on issues such as human rights, the fight against oppressive practices (such as apartheid South Africa, with Brian Mulroney continuing the approach),[2] and an autonomous policy on Cuba, thus playing to rather than at odds with the narrative of consensus.

At its core, this chapter asks the question of whether the projection of Canada's image in the world has changed because of the tilts found in the approach by the Chrétien/Martin and the Harper governments. At particular sites of the issue spectrum, the image of internal consensus has indeed been severely tested. Yet what is significant is that these tensions have not come to the fore with a focus on the instrumental components of the foreign policy agenda. Indeed, there remains some considerable agreement between Liberals and Conservatives (albeit less so with the New Democratic Party) on a wide number of key issues, not the least the significance of the American-Canadian relationship as the interest-oriented main game of Canadian foreign policy and on responses with economic diplomacy related not only to the North American Free Trade Agreement (NAFTA) and the subsequent the United States–Mexico–Canada Agreement (USMCA), but also on mega cross-regional trade arrangements.[3]

Rather than the instrumental substance of policy being a source of intense differentiation, the key points of division center on a clash of symbolic identity-oriented narratives grounded in the past. During the Chrétien government years, the most significant of these splits came on questions of like-mindedness on specific albeit highly normatively driven niche issues, most particularly those animated on land mines and the International Criminal Court (ICC) by Chrétien and Foreign Minister Lloyd Axworthy.[4] The question of who and what was Canada 'within' the world was grounded on the animation of a particular set of values, an approach magnified by the Martin government's push for a comprehensive 'World [that] We Want.'[5]

Notwithstanding some expectations that there would be a radical shift when the Harper Conservatives came into office, the main point of differentiation, in practice, was not so much on the substantive contours of foreign policy (although the like-minded question continued to be prominent, especially on questions relating to Israel and Iran), but on reshaping the ideological context of Canada's position in the world. In a concerted

effort to reformulate the historical image of Canada, the Harper government made it a priority to downplay Liberal branding (including the
emphasis on peacekeeping and normative niches of the Axworthy years)
and play up Canada's robust military performance, dating back to earlier
eras.

As noted, however, this battle to see 'whose story wins'[6] was largely
disengaged from the fundamental operational practice of foreign policy—
it did not interfere with core concerns. While clashes in style as
expressed significantly in expressions of public diplomacy should not
be ignored, they should not be embellished beyond recognition, either.
Lloyd Axworthy did not drive the main game of Canadian foreign policy,
nor did the 'values-projection' project of the Martin government heavily
impact issues such as Afghanistan. The Harper government, for its part,
adopted a narrower and traditional view of like-mindedness opposed to
pushing advances global governance approach. Self-selected friends and
organizations (NATO for example) were chosen over the United Nations.

Although the core of this chapter looks back at the similarities
and differences between the Chrétien/Martin and the Harper governments, the dualistic theme is stretched out with reference to the Justin
Trudeau government. As in the earlier period, significant differences
can be parceled out between the Harper and Trudeau government's
approaches to symbolic/identity issues. The use (or non-use) of representative symbols is illustrative here. In 2011, the Harper government—more
precisely, Foreign Minister John Baird—ordered that a portrait of the
Queen be put in the departmental building on Sussex Drive in Ottawa, in
the place of two paintings by modern Quebec artist, Alfred Pellan. Baird
also played up the 'John Diefenbaker Defender of Human Rights and
Freedom Award' at the expense of the Thérèse Casgrain Volunteer Award.
The Trudeau government reversed the moves, removing the Queen's
portrait and restoring the Pellan paintings just five days after being sworn
in. Moreover, the Thérèse Casgrain Volunteer Award was restored,[7] while
the Diefenbaker award was placed in limbo.

On the main issues of foreign policy relating to instrumental or material purposes, however, any contrasts narrowed appreciably. While some
nuances can be found between the Harper and the Trudeau governments
in the security domain, when it comes to economic policy, it is the paral-
lels that are striking. The Trudeau Liberals embraced a wide variety of
trade agreements and have managed the renegotiation of NAFTA with
the Trump administration in a manner that borrows heavily from earlier
playbooks.

GROWING TENSIONS AROUND LIKE-MINDEDNESS

A clear example of the hold of consensus was the reluctance of Prime Minister Harper to put aside the middle power notion. In an address to the Council on Foreign Relations on September 25, 2007, Harper noted that the country could work, 'with other middle powers. Canada can and Canada is making a real contribution to protecting and projecting our collective interests, while serving as a model of a prosperous, democratic, and compassionate society, independent yet open to the world.'[8]

At the same time, however, this language makes it clear that Harper was pushing a slightly different narrative. Canada intended to lead by example. Core interests mattered. The like-minded countries that Canada was 'with' were explicitly represented as democracies.

The middle power notion as depicted by Harper was not, then, that of an upgraded middle power, but rather, a model power—with ambitions that found outlets in dramatic initiatives/connections with transnational society. A primary example of this thrust is a book by Jennifer Welsh, At *Home in the World: Canada's Global Vision for the 21st Century* (2004). *At Home in the World* is framed by the aspiration that Canada should be a model international citizen. Another example of this idea comes from Michael Byers, of the University of British Columbia, in his book, *Intent for a Nation: What Is Canada For?* (2007). The model citizen advocates to look instead to a post-colonial Canada; they ought to have a deep distrust for followership—although this idea is more robustly stated by Byers than by Welsh. What both advocate is a mode of cosmopolitan globalism, where Canadians as individuals transcend state-centric nationalism.

Certainly, amid this type of declaratory statement, the strong current of polarization concerning Canadian foreign policy—even predating PM Harper's government—should not be overlooked. In the place of the consensus orientation, what played out was a rich but decisive clash.

In policy terms, the clash of analysis intersects with key areas of Canadian foreign policy, which were animated through the 1990s but greatly magnified in the period after 9/11. The first sign of the narratives departing the multilateral arena is found in the so-called Axworthy doctrine—with its emphasis on mixed coalitions, soft power, and human security. The most dynamic expressions of this narrative come on the issues of land mines, the ICC, and the advance of the Responsibility to Protect (R2P). The narrative of the Axworthy doctrine puts orthodox conceptions of security and national interest on the defensive; at the same time, it is an implicit criticism of traditional Pearsonian conceptions of middle power diplomacy, deeming this approach too slow and too cautious.

Where Axworthy departed from the established tenets of the past was in his impatience with the static quality of the traditional forms of like-mindedness. Explicitly, he wanted to liberate the like-mindedness concept from its identification with the fixed stability-driven worldview of the Pearson era to a more fluid focus on ad hoc, normality-driven, and issue-specific coalitions of the willing. This impatience was a long-standing condition, which can be traced back to Axworthy's younger days as a critical observer of Pearson's 'worth[y]' but 'grey and oh so solid' diplomacy. As neatly captured, for instance, in a series of newspaper articles that Axworthy wrote for the *Winnipeg Free Press* in September 1965, this sense of impatience pointed toward diplomacy that was noisier and directed towards a wider public audience.[9]

In intellectual terms, traditional voices argued that Canada's aspirations needed to be routed through another fork in the road, not as a pathfinder state but as a state that should bond with those countries it has long been comfortable with—above all the Anglo-sphere. Such a division highlights, among other things, the completely different use of historical analysis. The traditional perspective looks back to the glories of the past, whether World War I or World War II, when Canada was seen as a distinctly powerful global figure. Most notably, these moments are played out through battles where Canadian soldiers have played a key role, such as Vimy Ridge and the D-Day Invasion.

By identifying itself with a multifaceted group of high-minded but not pivotal like-minded actors, it is argued, Canada has moved away from a more appropriate centripetal approach to the margins of diplomacy. This sense that Canada's coalition behavior is reducing its status comes out most forcefully in Conrad Black's stinging critique of this diplomatic pattern: 'Canadians tend to feel keenly that Canada is on the verge of becoming a country of the first rank but it is not widely perceived to be so. To be at the forefront of a large group of secondary powers such as the Scandinavians and the Dutch and even the Australians is something of an underachievement.'[10]

Voices of opposition reacted vigorously to an approach that they saw as a sham. In Denis Stairs' words, 'speak loudly and carry a bent twig.'[11] For some, the offense was that this narrative betrayed Canada's alternative allies—preferring the small and the virtuous to the robust and reliable. For others it was perceived hypocrisy, in that Canada was viewed as running down its military when there were cases—such as Kosovo, where human security was on the line—in which the military was required. The force of this backlash became so strong that new organizations began to spring up—especially, the Canadian Defense and Foreign Policy Institute, which encompasses the most robust of the traditionalists, including David Bercuson and Jack Granatstein, as well as more nuanced observers, such as Kim Nossal, Denis Stairs, and Gordon Smith, in their ranks.

The second clash of narratives straddles the time before and after 9/11 and is focused on the Canadian border with the United States. The narrative of consensus extended to this domain, with discourse championing the longest undefended border in the world. While Liberals might have opposed the Canada-US FTA in the 1980s, their legacy suggests a tendency toward cooperating and ceding to American interests, including the Auto Pact, which managed trade between major automobile companies with production plants on both sides of the Canada-US border. With the pressure for securitization of the border, however, the narratives diverged once again.

The model citizen advocates resisted most, if not all, forms of accommodation to this emerging agenda—a tendency that became magnified after 9/11. Calls for responses that reflected the realities of the security situation were met with strong opposition to several sensitive items, including armed guards on planes and finger-printing. Alternatively, traditionalists—or realists—called for new forms of security perimeters, calls that were amplified by leading members of the business community.

The departure from the core ingredients of foreign policy, however, was never as pronounced as the optional extras. Certainly, the contrast between the Axworthy doctrine and the approach taken by John Manley in the post-9/11 environment on niche issues is striking. Whereas Axworthy pushed away from the consensus, Manley and the central agencies of the Canadian government aimed to consolidate it via the Canada-US Smart Border Declaration in 2003 and beyond.

But stresses on this consensus continue and are reinforced by the perceived needs of the model citizen advocates: more attention to human rights issues, punctuated by the backlash against renditions (most notably, the Arar case, where a Canadian of Syrian descent was stopped in New York and transported to a Syrian jail via Jordan), and ethnic profiling. On the other hand, the perception of the traditionalists emphasizes a continued need to fill cracks in the security perimeter through arming officials on the border, etc.

It must also be acknowledged that another clash of narratives, albeit exaggerated, did occur. This conflict was purportedly over the weight given to values compared with national interest in Canadian foreign policy. In many ways, this was a false debate, as shown by the Harper government's preference for values on many foreign policy issues—the values of democracy and human rights, especially.[12] Certainly, it is noteworthy how often Prime Minister Harper has invoked these values in the context of the Afghanistan mission: On the day after the 2006 federal election, he said: 'We will continue to help defend our values and democratic ideals around the world – as so courageously demonstrated by those young Canadian soldiers who are serving and who have sacrificed in Afghanistan.'[13] In other ways, it was simply an echo of the larger debate, juxtaposing a Canada that can be counted on in tough situations against a more moralistic Canada.

Though exaggerated, the intensity of this debate should not be discounted. On the one hand, a model citizen advocate such as Michael Byers could underscore the power of imagination—the foundation of what he terms 'Intent for a Nation.' On the other side, traditional realists scoffed at what they considered the pretense of such sentiments. As Jack Granatstein asserted: 'We want our nation to be a good international citizen, but it can't if we have no resources to employ abroad...It is time to put our nation's interests first.'[14] Such a call was echoed firmly by the so-called wise men of the older generation of diplomats—most notably, Derek Burney and Allan Gotlieb, who had been instrumental in reshaping Canada's public diplomacy in their roles as ambassadors to the United States in the 1980s and 1990s.[15]

If all of these issues are significant in highlighting the clash of analysis in Canadian foreign policy, it is through Afghanistan that largely symbolic references to different types of historical narratives are most explicit. For the model citizen advocates, though, the crucial narrative about Anglo-sphere solidarity—the common element of which has been Canada's support of the United States and the UK—is one of neo-colonialism. One such alternative narrative showcases not the glories of D-Day but the defeats of earlier interventions in support of the UK in the Anglo-Boer war. Another narrative compares the argument in support of the Afghanistan mission to support for joining the Vietnam War in the 1960s.

Afghanistan also most clearly brings in the element of high politics to Canadian foreign policy. As a highly detailed book by Janice Gross Stein and Eugene Lang, *The Unexpected War*, reaffirms, PM Martin's decision-making approach to Afghanistan was highly reactive: He did not grab ownership of Afghanistan. Afghanistan was, in the words of Prime Minister Martin's former chief of staff, Tim Murphy, 'something we had to do more than something we wanted to do.'[16]

What the Harper government did was to try to contrast its own approach with that of Martin on a number of significant criteria. Whereas the Martin approach was hyperactive across a diffuse set of policy initiatives, the Harper government chose to concentrate on core concerns. If the Martin government's weak point was its tendency to 'review not do,' the Harper government wanted from the outset to rebrand Canada in a more stand-up image, as a country that was action-oriented and muscular.

In his paper, 'Mr. Harper Goes to War: Canada, Afghanistan and the return of "High Politics" in Canadian Foreign Policy,'[17] Duane Bratt has explored the question of why PM Harper was prepared to ramp up the Canadian mission, as much symbolically as instrumentally, to the point where it is often called, 'Mr. Harper's War.' The 'how' is very connected with PM Harper's willingness to go to the front lines in Afghanistan, complete with his statements that, 'we don't make a commitment and then run away at the first sign of trouble.'[18] Still, if Harper extended and expanded the mission, Canada's commitment to ISAF around Kandahar was initiated by the Martin government.

The motivating principle that shaped the worldview of the Martin government was that of R2P, the concept put into play in large part by Canadian entrepreneurship and intellectual support via the Commission on State Sovereignty and Intervention. Indeed, R2P is a rare case where an issue has been passed on from one government to another: It was introduced by Lloyd Axworthy under the Chrétien government and taken up by Paul Martin (former PM Chrétien's archrival). Potential and performance, however, remained two different matters. In the case of the R2P, there was little tangible evidence to show for this ambitious approach. For all of its good talk, above all the push for humanitarian intervention on Darfur, PM Martin's government was widely judged to have generated far more promises than delivery by its 2006 electoral defeat.

Yet, it would be wrong to ignore the fact that sections of Canadian society have continuously laid out a strong normative claim for 'doing something' in Afghanistan. This sentiment was especially strong among mainstream women's groups, as the oppressive nature of the Taliban's gender war became more visible.[19] To some extent, nonetheless, this idealism has been complicated by the increasingly polarized view of the mission. To the opponents of the extension of the mission, the idealism has been contaminated. To them, the hopes of the Bonn process—with its framework for power-sharing, a constitution, elections, and other expressions of a democratic impulse—seem a very distant memory.

To return to the perspective of one of the most vociferous critics, Michael Byers takes issue with any positive interpretation of the Karzai government. In a presentation he made to Members of Parliament, Byers stated, 'some of the most important posts in the Afghan government are held by former warlords. Some of them stand accused...of heinous crimes, and of siphoning of billions of dollars of foreign aid.'[20] Byers, in a more sustained fashion, has also expressed his disdain for some of the practices he takes Canadian forces to have overlooked if not actively participated in—for one, the transfer by Canadian Special Forces of detainees to US custody without scrutiny or approbation.

In taking on this line of argument, links are made, rightly or wrongly, between normative deficiencies at home—as found most notably in the Arar case—and abroad. Defenders of the mission believe that Canadian feminists, in particular, should lend accentuated support for the Canadian mission. Jack Granatstein pointedly asks why there should be so much enthusiasm for other forms of intervention, above all on Darfur (an enthusiasm that Michael Byers shared) and not on Afghanistan. In his own reflections on this differentiation, Granatstein suggests that, 'there are a number of pathologies at work here. One is that Darfur [is to] be a UN peace enforcement mission, and the United Nations and peace-keeping in any variety are, by definition, good. Afghanistan, by contrast, is seen by the left as a US war, aided and abetted by NATO.'[21]

Such a view also merges the rebranding efforts by analysts (such as Granatstein) with those of key practitioners (such as General Rick Hillier) to dispel the image of Canada as an UN-centric peacekeeper and facilitate its return to a more militaristic reputation. The motor for this rebranding approach was national pride, as Canada moved in its deployment in Afghanistan to become part of NATO's inner circle and as the International Security Assistance Force (ISAF) gradually spread its coverage beyond Kabul.

Nonetheless, bureaucratic self-interest was married to national interest: Canada was back and so was the Canadian military. The opportunities open to the Department of National Defence, in terms of both prestige and material resources, by going big into Afghanistan are obvious. After years of being held back by their political masters, instead of being lectured by NATO officials about Canada's under-performance, Canada could lecture other NATO members about the need to pull their weight.[22]

With big opportunities come big risks, however. At the forefront of these risks were the physical dangers faced by the Canadian military and Canadian state officials, more generally; the death of 158 military personnel and one diplomat (Glyn Berry from DFAIT) is a stark testament to this fact.[23] It is well publicized that Canadian military engagement in Afghanistan—as showcased both by the decision in August 2005 to send 2300 military personnel as part of Task Force Afghanistan to Kandahar and the onset of Operation Archer—is their largest since the Korean War.

Less publicized, at least outside of Canada, is the fact that Canada's losses of military personnel are of a disproportionate number (158, plus the one diplomat) to the level suffered by other states that have engaged in both Afghanistan and Iraq. The comparative example is of Australia, which, outside of one case of suicide in its military ranks, did not face one fatal casualty while maintaining a high reputation in terms of commitment and capabilities.[24]

Canadian involvement in Libya reinforced the emphasis on reassurance among key allies while holding a comparatively stronger economic position, particularly with the unfolding of the Eurozone crisis and its impact on the defense spending of European NATO allies. Canada experienced significantly less of a budgetary hindrance than did other G-8/NATO countries in the wake of the financial crisis and was thus strategically positioned to bolster the confidence of its allies by playing a more visible role in collective defense missions.

Canada's enhanced efforts were spelled out in the decision to participate in the Libyan Contact group. Although in some ways running parallel to the normative orientation of Responsibility to Protect under the Axworthy approach, the key divergence with R2P was that the NATO-led mission sought not only to protect the security of Libyan citizens, but also to carry out a full-scale elimination of the Gaddafi regime, on which both NATO and rebel forces converged.[25] This difference also reflects a key component of the Libyan conflict insofar that NATO played a supporting role by facilitating the rebel advance.

Through the rest of the Libya intervention, Canada's focus concentrated on NATO as opposed to the UN, illustrating the comparative privileging of the two international organizations.[26] Indeed, in overall terms, during the Harper years, Canada made a point of channeling concrete efforts into organizations it deemed to be more significant, rather than posturing in organizations with decidedly less significance. The efforts channeled into the NATO-led mission on Libya stood in stark contrast to the comparative disengagement with the UN, a point reinforced by the unprecedented failure by Canada in its bid to win a temporary seat on the UN Security Council in 2010.

THE EMBEDDED IMPORTANCE OF SYMBOLISM

These departures by the Harper government do not exhaust the areas of tension in terms of the narrative of consensus. If there were significant tilts about the definition of like-mindedness, there were also some sharp differences on un-like-mindedness. Specifically, there was a greater focus not only on who Canada was with, but on who and what Canada was against. Solidarity with the UK and Australia, as well as Israel, was played up. Most decisively, the Harper government made the unilateral move of cutting off all direct diplomatic ties with Iran, complete with the sudden closing of the embassy and the expulsion of all Iranian diplomatic personnel from Canada in September of 2012.

Such actions again bent but did not mark a complete break with Canada's operational practice, considering the Canadian embassy had previously been closed for eight years following the 'Canadian caper,' which involved getting American diplomatic personnel out of Tehran in 1980. This view of continuity, as opposed to change, was reinforced by estimates that the 'hard' capacity of Canada had not expanded appreciably during the Harper years.[27] The major shift was in the narrative of Canada's position in the world via an effort to rebrand Canada according to a markedly different historical story.

Nonetheless, the concerted focus of the Harper government was not in setting accurate guidelines for future policy but in providing a firm template about what Canada had accomplished in the past. As a check against the narrative that Canada was the first peacekeeper, updated by the normatively oriented initiatives of the late 1990s, the Harper government instead emphasized a record of muscular accomplishments.

Rather than use the D-Day ceremonies of June 6, 2014, to laud the accomplishments of global order post-War, Harper stuck to the main script concerning hard capacity: 'Such was the nature of the Canadian Army, such was their intensely aggressive fighting spirit, that during the Battle of Normandy that followed D-Day, they would suffer the most casualties of any division in the wider British Army Group. As a Canadian, reflecting on this achievement I can only feel two emotions that are not usually reckoned together: fierce pride and the deepest humility.'[28]

In memorialization, there was a fundamental shift. The main site for Liberals was Reconciliation, as demonstrated by the Peacekeeping Monument in Ottawa (completed in 1992) with the 1956 quote from Lester Person on its base: 'We need action not only to end the fighting but to make the peace... My own government would be glad to recommend Canadian participation in such a United Nations force, a truly international peace and police force.'

The Harper Conservatives went back further, with a focus for example on the Canadian History Museum celebration of older war time achievements notwithstanding some significant indications that public support for these events was over-estimated. As one journalist put it: 'When it comes to putting a patriotic gloss on the past, Conservatives regard their $28-million War of 1812 commemorations as the gold standard. Yet a poll early this year, conducted for the Institute for Research of Public policy, found that just 28.6 per cent of Canadians supported those celebrations, far below the 47.1 per cent who would have favoured a celebration of the Charter of Rights and Freedoms.'[29]

While the record for hard capacity was lauded, however, the mechanism for different sorts of soft power was eroded. In terms of physical sites, while the use of the Canadian Museum of History was closely managed, the 'dismantling of Library and Archives Canada, the main repository of the nation's memory took place.'[30] In 2009, as another sign of this trend, Toronto City Centre Airport was renamed after Billy Bishop, World War I flying ace. In 2007, the stretch of Highway 401 between and the intersection of the Don Valley Parkway and Highway 404 in Toronto became the Highway of Heroes (French: Autoroute des héros), in honor of Canadian soldiers who have died, with bridges along the 401 named after individual soldiers.

Going beyond the sites for an alternative form of national branding, a number of critics return to the theme expounded by the model citizen advocates—that the dominance of the narrative about Anglo-sphere solidarity reflects a neo-colonialism that marginalizes—even eliminates—other narratives that should be included not only in the portrayal of Canadian history at home but also in a creative form of public diplomacy. In examining the 2013 Conservative throne speech, Alain Noel points to the gaps in the ascendant orthodoxy: 'Only wars moved this country during the 20th century. There was no fight for Aboriginal rights and self-determination, no mobilization over female suffrage or reproductive rights, no labour movement, no welfare state, no official bilingualism or multiculturalism, no Charter of Rights and, for all practical purposes, no Québec...Am I making too much of a short speech? Not really. All the historical events that the federal government plans to celebrate in the coming years have to do with Confederation or with wars, with the exception of a memorial to the victims of communism, which indeed also relates to a war, the Cold War. Step by step, the government is rewriting the history of Canada, to downplay its progressive, liberal, or multinational dimensions and to highlight instead its conservative, royalist, and military origins.'[31]

Other critical commentators also showcase how the politics of symbolism privilege dominant messages (such as the commemorations of Vimy Ridge on the new \$20 bill) while excluding others. Again, this is viewed not only as a source of concern for domestic purposes but also as a defect in global branding. As Yasmeen Abu-Laban highlights: 'What we can see with the Harper conservatives is a pattern in which military and patriotic history is being valorized over social history and multicultural citizenship.'[32] Or, in Tasha Kheiriddin's words: 'Harper's remarks were perhaps more notable for what they did not mention: multiculturalism, medicare, peacekeeping, national unity, the Charter of Rights and Freedoms.'[33]

INSTRUMENTAL BENDING/SYMBOLIC BREAKING

Some of the shifts in the government of Prime Minister Justin Trudeau indicate that we are moving toward a different style of Canadian foreign policy. On Israel, Trudeau has signaled that Harper government's close 'likeminded' embrace will be eased, and that Canada will not avoid sensitive issues. As Trudeau noted in a town hall on foreign policy, 'there are times we will disagree with our friends, but we will stand by our friends. We've all had that friend we've had to do that for.' However, besides the replacement of the Harper-appointed Canadian ambassador to Israel, the implications of this shift—serious or not—have yet to be tested.[34] Although they expressed reservations about the form and intent of a motion put forward by the Conservative opposition calling for the condemnation of the global Boycott, Divestment, and Sanctions movement the Liberals overwhelmingly supported it in substance.[35]

More tangibly, the Trudeau government has indicated that it has found fault with the 'un-likeminded' approach taken against Iran. In one detailed speech (complete with a call for a more representational form of public diplomacy), during his time as foreign minister, Stéphane Dion called for an approach based on constructive engagement: 'Canada's embassy in Iran has been closed for over three years. With which results? Is it right to need to count on Italy to protect our interests in this country? Let's not forget that the world was lucky that Canada had an embassy in Iran at the end of the 1970s so it could come to the aid of the American hostages. Two films have been made about this, one not very good, made by Hollywood, and the other, much better, called Escape from Iran: The Canadian Caper.'[36]

However, it is worthwhile to mention that Dion went to great pains in another speech to signal that the shift is not intended to be a complete break. He stated before the UN that: 'Canada must return to Iran to play a useful role in that region of the world, while remaining vigilant about embassy security issues in Tehran and elsewhere. We are being asked by all sides to reengage, and we are doing so. But this does not mean we will be silent or inactive when we see Iran move in the wrong direction. We will maintain our firm commitment to the human rights of Iranians. Canada will continue to steadfastly oppose Iran's support for terrorist organizations, its threats toward Israel and its ballistic missile program, while also monitoring Iran's compliance with its obligations under the Joint Comprehensive Plan of Action.'[37]

While they should not be ignored, the differences on issues of substance between the Liberals and Conservatives should also not be exaggerated. As in the past,[38] the Trudeau government conducted the NAFTA re-negotiations in a cautious, managerial fashion.[39] Indeed, an appreciation of the need to cross traditional boundaries is highlighted by the Trudeau Liberals' willingness to utilize the expertise of Derek Burney and Brian Mulroney, with a particular focus on ensuring the continuity of Chapter 19 as a dispute resolution mechanism. Even in the context of the 'trade war' on steel and aluminum in mid-2018, retaliation was conducted within strict boundaries. In the words of one senior diplomat: 'This government has been remarkably constructive...They have done everything humanly possible to deal rationally with this Trump administration.'[40]

The nub of the bipartisan split is less on substance than on symbolism. Indeed, symbolism (with frequent references to some past 'golden age') becomes a proxy for highlighting their differences without compromising policy space amid a complex agenda. For the Conservatives, the aim is to get Canada's history right, less as a means to direct policy in the future than a vehicle to demean the Liberal's own dominant narrative from the past. As one insightful journalist put it in 2015, just before the federal election: 'Canadians will have their first chance to vote on a plausible new contender for the national myth, an ideal that is equally visionary and based on morals, but colder, more cynical, solitary, realist, and militaristic. The coming election will highlight the shift. Liberals, once moral visionaries...of a sort abroad, have become pragmatic critics at home, while Conservatives, once so keen to call out sanctimony in those who see Canada as a "Boy Scout imperialist, the busybody of international politics," are now preoccupied with their own values and visions.'[41]

For the Liberals, being in office means a renewed opportunity to embellish the 'orthodox' image of Canada in the world, led in earlier years by activist prime ministers across party lines. As Foreign Minister Dion reiterated at the UN: 'The world needs a more active and more engaged Canada. That is what the Prime Minister, myself and other Canadian ministers have been hearing wherever we go...This plea for Canada's active return to multilateral action is rooted in our history. In the past, Canada was a key multilateral player. From Lester B. Pearson's leadership in resolving the Suez Crisis, to Brian Mulroney's determination in the struggle against apartheid in South Africa, to Jean Chrétien's decisive action for a ban on antipersonnel landmines and cluster munitions and the creation of the International Criminal Court, Canada has played a critical role. Today, we need to put our collective shoulder to the wheel once again.'[42]

Since the replacement of Dion by Chrystia Freeland as foreign minister, the contrast between the symbolic and the instrumental elements has become more accentuated. Trudeau talked in October 2015 about 'Canada's global pivot' without any explicit reference to the middle power model.[43] By 2017, in contradistinction, as witnessed in a major speech by Freeland, the Trudeau government embraced the middle power model in a more fulsome manner. On the one hand, it emphasized the necessity for

Canada to work continually with like-minded coalition partners, in that its ability to act alone 'is limited.' On the other hand, it placed normative purpose at the forefront, connecting self-interest and progressive norms: 'For we are safer and more prosperous...when more of the world shares Canadian values.'[44]

Yet on the instrumental side, the points of comparison have narrowed further. While in declaratory language differentiating Canada from Donald Trump's United States, in operational terms, Canada has done little to irritate Trump or his administration. On security issues, the Trudeau government has taken a hard stance defending Ukraine's sovereignty; it moved from words to action in sending several hundred soldiers to lead a multinational force in Latvia.[45]

The Conservatives, under the leadership of Andrew Scheer, attempted to differentiate their approach from the Liberals by highlighting a loyalty to core like-minded countries and values. Conversely, they emphasized an explicit dissociation from countries deemed un-likeminded. Notably, Scheer argued during the 2019 election that: 'It's time for Canada to put our money where our mouth is and only use foreign aid to support the Canadian values we hold dear.'[46]

Yet on instrumental issue related to material interests, the Conservatives did not break from the embedded consensus. Although Scheer made ritualistic claims that he would have done a better job than Trudeau in renegotiating NAFTA, this was a peripheral issue during the election. While Scheer indicated that 'repressive regimes' would be stigmatized, the focus was on Iran and Korea, countries with little economic importance to Canada.[47]

All of this analysis showcases a stark duality existing within Canadian foreign policy. Partisanship differences exist. Nonetheless, it is the boundaries of this partisanship that are so striking. On symbolic issues, there is a highly visible divide between Liberals and Conservatives, a split that has hardened over the decades. On instrumental issues, in particular, those that are concentrated on the main game of Canada-US relations and other related materially driven issues, there is a surprisingly high degree of operational parallelism. In other words, where the substance of policy matters most, a consensus has held. Yet, if the symbolic contest is not about the core substance of Canadian foreign policy, it does concern the projection of Canadian identity. So, if these issues play out on the margins of operational practice, they are still important in framing who and what is Canada 'within' the world.

NOTES

1. For some interpretations of these trends see Tom Keating, *Canada and World Order: The Multilateralist Tradition in Canadian Foreign Policy.* 3rd edition, Toronto: OUP, 2013; Andrew F. Cooper, *Canadian Foreign Policy: Old Habits and New Directions*, Scarborough: Prentice Hall, 1997; Andrew F. Cooper, 'In Search of Niches: Saying 'Yes' and Saying 'No' in Canada's International Relations,' *Canadian Foreign Policy*, 3, Winter 1995: 1–13.

2. On Mulroney's activism see Fen Osler Hampson, *Master of Persuasion: Brian Mulroney's Global Legacy*, Toronto: Penguin Random House, 2018.

3. On the differentiation between the manner by which it focused on the main game on NAFTA and international activism see Andrew F. Cooper, 'NAFTA and the Politics of Regional Trade,' in Brian Hocking and Steven McGuire, eds., *Trade Politics: Actors, Issues and Processes,* London: Routledge, 1999: 229–244.

4. Lloyd Axworthy, "Canada and Human Security: The Need for Leadership," *International Journal*, 52, 2, 1997: 183. See also Andrew F. Cooper, 'Stretching the Model of 'Coalitions of the Willing,'" in Andrew F. Cooper, Brian Hocking and William Maley, eds., *Diplomacy and Global Governance: Worlds Apart?*, London: Palgrave, 2008: 257–270.

5. Bill Graham, speech to the International Press Freedom Awards, Toronto, 13 November 2002, quoted in Kim Richard Nossal, 'The World We Want'? The Purposeful Confusion of Values, Goals, and Interests in Canadian Foreign Policy,' http://www.cdfai.org.previewmysite.com/PDF/The%20World%20We%20Want.pdf.

6. Joseph Nye, *Soft Power: The Means to Success in World Politics*, New York: Public Affairs, 2004: 106.

7. Dean Beeb, 'Diefenbaker Award Missing in Action After Liberals Take over,' 5 March 2017, available at http://www.cbc.ca/news/politics/diefenbaker-award-stephen-harper-john-baird-human-rights-casgrain-liberals-trudeau-1.4007086.

8. For the full transcript of Prime Minister Harper's address, see http://www.cfr.org/publication/14315/conversation_with_stephen_harper_rush_transcript_federal_news_service.html.

9. Lloyd Axworthy, 'Canada's Role as a Middle Power,' *Winnipeg Free Press*, 8–9 September 1965.

10. Conrad Black, 'Taking Canada Seriously,' *International Journal,* 53, 1, 1997–1998: 1.

11. These words are the title of an Institute for Research on Public Policy report that Denis Stairs produced in 2001, entitled 'Canada in the 1990s: Speak Loudly and Carry a Bent Twig,' available at http://www.irpp.org/po/archive/jan01/stairs.pdf.

12. Prime Minister Harper's position in this regard is reflected in his dealings with China, where he has advocated for human rights and democracy at the expense of deeper trade integration. For more information see Scott Deveau and Brian Laghi, 'PM Says He Won't Sell Out Human Rights,' *The Globe and Mail*, 15 November 2005, available at http://www.theglobeandmail.com/servlet/story/RTGAM.20061115.wchina1115/BNStory/National.

13. Quoted in John Kirton, 'Canada's New Government's Foreign Policy and the G8 St. Petersburg Summit,' available at https://tspace.library.utoronto.ca/bitstream/1807/4819/1/kirton_060125.html.

14. J.L. Granatstein, *Whose War Is It? How Canada Can Survive in the Post-9/11 World*, Toronto: HarperCollins, 2007: 4.

15. Allan Gotlieb, 'Romanticism and Realism in Canada's Foreign Policy,' *C.D. Howe Institute Benefactors Lecture*, Toronto, Canada, 3 November 2004; Derek Burney, 'Foreign Policy: More Coherence, Less Pretence,' *Simon Reisman Lecture in International Trade Policy*, Carleton University, Ottawa, Canada, 14 March 2005. On Gotlieb's earlier role in managing the main game of Canada-US relations, see Andrew F. Cooper, 'Playing by New Rules: Allan Gotlieb, Public Diplomacy, and the Management of Canada-US Relations,' *Fletcher Forum of World Affairs*, 14, Fall 1989: 93–110.

16. As quoted in John Turley-Ewart, 'Manley Report Takes a Dig at Paul Martin,' *The National Post*, 22 January 2008, available at http://network.nationalpost.com/np/blogs/fullcomment/archive/2008/01/22/john-turley-ewart-manley-s-report-takes-a-dig-at-paul-martin.aspx.

17. Duane Bratt, 'Mr. Harper Goes to War: Canada, Afghanistan, and the Return of 'High Politics' in Canadian Foreign Policy,' available at http://www.cpsa-acsp.ca/papers-2007/Bratt.pdf Presented at the 79th Annual Conference of the Canadian Political Science Association, 30 May–1 June 2007, https://www.cpsa-acsp.ca/papers-2007/Bratt.pdf.

18. As quoted in a speech to Canadian troops in Kandahar on 13 March 2006. For more information see, CBC News 'Canada Committed to Afghan Mission, Harper Tells Troops,' 13 March 2006, available at http://www.cbc.ca/world/story/2006/03/13/harper_afghanistan060313.html.

19. See the book by Sally Armstrong, the former editor of Homemaker's magazine, *Veiled Threats*, Toronto: Penguin Canada, 2003.

20. As quoted in a speech to Members of Parliament and Senators on 5 October 2006. For more information see Michael Byers, 'Afghanistan: Wrong Mission for Canada,' 6 October 2006, available at http://thetyee.ca/Views/2006/10/06/Afghanistan/.

21. J.L. Granatstein, 'The Left, Feminists and Afghanistan,' *The Hamilton Spectator*, 15 January 2007.

22. CBC News, 'Canada Handling More Than Its Share in Afghanistan: O'Conner,' 7 September 2003.
23. Gar Pardy, 'When Diplomacy Turns Deadly,' *Diplomat & International Canada*," 20–21 May–June 2006.
24. If, however, Retired Maj.-Gen. Lewis MacKenzie, is correct, Canada is required to pay a higher price in terms of physical risk, precisely because it is seen as a country that scaled back on these risks for too long: 'You don't get credit on these missions unless the potential is there to bleed…You've got to be on the ground, you've got to be there taking high risk.' Quoted in Kathleen Harris, 'Sitting with the Big Boys: Harper Recast Foreign Policy,' *Winnipeg Sun*, 7 September 2006.
25. Kevin Boreham, 'Libya and R2P: The Limits of Responsibility,' *East Asia Forum*, 31 March 2011, http://www.eastasiaforum.org/2011/03/31/libya-and-r2p-the-limits-of-responsibility/.
26. J.L. Granatstein, 'Harper's Foreign Policies Have Made Canada a World Player,' *National Post*. Don Mills, ON, Canada, 30 January 2012, Online edition, sec. Full Comment, http://fullcomment.nationalpost.com/2012/01/30/jack-granatstein-harpers-foreign-policies-have-made-canada-a-world-player/.
27. Jeffrey Simpson, 'The Harper Government Loves the Military—In Theory,' *The Globe and Mail*, 28 June 2014.
28. Text of Stephen Harper's speech at D-Day ceremonies: 6 June 2014, http://toronto.citynews.ca/2014/06/06/text-of-stephen-harpers-speech-at-d-day-ceremonies/.
29. Harper pointedly declined to do anything to mark the 30th birthday of the Charter, Liberal icon Pierre Trudeau's signature achievement. John Geddes, 'How Stephen Harper Is Rewriting History,' *Macleans*, 29 July 2013.
30. Yves Frenette, 'L'embrigadement du passe canadien: les politiques memo-rielles du gouvernement Harper,' *Canadian Journal of History*, 49, 1, 2014: 31.
31. Alain, Noel. 'History Under Harper: Leaving Québec, and Much Else, Outside Canada,' *Labour/Le Travail*, 73, 1, 2014: 210–212.
32. Yasmeen Abu Laban, 'The Politics of History Under Harper,' *Labour/Le Travail* 73, 1, 2014: 215–217.
33. Tasha Kheiriddin, 'Harper's Canada Day Speech and the Canadian Identity,' *iPolitics*, 2 July 2015.
34. Amanda Connolly, 'Is Trudeau Getting Ready to Drop Ambassador to Israel Vivian Bercovici?' *Politics*, 11 March 2016, https://ipolitics.ca/2016/03/11/is-trudeau-getting-ready-to-drop-ambassador-to-israel-vivian-bercovici/.
35. CTV News, 'Trudeau Backs Motion Condemning Boycott Israel Movement, Some Liberals Balk,' 11 February 2016, http://www.ctvnews.

ca/politics/trudeau-backs-motion-condemning-boycott-israel-movement-some-liberals-balk-1.2788346.

36. Address by Minister Dion at the Canada in Global Affairs, New Challenges, New Ways international conference: 29 March 2016—Ottawa, ON, https://www.canada.ca/en/global-affairs/news/2016/04/add ress-by-minister-dion-at-the-canada-in-global-affairs-new-challenges-new-ways-international-conference.html?=undefined&.

37. Address by Minister Dion to United Nations Security Council: 16 March 2016—New York, NY, http://www.timesofisrael.com/severing-iran-ties-did-nothing-for-us-new-canadian-fm-says/?fb_comment_id=994789277 284149_994950120601398#ff2cfba38c2f4a.

38. Cooper, 'NAFTA and the Politics of Regional Trade,' 229–244.

39. On this traditional managerial style see Cooper, 'Playing by New Rules: Allan Gotlieb, Public Diplomacy, and the Management of Canada-US Relations,' 93–110.

40. John Ivison, 'For all Trudeau's Efforts to Be the Trump Whisperer, Canada Is Now Fighting a Trade War,' National Post, 31 May 2018, http://nationalpost.com/news/politics/john-ivison-steel-tar iffs-deal-a-blow-to-trudeaus-reputation-as-the-trump-whisperer.

41. Joseph Brean, 'After Half a Century of Liberal Internationalism, Tories Have Forged a New Foreign Policy Myth,' National Post, 2 January 2015, http://news.nationalpost.com/news/canada/after-half-a-century-of-liberal-internationalism-tories-have-forged-a-new-colder-realist-foreign-policy-myth.

42. Address by Minister Dion to United Nations Security Council: 16 March 2016—New York, NY, http://www.timesofisrael.com/severing-iran-ties-did-nothing-for-us-new-canadian-fm-says/?fb_comment_id=994789277 284149_994950120601398#ff2cfba38c2f4a.

43. CP, "PM to Davos: 'Know Canadians for Our Resourcefulness,'" 20 January 2016, http://www.macleans.ca/news/canada/what-justin-tru deau-plans-to-tell-davos/.

44. 'Address by Minister Freeland on Canada's Foreign Policy Priorities,' 6 June 2017, https://www.canada.ca/en/global-affairs/news/2017/06/ address_by_ministerfreelandoncanadasforeignpolicypriorities.html.

45. Paul Wells, 'Trudeau Channels Harper on Ukraine,' 29 June 2016, http://thechronicleherald.ca/opinion/1376400-wells-trudeau-cha nnels-harper-on-ukraine.

46. CP, 'Scheer Would Cut Foreign Aid by 25%, Focus Help on Kids in Conflict Zones,' 1 October 2019, https://www.bnnbloomberg.ca/sch eer-would-cut-foreign-aid-by-25-focus-help-on-kids-in-conflict-zones-1. 1324671.

47. Mike Blanchfield, 'Scheer, Trudeau Draw Blinds on Foreign Policy and Focus on Pocket-Book Politics,' 6 October 2019, https://nationalp ost.com/news/politics/election-2019/scheer-trudeau-draw-blinds-on-for eign-policy-and-focus-on-pocket-book-politics.

CHAPTER 9

The Return of Trudeaumania: A Public Diplomacy Shift in Foreign and Defence Policy?

Stéfanie von Hlatky

He's young, he's attractive, he loves pandas and yoga. Prime Minister Justin Trudeau had the world at hello. In terms of public diplomacy, Trudeau had a successful start: he had a lot of media coverage internationally and it was overwhelmingly positive. In Canada, however, media outlets were expressing some scepticism: "Does Justin Trudeau Risk Being Overexposed?" read a 2016 *Maclean*'s headline, during Trudeau's first year as Prime Minister.[1] Even before becoming Prime Minister, Trudeau was getting a lot of media coverage, but it was more national in scope. In 2013, one journalist remarked that "...the Liberal leader-to-be gets more ink than would a chance meeting of the newly minted pope, Justin Bieber and Ikea monkey".[2] Some say he is lucky, others caution about the buzz pushing public expectations to unattainable heights. There is no doubt that the Prime Minister's popularity has

S. von Hlatky (✉)
Queen's University, Kingston, ON, Canada
e-mail: svh@queensu.ca

© The Author(s) 2021
N. J. Cull and M. K. Hawes (eds.), *Canada's Public Diplomacy*,
Palgrave Macmillan Series in Global Public Diplomacy,
https://doi.org/10.1007/978-3-319-62015-2_9

increased Canada's visibility on the world stage. Internationally, this created a window of opportunity for Canada to regain its moral high ground through traditional honest brokerage, after the aloofness of Prime Minister Stephen Harper. In the realm of foreign and defence policy, the focus of this chapter, the Liberal government has turned to pursuits that have in the past been the hallmarks of Canada's international reputation, like multilateral diplomacy and peacekeeping.

The first decisive shift was to put an end to Canada's combat mission in Syria and Iraq as part of Operation Impact.[3] Refuelling fighter jets and providing coordinates through aerial reconnaissance were deemed acceptable by the new government, but not carrying out airstrikes themselves. Beyond that decision, has Justin Trudeau made enough substantial changes to Canada's international policy to alter its image and status on the world stage? Will this Liberal government be able to reap the benefits of Trudeaumania through tangible gains, like securing key positions in international organizations? This chapter examines the foreign and defence policy actions taken by Justin Trudeau through the prism of his first year, identifying the important themes and priorities in diplomacy and defence. By focusing on these portfolios, the chapter examines the Liberals' global engagement strategies to provide an assessment of shifting trends in public diplomacy.

Framework

Since the beginning of his first term, Prime Minister Trudeau has declared to the world that Canada "is back" and that the country is "here to help".[4] This is the message he took to the UN General Assembly on September 20, 2016. Trudeau emphasized Canada's soft power image, talking about diversity, refugees, engagement through international organizations and the importance of action on climate change. The tone was at times moralistic, for instance, when listing what Canada has gotten "right", but Trudeau also expressed a sense of collective shame when talking about the country's strained relations with Indigenous peoples. The emphasis, oddly enough for a platform like the UN General Assembly, was decidedly domestic in focus. Usually, UN General Assembly meetings are opportunities for high-level summitry and leaders attempt to refine their national role conceptions by articulating how they will contribute to solving the world's most pressing crises and security challenges. These national role conceptions are also presented in the most favourable light possible in order to win over international audiences.[5]

To assess Canada's global engagement strategies and its effects, this section introduces some conceptual guidelines for the analysis. Since the focus of the chapter is on foreign and defence policy, the primary task will be to describe the balance between soft power and hard power issues that the government has attempted to strike.[6] Canada, as a middle power, has always been dependent on soft power to increase its power position in international politics.[7] Soft power is understood here as foreign and defence policy strategies that do not require the use of force and that strongly rely on domestic and international support. Hard power will refer to the opposite and draw on examples where Canada uses force or coercive capabilities to achieve its political aims. At the outset, however, the Liberal government can make a claim to legitimacy for both soft and hard power aspects of its international policy because the development of key policy priorities has been developed and articulated as the result of public and stakeholder consultations.[8] On the defence front, for instance, the Department of National Defence orchestrated nationwide consultations with the public (#defenceconsults), IPSOS-run roundtables with stakeholders and experts, as well as an online forum so that anyone could send in detailed written submissions. Over 20,200 submissions were received through the online portal and 4700 people participated in the virtual discussion forum. The resulting defence policy, *Strong, Secure and Engaged* released in 2017, can thus claim that it reflects the preferences of Canadians, even if in practice, the policy parameters have already been set in the mandate letter, announcements on various deployments (Operation Impact, Operation Reassurance and peace support operations), as well as a budgetary constraints.[9] What, then, are the reliable pieces of evidence we can point to in order to make sense of Canadian foreign and defence priorities? How are these priorities linked to the government's public diplomacy efforts?

Drawing from Joseph Nye's work on soft power, hard power and public diplomacy, the sources of evidence used for this analysis are three-fold: 1) early communication from the Prime Minister's Office and his staff on Canadian foreign and defence policy priorities; 2) the recurrence of core themes as reiterated in major speeches, the ministers' mandate letters and, when available, policy documents; 3) the identification of key bilateral or multilateral relationships based on their prioritization by the Prime Minister during his first year.[10] The two priorities that I have identified for further discussion below, which have direct implications for foreign and defence policy, are the nexus of gender and security, as an example of soft power, and peacekeeping as an example of hard power. Both priorities are discussed in reference to global engagement as the *leitmotif* of Trudeau's international policy.

GLOBAL ENGAGEMENT

Since taking office, the Prime Minister has been active on major international platforms, such as the G7, the UN General Assembly and NATO Summits, but has also sought partnerships with activists and a plethora of non-state actors, seeking to promote greater state-society interactions as part of his diplomatic strategy.[11] Having Bono and Bill Gates by his side during the Global Fund Conference, for instance, has not hurt Trudeau's popularity.[12] One gets a sense that Canada is becoming a top-shelf brand and that every angle and every tweet is being carefully managed to enhance Trudeau's appeal, though admittedly, his diplomatic trip to India and old pictures of him in blackface resurfacing have tarnished his image.[13] Beyond the flashy photo ops, however, one wonders how the government has articulated a vision of global engagement and how foreign policy performance might be assessed over the course of his two terms.

The report on Plans and Priorities (2016–2017) is a good place to start, as it laid out initial benchmarks. It states that "...our priority is re-energizing Canada's leadership and constructive engagement on key international issues and in multilateral institutions".[14] What is striking about the policy language chosen is the insistence that the entire process has to be "re-engaged", "re-energized" and "renewed", all terms that imply that these connections had been ignored under the previous government. In then Minister of Foreign Affairs Stéphane Dion's mandate letter, there is also a sense that Prime Minister Trudeau wants to press the reset button with the world: "As Minister of Foreign Affairs, your overarching goal will be to *restore constructive Canadian leadership* in the world and to advance Canada's interests. This renewed leadership will serve our security and economic interests, but it will also support the deeply held Canadian desire to make a real and valuable contribution to a more peaceful and prosperous world [emphasis added]".[15] The letter goes on to underscore the importance of diplomacy, to "Revitalize Canada's public diplomacy, stakeholder engagement, and cooperation with partners in Canada and abroad".[16] And finally, the letter specifies the specific issues that will be the focus of the new government's efforts, as delegated to Global Affairs Canada, namely climate change, UN peace operations, human rights, the Arms Trade Treaty, as well as cultural promotion.[17]

More specifically, how can we examine Canada's global engagement strategies under Trudeau as channelled through Global Affairs Canada (GAC)? In terms of GAC's stated priorities, public diplomacy is featured under the banner of "diplomacy, advocacy and international agreement" where the key strategic outcome is focused on shaping the global agenda to further Canada's interests and values. How can that be measured beyond the initial funding allocation of approximately $950 million? The guiding document for putting this strategy into action specifies a number of expected results and performance indicators. The global engagement strategies are primarily measured by the ability of Canada to reach and engage foreign decision-makers through events, summits and outreach programs. The ultimate outcome is influence, but it has always proven elusive to measure.[18]

To evaluate influence, GAC uses support for Canadian positions as a proxy, as demonstrated in the content of bilateral and multilateral agreements, negotiations and initiatives, while identifying the UN, G7, G20, NATO and La Francophonie as the forums through which these efforts will be prioritized.[19] A number of countries are also mentioned as important target countries for Canada's global engagement strategy, namely Syria, Iraq, Ukraine, Afghanistan and countries in the Sahel region. Here the metrics get a little more difficult to assess as the government will rely on an evaluation of how foreign decision-makers take account of Canadian positions in their decisions and actions. To be effective, Trudeau and his Ministers thus have to invest a lot in official visits and public diplomacy, also identifying new ways through which government representatives will interact with their counterparts abroad and make a positive impression on foreign publics. It is obvious that Trudeau's summitry agenda was particularly busy during his first ten months in office, with fifteen official trips in Turkey, the Philippines, the UK, Malta, France, Switzerland, the US, Japan, Poland, Ukraine and China, and then got sidetracked by President Donald J. Trump's election, the renegotiation of NAFTA and, in his second term, the management of the global pandemic crisis.[20]

On foreign policy issues that intersect with defence, the metrics are more complex still. The list of such issues includes:

- Working with allies on non-proliferation, arms control, disarmament and weapons of mass destruction threat reduction issues, as well as space security and civil nuclear cooperation;
- Strengthening multilateral frameworks and operational capacities to address international conflicts and crises, including peace operations, as well as terrorism, crime and radicalization; and
- Advancing the multilateral agendas for Women, Peace and Security and Protection of Civilians in conflict.[21]

The remainder of this chapter picks up on two of those items, the Women, Peace and Security agenda, since gender and diversity are cross-cutting issues under the Trudeau government and peace support operations because it is a priority issue that also signifies a clear break with the previous government, therefore enabling us to comment on some of the distinctive aspect of Trudeau's international policy.

GENDER AND DIVERSITY

When Prime Minister Justin Trudeau appointed a gender-balanced Cabinet after his 2015 election, the accomplishment was framed as self-evident: "because it's 2015" is the answer he gave to justify his choice. Trudeau's insistence on gender equality and greater diversity was reiterated during his speech at the 2016 UN General Assembly but was also backed up by a commitment to fund more consistent gender-based analysis through Status of Women Canada (now Women and Gender Equality Canada). The small department developed a tool called GBA+ which the new government is investing in, so that gender analysis can be tailored to specific departments and agencies. The Canadian Armed Forces (CAF) also received a formal guidance from the Chief of the Defence Staff (CDS), General Jonathan Vance, mandating members of the CAF to take the GBA+ training. The CAF is also overseeing the entire curriculum of professional military education to make sure gender perspectives will be included. Moreover, the CDS announced the appointment of gender advisors that can advise military leadership on how to incorporate a gender perspective in operational planning and missions. The stated intention of incorporating gender considerations into the practices of the Canadian Armed Forces has translated into a series of reforms, with implications for public diplomacy since Canada is showcasing these changes under the rhetorical guise of sharing good practices with other nations and partners. This culminated in General Vance taking up the role of Chair of the Women, Peace and Security Chief of Defence Network in 2019.[22]

On the policy side, Global Affairs Canada embarked in consultations with stakeholders and experts to rethink the way it engages in reporting for its action plan on the implementation of United Nations Security Council (UNSC) Resolutions on Women, Peace and Security. DND also organized a roundtable on gender as part of the defence policy review consultation process. The national action plan reporting exercise relies on collecting data from relevant government organizations with an international security mandate (GAC, DND, the Royal Canadian Mounted Police) on their gender balance, how departments and agencies mainstream gender in their programming, as well as contributions to eradicate sexual and gender-based violence.[23] This incorporation of gender perspectives into international policy, security and defence is consistent with Canada's commitment to implement Resolution 1325 and follow-on resolutions, though the government's efforts were heavily criticized under Harper.[24] The national action plans have international significance because it is a benchmarking tool across the UN to measure implementation of 1325. These reports are scrutinized by non-governmental organizations and activists that produce independent assessments of countries' performance.[25]

In terms of background, in 2000, the United Nations Security Council recognized that gender analysis was important to better understand conflict dynamics. Through UNSC Resolution 1325 and the cognate resolutions that followed, both civilian decision-makers and military leaders were urged to think about how conflict dynamics impact men, women, boys and girls differently. This kind of analysis, if done properly, leads to major changes in the way programmes are delivered and how military operations are carried out, not to mention how they are framed for public consumption internationally.[26] Indeed, the resolution built on mounting evidence that including more women in peace processes translates into better and more stable outcomes.[27] This evidence-based case also became a driving narrative for the United Nations Department of Peacekeeping Operations (now the Department of Peace Operations) which called on troop-contributing nations to include more women as part of their peacekeeping force.[28] This "gender turn" in military issues and the Women, Peace and Security agenda more broadly speaking slowly brought gender issues closer to the mainstream of international politics and communities of practice across government, the armed forces and international organizations.[29] Nor is this increased attention to gender specific to the practice of international security. Gender issues are trending. From Sheryl Sandberg to Malala Yousafzai, there is a global push to engage in discussion about female leadership, gender dynamics and questioning the boundaries of traditionally-male spheres of influence.

This push is gaining momentum and Trudeau has made gender and diversity central themes of his lexicon on both domestic and international platforms. Trudeau has integrated this key message for Canadians, through his electoral campaigns and speeches as Prime Minister, and has adapted his take on gender equality and diversity for international audiences via the United Nations, the G7, NATO and other high visibility platforms. Moreover, Canada's success in securing the appointment of Lieutenant-General Chris Whitecross as the Commandant of the NATO Defence College in Rome is the result of intense lobbying efforts on the part of Canada where the case for promoting female leadership was one of the decisive arguments to win over the support of a majority of military permanent representatives.[30] At NATO, Trudeau pledged a financial commitment to support the work of the Women, Peace and Security office and domestically, the post of Women, Peace and Security Ambassador was created. The next section turns to the military instrument and examines how peacekeeping is once again part of Canada's defence priorities, at least on paper.

PEACEKEEPING AND MILITARY COOPERATION

Although peace support operations represent a somewhat softer side of defence, it is still unequivocally in the hard power category, since it resorts to armed force to support political objectives and because the new peacekeeping can be more coercive than humanitarian.[31] This is a point that has been stressed by the Defence Minister, Harjit Sajjan on several occasions, as he attempts to manage public expectations about what peace support might look like in countries like Mali, South Sudan or the Central African Republic.[32] The Minister participated in the Peacekeeping Summit in London and then hosted the UN Peacekeeping Defence Ministerial in Vancouver in 2017, which led to the adoption of the Vancouver Principles on Peacekeeping and the Prevention of the Recruitment and Use of

Child Soldiers and the solicitation of national pledges to support peace-keeping missions. Conspicuously absent were Canada's own contributions to peacekeeping missions, through Operation Presence, which only materialized in 2018, as CAF personnel were deployed to Mali. Yes in both the Minister's mandate letter and in the Prime Minister's Throne Speech, at the beginning of Trudeau's first term, a return to peacekeeping was clearly emphasized as part of the core missions the Canadian Armed Forces will be asked to undertake:

> [...] protect Canadian sovereignty, defend North America, provide disaster relief, conduct search and rescue, *support United Nations peace operations*, and contribute to the security of our allies and to allied and coalition operations abroad [emphasis added].[33]

Under the Harper government, from 2006 to 2015, the government had primarily focused on allied and coalition operations, striving for greater interoperability as part of a select group of powerful allies and contributing to deterring threats in the Euro-Atlantic area, efforts that were ramped up after the Ukrainian crisis in 2014.[34] The current government maintains those commitments, though it changed the nature of Canada's contribution to coalition operations in Iraq and Syria. It is in the context of existing interventions in the Middle East and Europe that the Trudeau government has pledged to renew Canada's contribution to UN peace operations. The throne speech also emphasized peace support operations, with Prime Minister Justin Trudeau promising that "the government will renew Canada's commitment to the United Nations peacekeeping operations, and will continue to work with its allies in the fight against terrorism".[35] What the renewal of peacekeeping entails took several years to take form, though Canada did announce a pledge of $450 million and 600 troops for peace support operations in 2016.[36] Even with a contribution to Mali in 2018–2019 and then Uganda in 2019–2020, Canada's peacekeeping footprint remains light, by historical standards.

If Canada is to renew its commitment to UN peace operations, it might have to rebalance some of its assets away from Europe and Iraq to instead support peace operations in Africa—where about half of ongoing peacekeeping operations are located.[37] Canada played a role in the UN Stabilization Mission in Haiti (MINUSTAH) but this mission has since ended in October of 2017. As for other potential peace operations in the Americas, the CAF simply does not have the linguistic comparative advantage, as it did in Haiti.

Then, there is the possibility of a peacekeeping role in Africa or the Middle East. The demand is already strong in both regions, as shown in Table 9.1. The CAF could act as force multipliers if they were deployed alongside traditional troop-contributing countries, like Bangladesh, Rwanda or Jordan. This kind of peacekeeping train-and-assist role for the CAF would not require large numbers of deployed personnel but could make a real difference on the ground by sharing their expertise with partner countries. There are urgent needs in the Central African

Table 9.1 List of current UN peacekeeping operations

Name of operation	Location
United Nations Mission for the Referendum in Western Sahara (MINURSO)	Western Sahara
United Nations Multidimensional Integrated Stabilization Mission in the Central African Republic (MINUSCA)	Central African Republic
United Nations Multidimensional Integrated Stabilization Mission in Mali (MINUSMA)	Mali
United Nations Organization Stabilization Mission in the Democratic Republic of the Congo (MONUSCO)	Democratic Republic of the Congo
African Union-United Nations Hybrid Operation in Darfur (UNAMID)	Darfur
United Nations Disengagement Observer Force (UNDOF)	Syria
United Nations Peacekeeping Force in Cyprus (UNFICYP)	Cyprus
United Nations Interim Force in Lebanon (UNIFIL)	Lebanon
United Nations Interim Security Force for Abyei (UNISFA)	Sudan
United Nations Mission in the Republic of South Sudan (UNMISS)	South Sudan
United Nations Interim Administration Mission in Kosovo (UNMIK)	Kosovo
United Nations Military Observer Group in India and Pakistan (UNMOGIP)	Pakistan
United Nations Truce Supervision Organization (UNTSO)	Middle East

Source Department for Peacekeeping Operations

Republic and Mali, given the shifting political and security situation. A renewed peacekeeping role along these guidelines will require a modest increase in the number of Canadian peacekeepers, but no one will expect Canada to rival the top troop-contributing countries in terms of numbers. What the CAF can offer is specialized expertise and advanced capabilities that can lead to the qualitative improvements of existing or future missions. Still, the Canadian government would have to do better than having very limited (in scope and in time) peacekeeping contributions, as it currently does. So far, Trudeau and his Ministers have been making the case for a return to peacekeeping but the calculations of what this reengagement should be are overly cautious.

Even with a very modest increase in deployed peacekeeping troops, Canada can still play a greater role in peacekeeping by boosting its training intake in Canada.[38] The demand for training is growing as the requirements of peace support operations get more complex. Peacekeepers are now expected to be well versed in international law, human rights, as well as gender and cultural awareness. Canada can offer this kind of training in existing facilities, such as the Peace Support Training Centre in Kingston, Ontario. With more resources dedicated to those facilities and training personnel, Canada could grow its intake, translating its peacekeeping expertise into a global network of defence cooperation.

Another reason why the demand for training is likely to increase is the number of high-profile sexual misconduct scandals that have harmed the reputation of peacekeeping and of the United Nations. Since eradicating sexual misconduct is a Canadian priority, as made clear by the CDS's decision to launch Operation Honour at the very beginning of his mandate, the timing seems appropriate. Taking an active stance in training, with an emphasis on achieving the highest professional standard of conduct for peacekeepers worldwide and additional training on the prevention of conflict-related sexual and gender-based violence, would be a meaningful way to show that the CAF are viewing Op Honour seriously and taking action in a constructive way, both domestically and internationally.

In sum, Trudeau's insistence that Canada play a role in UN peace support operations is a theme that has been front and centre across Trudeau's two terms, yet words have been more visible than the deeds. What is clear is that peacekeeping remains a popular concept in Canada, one which is deeply tied to the country's foreign policy history and Pearsonian legacy. Other countries also view Canada as the quintessential peacekeeping nation, despite the apparent withdrawal from peace support operations since the early 2000s. However, peace support operations have changed. A return to peacekeeping may now look like a riskier proposition than it did when Trudeau was trying to downplay Canada's combat role in favour of a softer military role focused on train-and-assist missions and defence cooperation.[39]

CONCLUSION

This chapter has highlighted Prime Minister Trudeau's foreign and defence policy narratives. By focusing on key priorities, across the spectrum of both soft and hard power, it is possible to assess the impact, in terms of funding priorities and how the core messages have been articulated internationally and translated into action. The chapter has been able to infer the government's policy intent from early documents, speeches and funding commitments, but it is worth thinking in greater depth about how some of the main policy outcomes might be measured. It would be easy to declare success by pointing to Trudeau's extensive media coverage and the budgetary decisions he has made to back up the liberal international policy agenda, however, it leaves us with an incomplete picture. Has Trudeau's foreign and defence policy shifts led to an improvement in international perceptions of Canada, which have always been quite favourable, even under Harper?[40] If polling data on international attitudes towards Canada are not a good predictor of Trudeau's public diplomacy success, then what is? Domestically, however, Trudeau lost some of his edge, as he was only re-elected with a minority government in 2019.

In terms of investments, Canada is like other countries in that it spends more on hard power than it does on soft power internationally. The defence budget, though stagnant at a little more than 1% of the GDP (21.6 billion), dwarfs the budget of Global Affairs Canada, which includes the international development portfolio. In terms of both size and funding, there is an asymmetry there that no government is likely to fundamentally transform.[41]

What is clear, however, is that public diplomacy has now become a cross-cutting issue, it has been mainstreamed in the way Trudeau and his team of Ministers carry out their foreign and defence policy mandates. Global engagement has been pursued through summitry and pledges to showcase Canada's tangible commitments to international peace and security, gestures that have been carefully documented and disseminated via Twitter, Facebook and clever photo ops. While Trump has out-tweeted Trudeau on more than one occasion, there is no question about who is winning the international popularity contest.

NOTES

1. Martin Patriquin, "Does Justin Trudeau Risk Being Overexposed?" *Maclean's*, 26 August 2016. Online: http://www.macleans.ca/politics/does-justin-trudeau-risk-being-overexposed/.
2. Warren Kinsella, "Are You Sick of Media Coverage About Justin Trudeau," *Toronto Sun*, 8 April 2013.
3. National Defence and the Canadian Armed Forces, "Operation Impact." Online: http://www.forces.gc.ca/en/operations-abroad-current/op-imp act.page.
4. Justin Trudeau, *Address to the 71st Session of the United Nations General Assembly* (New York: United Nations Headquarters, 20 September 2016).
5. Kal J. Holsti, "National Role Conceptions in the Study of Foreign Policy," *International Studies Quarterly* 14, 3 (1970): 233–309; Justin Massie, "Making Sense of Canada's 'Irrational' International Security Policy: A Tale of Three Strategic Culture," *International Journal* 64, 3 (2009): 624–645.
6. The definitions of soft power and hard power presented here are adapted from, Joseph S. Nye, "Public Diplomacy and Soft Power." *Annals of the American Academy of Political and Social Sciences* 616, 1 (March 2008): 94–109.
7. If it is true for the US, the logic is even more compelling for Canada. See Ernest J. Wilson III, "Hard Power, Soft Power, Smart Power," *Annals of the American Academy of Political and Social Science* 616, 1 (March 2008): 110–124.
8. Marie-Danielle Smith, "Consultations, Consultations, Consultations: The Liberal Government Wants to Hear from this Summer," *National Post*, 10 June 2016. Online: http://news.nationalpost.com/news/canada/can adian-politics/consultations-consultations-consultations-the-liberal-gov ernment-wants-to-hear-from-you-this-summer.
9. The policy is available online: https://www.canada.ca/content/dam/dnd-mdn/documents/reports/2018/strong-secure-engaged/canada-def ence-policy-report.pdf.
10. Nye, "Public Diplomacy and Soft Power," 101.
11. Ole J. Sending, Vincent Pouliot, and Iver B. Neumann, "The Future of Diplomacy: Changing Practices, Evolving Relationships," *International Journal* 66, 3 (2011): 527–542.

12. "Bono Sings Canada's Praises at Global Fund Conference in Montreal," *The Canadian Press*, 17 September 2016. Online: http://www.huffingto npost.ca/2016/09/17/rock-star-bono-praises-canada-as-a-global-leader-at-montreal-aids-conference_n_12062426.html.

13. Rasmus Kjaergaard Rasmussen and Henrik Merkelsen, "The New PR of States: How Nation Branding Practices Affect the Security Function of Public Diplomacy," *Public Relations Review* 38, 5 (2012): 810–818.

14. Global Affairs Canada, *Report on Plans and Priorities 2016–2017*. Online: http://www.international.gc.ca/departmentministere/plans/rpp/rpp_1617.aspx?lang=eng.

15. Justin Trudeau, *Minister of Foreign Affairs Mandate Letter (2015)*. Online: http://pm.gc.ca/eng/minister-foreign-affairs-mandate-letter.

16. Ibid.

17. Ibid.

18. James Pamment, "Articulating Influence: Toward a Research Agenda for Interpreting the Evaluation of Soft Power, Public Diplomacy and Nation Brands," *Public Relations Review* 40, 1 (2014): 50–59.

19. Global Affairs Canada, *Report on Plans and Priorities 2016–2017*. Online: http://www.international.gc.ca/departmentministere/plans/rpp/rpp_1617.aspx?lang=eng.

20. All trips are listed on the Prime Minister's official page. Online: http://pm.gc.ca/eng/news.

21. Global Affairs Canada, *Report on Plans and Priorities 2016–2017*.

22. For more information on this network: https://www.wpschods.com.

23. Global Affairs Canada, *2013–2014 Progress Report—Canada's Action Plan for the Implementation of United Nations Security Council Resolution on Women, Peace and Security*. Online: http://www.international.gc.ca/start-gtsr/women_report_2013-2014_rapport_femmes.aspx?lang=eng&pedisable=true.

24. Rebecca Tiessen, "Gender Essentialism and the Discourse of Canadian Foreign Aid Commitments to Women, Peace and Security," *International Journal* 70, 1 (March 2015): 84–100; Rebecca Tiessen and Krystel Carrier, "The Erasure of Gender in Canadian Foreign Policy Under the Harper Conservatives: The Significance of the Discursive Shift from Gender Equality' to Equality Between Women and Men," *Canadian Foreign Policy Journal* 21, 2 (February 2015): 95–111.

25. Inclusive Security, *Assessment of Canada's Action Plan for the Implementation of United Nations Security Council Resolutions on Women, Peace and Security 2010–2016* (September 2014). Online: http://www.international.gc.ca/start-gtsr/assets/pdfs/Canada_Action_Plan_Women_Peace_Security-2010-2016.pdf.

26. See special issue "A Systematic Understanding of Gender, Peace, and Security: Implementing 1325," *International Interactions* 39, 4 (2013): 425–619.

27. One of the pioneering articles examining this relationship is Mark Tessler and Ina Warriner, "Gender, Feminism, and Attitudes Toward International Conflict: Exploring Relationships with Survey Data from the Middle East," *World Politics* 49, 2 (1997): 250–281.

28. See UN Peacekeeping's featured page "Women in Peacekeeping," online: http://www.un.org/en/peacekeeping/issues/women/womeni npk.shtml.

29. Stéfanie von Hlatky, "The Gender Turn in Canadian Military Interventions," in Fen Osler Hampson and Stephen M. Saideman (eds.), *Canada Among Nations* (Waterloo: Centre for International Governance Innovation, 2015).

30. Interview with members of the Canadian delegation at NATO (Brussels, 6–8 September 2016).

31. Brooke A. Smith-Windsor, "Hard Power, Softer Power Reconsidered," *Canadian Military Journal* (Autumn 2000): 51–56.

32. "Harjit Sajjan's New Peacekeeping Is 'Force If Needed'," *The Globe and Mail*, 14 September 2016. Online: http://www.theglobeandmail.com/opinion/editorials/harjit-sajjans-new-peacekeeping-is-force-if-needed/art icle31887686/.

33. Justin Trudeau, *Minister of National Defence Mandate Letter*, 2015. http://pm.gc.ca/eng/minister-national-defence-mandate-letter#sthash.NYjDu5tj.dpuf.

34. As argued in Stéfanie von Hlatky, "Trudeau's Promises: From Coalition Operations to Peacekeeping and Beyond," *CDA Institute Analysis* (June 2016), 8 pages.

35. *Speech from the Throne*, 4 December 2015. http://speech.gc.ca.

36. Murray Brewster, "Liberals Commit $450M, Up to 600 Troops to UN Peacekeeping Missions," *The Globe and Mail*, 26 August 2016. Online: http://www.cbc.ca/news/politics/canada-peacekeeping-announ cement-1.3736593.

37. United Nations, "Peacekeeping Time Sheet," 30 April 2016. http://www.un.org/en/peacekeeping/resources/statistics/factsheet.shtml.

38. For a comprehensive discussion on peacekeeping training, see A. Walter Dorn and Joshua Libben, *Unprepared for Peace? The Decline of Canadian Peacekeeping Training (and What to Do About It)* (Canadian Centre for Policy Alternatives/Rideau Institute on International Affairs, 2016). http://www.operationspaix.net/DATA/DOCUMENT/8251~v~Unprepared_for_Peace_.pdf.

39. Alan Bloomfield and Kim Richard Nossal, "Towards an Explicative Understanding of Strategic Culture: The Cases of Australia and Canada," *Contemporary Security Policy* 28, 2 (2007): 286–307.
40. Lauren O'Neil, "Canada's Reputation Takes Top Spot in International Survey," *CBC News*, 16 July 2015. Online: http://www.cbc.ca/news/trending/canada-has-the-worlds-best-reputation-global-survey-shows-1.3155500.
41. Wilson III, "Hard Power, Soft Power, Smart Power."

CHAPTER 10

International Gifts and Public Diplomacy: Canada's Capital in 2017

Mark Kristmanson

I'm not giving this to a titled individual. I'm giving to the head of an extraordinary community with a long, long history. Through that person, I am linking up with a community and the deeds that are being done in the name of that community.

Albie Sachs 2016

What does the "Resolute" desk in the Oval Office have in common with New York's Statue of Liberty, Cairo's Opera House, and Iceland's Flatey Book? At first glance, this disparate set of objects would seem widely disconnected in time, space, and purpose—but for one underlying similarity: They are prominent examples of gift exchanges between nations. As Canada counted down to the 150th anniversary of its Confederation in 2017, I took the opportunity of USC's Centre on Public Diplomacy conference to reflect on international contributions to Canada's

M. Kristmanson (✉)
National Capital Commission, Ottawa, ON, Canada
e-mail: lmdk@kristmanson.com

© The Author(s) 2021
N. J. Cull and M. K. Hawes (eds.), *Canada's Public Diplomacy*,
Palgrave Macmillan Series in Global Public Diplomacy,
https://doi.org/10.1007/978-3-319-62015-2_10

capital and what international "diplomatic gifts" might contribute to our understanding of public diplomacy.

As Chief Executive Officer of the National Capital Commission (NCC), my day-to-day interactions with diplomatic missions to Canada vary from overseeing the guest residence for visiting heads of state to partnering in public diplomacy activities presented on the NCC's properties. The NCC works closely with heads of missions to help locate new chanceries, strengthen their security, and beautify their surroundings.[1] As the regulator of federal land use in the capital, the NCC grants land use and design approvals to diplomatic missions when the government's lands are involved. From time to time, the Commission hosts visits by their city mayors and ministers, as well as features their leading architects, planners, and thinkers in its Capital Urbanism Lab. Finally, as a founding member of the Capitals Alliance, an international association of capital cities formed in 2001, the NCC maintains contacts with other national capitals.

Yet, the impetus for this paper came to me from pondering a lesser known responsibility of the NCC: managing the Prime Minister's forfeited gifts. Like other countries, Canada's conflict of interest regulations set a threshold for such gifts—in our case, one thousand dollars—over which the items normally are forfeited and handed over to the NCC for retention or appropriate reassignment. I will discuss gifts given and received by leaders, in addition to state-to-state gifts, gifts of restitution, and international gifts from non-state actors. What I encourage through this paper is a deeper discussion on the role of gift exchange in public diplomacy. The following survey touches on anthropological insights but is rooted in the National Capital Commission's practical experience of public diplomacy activities in Canada's capital region and its view towards the 2017 sesquicentennial.

THE ANTHROPOLOGY OF THE GIFT

Marcel Mauss's 1925 *Essai sur le don*, known in English as *The Gift*, begins with an extract from Scandinavia's *Poetic Edda* that already, almost a millennium ago, succinctly captured the essence of gift exchange that Mauss would elaborate upon: the obligation to give, the obligation to receive, the obligation to reciprocate.[2] Reading the gift across the cultural anthropology of his day, Mauss draws from the *Edda* crucial themes of parity, reciprocity, the animism of gift objects, and the call upon recipients' "honour" whose extreme case is the potlatch, the apotheosis of gift-giving that he called *"prestation totale."*

For my purposes here, it is useful simply to concede that while certain gifts may be given purely in altruism, indeed, others arrive with veiled obligations.[3] Critics of international gift exchange often see only utility; "the goal is to offer gifts to potential enemies in order to establish a relationship, by placing them in debt," is a typical view.[4] Furthermore, writes Giarda Fiorindo:

> The belief in the magical power of gestures and tokens seems to have been forgotten as one-of-a-kind gifts of State are replaced by customized mugs and caps, souvenirs from tourist shops, and sterile objects of planned obsolescence. What was once a sublime portrait of thriving epochs is now a gadget of mediocrity: the diplomatic gift.[5]

There is some truth here, though I agree with Jacques Godbout that it is more interesting to seek out traces of altruism in apparently utilitarian gift exchanges rather than the reverse.[6] The intense century-long debate over altruism versus self-interest in gift-giving truly would seem moot if it is the case that all diplomatic gifts are exchanged mechanically—if staff members in one country select and package gifts simply for their homologues abroad eventually to dispose of them into archives, museums, or agencies, like the National Capital Commission.

On the other hand, this overlooks how difficult it can be to choose the right gift and how meaningful the "right gift" can be in the long term. For example, diplomatic gifts associated with extraordinary moments in history—such as Canada's role in liberating the Netherlands in 1944–1945—accrue deeper meanings and become nurtured in bilateral relations, even as the affected generations pass on. Moreover, personal gift exchanges between leaders sometimes do hold great meaning and emotion.[7]

Michael Taussig writes that thinking of the gift "as a 'system of exchange' sounds like something out of a gear box manual." What is at stake, he argues, "are the greatest human passions, the very nature of being a person, and the strange intimacies that giving establishes between things and personhood."[8] Efforts to minimize the importance of the gift in modern diplomacy, particularly among the English-speaking nations, run up against the residual force of archaic gift exchange.

The Australian government's policy clearly states, "Australia is not traditionally a gift-giving country."[9] Officials should make it plain to international counterparts that reciprocity should not be expected. Yet, as a journalist pointed out, the Australian Prime Minister and other senior officials presented diplomatic gifts worth 3.4 m Australian dollars between 2009 and 2014, indicating more generosity than the policy might suggest.[10] It seems even bureaucratic impersonality cannot contain the deep human compulsion to give and to receive gifts as the basis for building relations.

Leader-to-Leader Gifts

Routine disclosures of information regarding diplomatic gifts received by national leaders result in regular news articles on this subject in many countries enjoying a free press. Their bemusing examples can be telling about the personalities and cultural expressions of leaders and their countries. Reporters particularly enjoy mining the lists for the outlier gifts—discs of movies in unreadable formats, electronic gadgets, odd portraits, and custom painted surfboards, among others—and their headlines can be good fun: "Surfboard Diplomacy: Tony Abbot wants to ensure Barack Obama is Australia's best mate." In fact, today, anyone can go online and view the gifts received by the leaders of the United States, and many other nations, including Canada.[11]

The gift largesse of the Saudi Royal Family attracts media attention, their opulent gifts of jewelry and works of art almost always valued above the allowable thresholds for Western leaders. Every single item in the exquisite trove—diamond and emerald necklaces, earrings, rings, brooches, watches, and bracelets—given by the late Abdullah bin Abdulaziz Al-Saud, Custodian of the Two Holy Mosques, King of the Kingdom of Saudi Arabia, in 2014 to First Lady Michelle Obama and her children, as well as to Secretary of State John Kerry and his spouse, far exceeded the allowable limits. The most expensive item was valued at $780,000 and the total value of the gifts exceeded $2.2 m. "Non-acceptance," the report states, "would cause embarrassment to donor and U.S. Government." Once graciously received, the items were deposited with the National Archives and Records Administration.[12] Of the 42 forfeited gifts or gift sets received by the NCC since taking responsibility in 2012, three have been placed in Stornoway, the official residence of the Leader of the Official Opposition, and nine have been placed on loan with national museums, including exquisite diamond and sapphire jewelry received from the late Saudi King.[13]

Due to the low thresholds for leaders' acceptance of gifts in Canada, the United States, and other Western countries, many diplomatic gifts in fact pass directly from their personal possession into the hands of national institutions like the NCC and, as such, into the realm of *public* diplomacy.[14] The limits are known and thus, from the outset, many highly valuable gifts are intended to benefit the general public of the receiving nation. Gifting leaders with elephants, for example, would seem to exceed any realistic welcome as household pets. President Eisenhower may personally have accepted the Central African Republic's gift of "Dzimbo," a 440-pound baby elephant, but it was the American public who befriended him in Washington's National Zoo.[15]

More recently, Sri Lanka's President Maithripala Sirisena's gift of "Jumbo" to New Zealand's Prime Minister John Key raised environmentalists' ire, as this was (at least) the twelfth elephant given by Sri Lanka to a foreign nation in recognition of "excellent bilateral relations."[16] The practice of giving animals, fish, and birds extends back into the depths of time. China's famous "Panda diplomacy" began in the Tang Dynasty in the seventh century and, since it was revived in 1958, dozens of these bears have become the most lovable of Chinese ambassadors. By 1982, 23 pandas had been sent to 9 countries.[17]

A curious animal gift exchange between national leaders was the case of "Winston," a live platypus sent as a gift by the Australian government to Prime Minister Churchill during the darkest depths of World War II. In fact, it was the intended recipient himself who had telegraphed his keen hope to receive an exemplar of this rare species for his menagerie at Chartwell. As Natalie Lawrence explains, by 1942, the war had severely strained Australian-British cooperation, and the respective Prime Ministers, Curtin and Churchill, were deeply at odds. In her view, Churchill's solicitation of the platypus reactivated Anglo-Australian kinship at a critical moment, initiating a gift obligation that renewed a bond. Alas, Winston (the platypus) perished en route following the shock of a German submarine attack, but she argues that the intended gift nonetheless fulfilled Churchill's deeper diplomatic purpose by helping to sustain Anglo-Australian relations through a critical downturn.[18]

Leaders' summits are prominent occasions for gift exchanges. The leader of the host country is expected to offer gifts inflected with a tinge of national character: Camp David leather jackets (United States), bowls turned from the wood of sugar maples (Canada), Eiffel Tower letter openers (France). Some of these gifts, such as expensive Swiss watches or French fountain pens, were forfeited by Canada's Prime Ministers and have found their way into our collection.

In 2013, an Italian newspaper accused Russia of handing out intelligence-gathering USB gift pens to G20 delegates during the meeting near St. Petersburg. Russia was quick to deny both these reports of "Trojan horse pen drives" and a further claim that "delegations also received mobile phone recharging devices...capable of secretly tapping into emails, text messages and telephone calls."[19] True or not, these reports serve as a reminder that the word "gift," as Mauss warned, has danger encoded in its ancient Germanic roots, where it also meant *poison*. Drawing examples from literature, he cites the Rhine Gold, the Cup of Hagen, and the curses of Loki.[20] Indeed, the *Edda* does not shy away from reciprocity's darker side. The ancient poet took pains to explain how one should respond to ill intent: "People should meet smiles with smiles and lies with treachery." With those you trust, go often to exchange ideas and gifts, but address those in whom you have no confidence with "fair words but crafty heart, and repay treachery with lies... Gifts ought to be repaid in like coin."[21]

On a more cooperative note, the recent term, "gift-basket diplomacy", denotes a technique of breaking impasses in international summits by grouping the concessions of willing nations in a 'basket,' hoping to induce cooperation from recalcitrant parties. The term originated at the 2010 Washington Nuclear Security Summit as "a form of multilateral, voluntary commitment-making."[22]

Major State-to-State Gifts

The deep history of gifts between peoples and their leaders recedes into the mists of archaic gift exchange and blurs into adjacent meanings such as tribute, tithe, or ransom. Was Atahualpa's offering of gold—stacked in a room up to the height of his raised arm—to the conquistador Pizarro truly a gift-sharing, as the Inca king described it, or rather an extortionate ransom payment that would still fail to preserve his own life?[23]

In modern times, the trademark state-to-state gift is arguably the Statue of Liberty, presented to the people of the United States by the people of France (both governments left it to their respective citizens to raise the required amounts—the French for the statue, and Americans for its pediment). Originally proposed in the context of Philadelphia's 1876 Centennial Exposition, where Liberty first raised up her torch, it took a further decade to fully realize Frédéric Bartholdi's design, so brilliantly engineered on Bedloe's Island by Gustav Eiffel. This enduringly effective gift object still serves its public diplomacy objective today, underscoring the commonality of the democratic ideal between France and the United States.[24]

Proceeding from Atahualpa's and Liberty's raised arms, one finds Mussolini's gift of an ancient Roman column to the United States on the occasion of the 1934 Century of Progress World's Fair still standing in Chicago's Burnham Park. It commemorated Italo Balbo's 1933 arrival in the windy city at the head of a fleet of Italian flying boats. The intended propaganda message is evident enough in Il Duce's inscription, praising Roman victories and daring, circa 1934, "the 11th year of the fascist era."[25]

In the genre of international gifts serving propaganda (or at least promotional) purposes, one could mention the global diffusion of statuary celebrating South America's nationalist heroes: as will be shown below, Generals Bolivar and San Martin are both honored with statues in Ottawa. Likewise, a statue of Mahatma Gandhi graces our city as it does other world capitals. China's gift to Montreal in the 1970s of a Dr. Norman Bethune statue, in the idiom of his statues in China, touches upon both Bethune's under-recognition in his home country and the great honour still accorded to him by the Chinese people.[26] (Indeed, a CBC report states that Prime Minister Justin Trudeau traveling in China "presented Chinese President Xi Jinping and Premier Li Keqiang with two portrait medallions of Bethune made in the same run as the medallion his father, then Prime Minister Pierre Elliott Trudeau, presented to chairman Mao Zedong in 1973.")[27]

In a somber vein, the post-World War I decades also witnessed substantive memorials built as international gifts commemorating the tragic host of fallen soldiers, particularly from the allied nations to France and Belgium. Canada's gift to France of the haunting Vimy Ridge monument has an enduring place in Canadians' national consciousness. Likewise, through the Imperial War Graves Commission, Britain gifted Belgium with solemn memorials at the Menin Gate and Tyne Cot, as well as the Helles Memorial at Gallipoli, at Lake Doiran in Macedonia, and the largest, the Thiepval Memorial at the Somme. For their part, the Australians created a monument at Villers Bretonneux and the South

Africans created a monument and cemetery at Delville Wood.[28] Even today, these memorials are the sites for annual international exchanges and leaders' visits.

From a capital city perspective, it is the smaller, and often replicable, gifts that draw one's attention to *aller retour* patterns of reciprocity: the "Friendship Train" that brought an outpouring of gifts from American families to war-ravaged Europe was reciprocated by France in 1949 with forty-nine "*Merci* Boxcars" that delivered gifts gathered from the French people, one boxcar each for every state in the Union, and one shared by the District of Columbia and Hawaii. Some of the boxcars are still on display in state capitals as monuments commemorating this international exchange of good will.[29]

Shifting to the Cold War era, its heightened *prestations* of cultural diplomacy have been characterized as a propaganda struggle for target populations' hearts and minds, but they could be equally considered as an international gift exchange.[30] There is a trace of the potlatch in that era's cultural diplomacy programs wherein the total cultural capital of a nation seemed to be extravagantly and agonistically showered by each competing side upon the other, measured in touring orchestras and jazz bands. Danielle Fosler-Lussier astutely associates Cold War musical gift exchange with the idea of "inalienable gifts." Invoking Mauss, she says, "the giver expects reciprocity, and the recipient's obligation can be weighty and lasting." Yet, she continues, the "ephemeral nature of a musical performance makes it an unusual form of gift for consideration in these terms." Following Annette Weiner, she views music as an example of a paradoxical gift that "can be given away and yet kept at the same time," always imbued with ineffable qualities associated with its original owners.[31]

Post-1989, gifts carried new messages. Sections of the disassembled Berlin Wall found their way around the world as monuments to the victims of East Bloc communism, including Edwina Sandys' sculpture "Breakthrough" in Fulton, Missouri, created from wall sections gifted by the GDR. Its prominent site on the university campus is adjacent to where Winston Churchill, her grandfather, thundered his "iron curtain" speech in 1946.[32] Another section of the wall found its way to Ottawa where it is housed in the Canadian War Museum.

Other twentieth-century statuary gifts to capital cities include a large statue of Leif Ericsson given to Iceland by the United States on the 1000th anniversary of Iceland's parliament, the Althing, founded in 930 AD.[33] It seems remarkably intuitive that early inhabitants founded the world's first parliament in a dramatic crevasse that they could not have known is formed by the collision of east and west tectonic plates. Now a prominent Reykjavik landmark, the statue subtly emphasizes Ericsson as symbolizing a west-faring orientation for this famously ambivalent mid-Atlantic nation.

Major international gifts are also associated with national cultural institutions. In Ottawa, one thinks of the Dutch contribution of two fine Flentrop pipe organs to the National Arts Centre, Canada's national performing arts center, which opened in 1969. As Sarah Jennings writes, "The idea of an organ...materialized...in a gift from the Dutch people in memory of Canada's service in Holland during the war."[34] Likewise, international gifts were involved in the building of Washington's Kennedy Center for the Performing Arts: from Italy, 3700 tons of white Carrara marble, from Austria, Norway, and Ireland, a total of thirteen large chandeliers, from France, two Gobelin tapestries designed by Matisse, from Great Britain, a Barbara Hepworth bronze, from Belgium, giant mirrors, and art from twenty-two African nations. Japan's gift of $3 m paid for the Terrace Theatre designed by Philip Johnson.[35]

Japan also made a remarkable cultural gift to Egypt following the tragic 1971 fire that destroyed the storied Khedivial Opera House, dating back to the opening of the Suez Canal (and the historic African premiere of Verdi's *Aida*). As a result of President Mubarak's visit to Japan in 1983, the Japanese government pledged to rebuild Cairo's lost opera house; indeed, it reopened in 1988 with Egypt's first Kabuki presentation, performed in the presence of Prince Tomohito of Mikasa.[36] During President Reagan's 1988 visit to Australia, he pledged $5 m for the US Gallery at Sydney's Australian National Maritime Museum, and President George H. W. Bush inaugurated it in 1992.

Post-war academic discussion of international gifts was scaled up to consider the Marshall Plan and international development efforts. In terms of archaic obligations to give, receive, and reciprocate, scholars observed that rich donor nations like the United States and Canada tended to be too unilateral and prescriptive in their giving of aid.[37] More recently, China's impressive gifts to African countries included the $200 m African Union Headquarters that opened in Addis Ababa in 2012.[38] "Gifts don't come bigger than this," said the BBC's Will Ross, and rarely do they come better designed than this state-of-the-art complex, featuring

Ethiopia's highest building. African leaders interviewed by Ross appreciated that the Chinese had not specifically tied their gift to any reciprocal trade obligation.[39]

THE SPIRIT OF THE GIFT

As Weiner's work in the Trobriand Islands showed, a gift object can be charged with inalienable obligations. Referring to Maori society, Mauss explained that reciprocation vested in the spirit of the gift: "Even when abandoned by the giver, it still forms part of him who holds it," seeking a return to "its forest, its soil, its homeland." To give something is "to give a part of your self," he wrote:

> It retains a magical and religious hold over its recipient. The thing given is not inert...and strives to bring back to its original clan and homeland some equivalent to take its place.[40]

Without resorting to animism, it should be noted that a compulsion for "return" does form a to-and-fro pattern in international gift exchange. Returning to the Oval Office and the Resolute Desk, here is a remarkable object whose material and symbolic transformations reflect such a passage. In 1854, when the HMS *Resolute* was abandoned in the Arctic ice while seeking the lost Franklin expedition, its departing British crew had no idea that a Connecticut whaler would salvage the vessel and sail her home the following year. At this peak moment of tensions with Britain, the Americans' unexpected and magnanimous gift of the refurbished *Resolute*, complete with her polar bear figurehead, helped to calm diplomatic relations. Queen Victoria's subsequent reciprocation, in the gift of the desk to President Cleveland, carried the exchange back across the Atlantic. Fashioned from the ship's timbers after it was decommissioned in 1879, a companion desk was also built for the Queen's own collection.[41]

The return of objects is the subject of a polyglot literature. For example, legal debates regarding the so-called mistaken gift center on whether a gift given under some misapprehension—say, a false report of the recipient's poverty—should be subject to restitution when the truth is known.[42] I have found no example of a donor nation demanding the return of a *mistaken* gift, only nations seeking the restitution of property lost to, or stolen by, other nations over the course of history. Such objects, when they are occasionally returned to their original owners under legal compulsion or international pressure, are not truly gifts. If there is such a thing as a diplomatic *gift of restitution*, it is an object that is given back freely, even if as part of a diplomatic rationale.

The ceremonies in Reykjavik surrounding the arrival of the Flatey Book, or *Flateyjarbók*, from Copenhagen in 1971, had all the fanfare of international gift exchange. Thousands of Icelanders gathered on the quay, the national orchestra played, and the Danish Education Minister fumbled slightly as he conveyed the ancient volumes into the hands of his Icelandic counterpart. Thus ended the "Manuscript Affair" that had stressed Icelandic-Danish relations for more than twenty-five years.[43] The preceding century of reluctance to return these foundational texts in Norse culture while Iceland was Denmark's distant colony is far from unique in the European colonial context. Nonetheless, I suggest the repatriation of the manuscripts represented a "gift of restitution" because Denmark acted voluntarily and in the spirit of diplomacy, and knowingly set a precedent for similar cases in the future.

Not all returns of "national DNA" documents are reparations for colonial-era treasure hunting. During a visit to Canberra in 2007, Canada's Prime Minister presented his Australian counterpart with the earliest surviving document printed in Australia, a rare Sydney playbill from 1796. Its significance was noticed when it turned up in a nineteenth-century scrapbook donated to Library and Archives Canada in 1973. "We were thrilled to discover this extraordinary artifact," the Minister of Canadian Heritage stated, "and we are proud to return it in the spirit of the great friendship between our countries."[44]

Sub-National Gifts and Non-State Actors

There is a wide range of international and philanthropic gifts by subnational bodies and non-state actors that exceeds the scope of this paper. The Carnegie Foundation's remarkable international program to build libraries had a profound effect on Canadian adult education, and in Ottawa, the NCC created a lovely garden called the Rockeries featuring architectural relics from the former Carnegie Library building.[45]

The twin cities movement and city-to-city relations generally are the source of many gifts, often organized thematically (e.g., Japanese cherry blossoms and British red phone boxes). Twin-City gifts sometimes follow upon tragedies, such as the Orly air crash on June 3, 1962 that killed more than one hundred art lovers from Atlanta. In response to what was the worst air accident to date, the Louvre sent *Whistler's Mother*, a painting admired during the Atlanta group's visit, and Rodin's *The Shade*, as gifts from France to commemorate their loss. Atlanta, in turn, sent a bronze sculpture to its sister city, Toulouse, commemorating French citizens who perished in a deadly chemical explosion on September 21, 2001, ten days after the 9/11 attacks in New York.[46] Following Hurricane Katrina in 2005, Toulouse sent relief to Atlanta. French businesses had raised $23 m toward rebuilding schools destroyed by the hurricane, and the French Consul General announced that, despite diplomatic differences over the Iraq war, "friendships exist when times are tough."[47]

AN UNDELIVERED GIFT

As Canada approached its 150th anniversary in 2017, there was renewed interest in its Centennial celebrations of 1967. In that case, the most significant international gifts received were from the sixty-one countries represented at Montreal's Expo'67. The world's press agreed that participating nations had outdone themselves by funding exceptional pavilions, whose architectural innovation heralded a brilliant urban future, with American Buckminster Fuller's splendid geodesic dome topping most visitors' lists. It also raises a case of my final sub-category in this survey, the undelivered gift.

The visit of French President Charles de Gaulle, one of 92 heads of state who attended the fair, is not memorable for its diplomatic grace. His momentous "*Vive le Québec... libre*," uttered ex tempore to a huge crowd and carried on television, rocked French and English Canada, not to mention Canada–France relations, for years afterward. Prime Minister Lester Pearson called it "totally unacceptable," and Justice Minister Pierre Elliott Trudeau questioned the likely French reaction to a visiting Canadian leader shouting, "Brittany to the Bretons!"[48] Hitherto respected by Canadians as a wartime ally, the French President would not journey to Ottawa the next day to receive Pearson's gift of an unusual wood, silver, and ivory "presentation box" created by Ontario artist David Chavel. In fact, this undelivered gift would lie out of sight in a museum vault for decades.[49]

From the above, a series of generalizations begin to emerge regarding the gift and public diplomacy:

- That archaic principles of gift exchange persist despite attempts to subordinate them to bureaucratic rationality;
- The low thresholds for personal acceptance of gifts mean that most gift exchanges between leaders operate in the realm of *public* diplomacy, not in personal diplomatic rapports;
- That gift exchange is not uniformly magnanimous, but altruism often is present;
- There is an international "diplomatic gift landscape," especially in capital cities, that adds to their built form and symbolic character.

OTTAWA'S DIPLOMATIC GIFT LANDSCAPE

It is this last point I will develop in relation to international gifts occupying sites in Canada's capital. Of the twenty-one outdoor locations, one third are clustered near the Lester B. Pearson building, the headquarters of Global Affairs Canada on Sussex Drive. Just one is located on the Quebec side of the Ottawa River (an arch in Gatineau featuring a metal truss from the Eiffel Tower, Jacques Chirac's gift while he was Mayor of Paris). Three were gift projects led by national associations in Canada, with secondary participation from their countries of origin. The country most represented is the Kingdom of the Netherlands, with four locations, including the annual gift of tulip bulbs. Surprisingly, France and England, two of Canada's "founding nations," are absent, with the exception of the fountain in Confederation Park that stood in Trafalgar Square from 1843 to 1948 and was a gift to the National Gallery of Canada from the National Art Collection Fund of England.[50]

The reasons for these gifts are highly diverse—some associated with state visits, others promoting foreign heroes (Gandhi, Shevchenko, Bolivar, and San Martin), others still commemorating significant events (the Air India bombing, the assassination of the Turkish military attaché Col. Altikat) or introducing prominent sculptors (the *Musika* and *Aries* sculptures from Mexico). Some are military (Polish Army and Can-Loan) or institution-to-institution (Colonel By Fountain). Over the years, I was directly involved in Canada's reception of at least five of these gifts and can attest to the element of altruism involved on a personal level between leaders in each of them, even when a foreign policy objective lay behind the initiative.

For example, in re-dedicating and improving the Mackenzie–Papineau Battalion Monument, Spain's Ambassador to Canada sought to draw

Canadians' attention to the last remaining volunteers of the International Brigades, who served in the Spanish Civil War. He felt these Canadians were deserving of greater honor, and I was grateful for his invitation to speak along with the Deputy Minister of Foreign Affairs and International Trade at the rededication in October 2011. There, I met veteran Jules Paivio, the last surviving "MacPap," who passed away two years later at the age of 97. A Canadian architect, professor, and one-time soldier, it was largely his personal determination that had brought the monument into being.

The best-known and most enduring international gift in Canada's capital is the annual gift of tulip bulbs from the Kingdom of the Netherlands, given in recognition for Canada's role in the liberation of the Dutch people in 1944 and 1945. Particular to Ottawa was the sheltering the Dutch Royal Family during the war and the birth of Princess Margriet at the Ottawa Civic Hospital in 1943, in a room designated by parliament as Dutch sovereign territory. The family was safely housed in Stornoway (as mentioned above, this house is owned and operated by the NCC today as one of six official residences). Every year since 1945, the NCC has received 10,000 tulip bulbs as a contribution to the total annual planting of about one million bulbs each year. For the 2017 celebrations, the NCC partnered with the Embassy of the Kingdom of the Netherlands and a national hardware store chain to register a special tulip that beautifully evokes Canada's national flag. In total, 4.5 million of these bulbs bloomed across Canada, with 150,000 specially planted in the fourteen provincial and territorial capitals. Taken together, these tulip bulbs, in addition to the monuments and works of public art, create a distinct international background to the cultural landscape of the capital, a subliminal reminder to Canadians of cosmopolitan connections between their capital city and the world of nations.

Canada's sesquicentennial in 2017 provides an opportunity to enrich that cosmopolitanism by deepening ties with diplomatic missions in the capital. The NCC issued a call to heads of diplomatic missions through GAC's Chief of Protocol to invite expressions of interest in presenting PD projects in 2017 in a special pavilion, built by the Commission for this purpose on a prime site on Confederation Boulevard. The NCC provided this fully serviced 3200 square-foot exposition building to diplomatic missions, each presenting its respective program content for periods up to one month. The exhibits and activities highlight bilateral relations with Canada. Of twenty-eight expressions of interest received, ten projects crystallized into signed agreements, beginning with the United States on February 2, 2017, and ending with the Republic of the Philippines on December 11.[51]

The US Embassy in Ottawa was a vital force in the sesquicentennial, and early on, Ambassador Bruce Heyman sought my suggestion for a 2017 legacy project. Following the 9/11 attacks in 2001, his embassy's main entrance had been permanently closed and an entire section of Confederation Boulevard was fortified with an improvised security barrier. Ambassador Heyman liked the NCC's plan to reopen that entrance, remove the concrete security barrier, and replace it with attractive bike lanes and landscaping that provided deeper and stronger security measures. In short order, he was able to secure the necessary State Department funding as a 2017 gift to Canada. Completed with the support of the NCC, the City of Ottawa, and the Province of Ontario, the Mackenzie Avenue rehabilitation is a win-win for cyclists *and* heightened security, and a success for US public diplomacy in Canada.

In 2017, the NCC will complete the construction of a new international landmark in the capital: the National Holocaust Monument. Designed by an international team led by Lord Cultural Associates in Toronto, including New York architect Daniel Libeskind, Toronto photographer Edward Burtynsky, and Montreal landscape architect Claude Cormier, this powerful statement occupies a prominent site across from the Canadian War Museum.[52] No international gifts were expected or solicited in aid of this project, but a touching moment in public diplomacy occurred when the German Embassy hosted the Coalition of Progressive Canadian Muslim Organization's gift of a substantial donation to the National Holocaust Monument Development Council, composed of prominent Jewish Canadians.

The final international project I will mention is the launch in 2017 of the new Global Centre for Pluralism as one of the NCC's Confederation Pavilions. The Government of Canada, through the NCC, has provided the Aga Khan Foundation with this significant unused heritage asset on Sussex Drive to be renovated for this innovative institution to be located in Canada's capital. It was also one reason that, earlier this year, I attended the Center's fifth annual lecture at the Ismaili Centre in Toronto, providing the epilogue for this paper.

RITUALS OF INTERNATIONAL GIFT EXCHANGE

The congenial and intimate lecture by South African jurist Albie Sachs was neither *about* gifts, nor gift exchange rituals, nor public diplomacy. He raised grave and far-reaching issues arising from the emergence of South Africa's constitution from the struggle to overturn Apartheid. Yet, near the end of his talk, he stated his intention to present a gift to the Aga Khan—sitting directly ahead and below in the front row of the auditorium—and as he asked that it be brought up on the stage, he acknowledged a dilemma.

"Houston," he said, "I had a problem [laughter], let me tell you [the] education I underwent in resolving that problem." Emailing his wife the previous night, he had worried, "I'm a very staunch Republican. I don't like titles." South Africa's Constitutional Court had dispensed with "My Lord" and "My Lady," he wrote, "and we are not even called 'Honourable.'" As such, it was difficult for him to "use the appropriate form of address to the person to whom I want to hand the most precious product of South Africa...not gold...not diamonds...not even platinum...*our Bill of Rights*."

After sustained applause, Sachs allowed that he had fretted since breakfast "until about an hour ago" over the presentation of his gift. "Come on, Albie," he told himself, "it is protocol, it is good manners. Do it." He worried that the gift "would be without grace... You cannot give something just to be gracious." And yet, he was in the Aga Khan Museum, *his* house, and what gracious guest would not respect his title?

> Then, the way discoveries are made: just suddenly, "of course, of course. I'm not giving this document to a titled individual. I'm giving the document to the head of an extraordinary community with a long, long history. Through that person, I am linking up with a community and the deeds that are being done in the name of that community, and that is something very beautiful. It is very beautiful.

Here, the presentation of the gift opened up a space wherein incommensurable cultural practices and asymmetric power relations were bracketed off. In this moment, diplomacy and public diplomacy merged, with leaders encountering each other not only personally as individuals, but also as representatives of entire social formations and their histories. "I am overcoming...my egalitarianism...not because I am forced to," Sachs went on, "It is actually rather lovely that I am, as it were, leaping out of my particular circumscribed world view, which I will defend, if I am compelled."

As Sachs descended the stage holding the unfurled Bill of Rights, he asked the Aga Khan please not to rise, though he did so anyway, and the two men met standing in the aisle, jointly touching the document, holding it lightly in their fingers: "I'm going to say with joy," Sachs concluded, "*Your Highness*, please accept South Africa's most precious gift to the world and to yourselves. Thank you, Your Highness."[53]

Albie Sachs' "solution" to his problem demonstrated that diplomatic gifts have the potential to open up spaces of equivalence in asymmetrical power relations. This could be useful to public diplomacy initiatives inasmuch as the ability to navigate such asymmetries often determines their success or failure. Second, he crystallized a key concept: that the diplomatic gift can *focalize* the entire donor and recipient societies through the personal interaction of the leaders. This is what he found "rather lovely"— the alignment of the personal and collective through the ritual of the gift, an alignment that seems to exemplify the essence of public diplomacy.

NOTES

1. As the largest landholder in Ottawa, Ontario, and its twin city Gatineau, Quebec, the NCC is responsible for 200 square miles of federal lands, including parks, official residences, heritage buildings, and monuments. See www.ncc-ccn.ca.
2. Marcel Mauss, *The Gift: Forms and Function of Exchange in Archaic Societies*. London: Routledge & Kegan Paul, 1969.
3. Mauss's critique suggested that European modernity had lost track of gift exchange as an essentially positive and stabilizing basis for social welfare and peace between individuals and peoples. Subsequent debates, from Claude Levi-Strauss, to Pierre Bourdieu to Jacques Derrida, have turned on this question of gifting as altruism or obligation.
4. Cosimo Bizzarri, "The Power of Giving: How to Master the Evolving Art of Diplomatic Gifts." *Quartz*, 1 August 2016.
5. Giarda Fiorindo, *Tokens of Decadence*. Website: http://www.giadafiorindi. com/2016/03/31/tokens-of-decadence/ (Visited: 9 August 2016).
6. Jacques Godbout, *The World of the Gift*. Montreal and Kingston: McGill-Queen's University Press, 1998.
7. Ari Shapiro, "The Art (and Artlessness) of the Presidential Gift." *National Public Radio*, broadcast, 25 May 2011. President Bill Clinton's gift to

Nelson Mandela of a scrapbook containing boxing memorabilia—assiduously collected under Clinton's supervision—was especially meaningful to both giver and recipient.

8. Michael Taussig, *Mimesis and Alterity: A Particular History of the Senses.* London: Routledge, 1991, p. 92.

9. Government of Australia: *Guidelines Relating to Official Gifts Received,* Website: http://www.maps.finance.gov.au/entitlements_handbooks/min isters-of-state/Appendix_C_Guidelines_relating_to_Official_Gifts_Rec eived.asp2 (Visited: 3 July 2016). Article 2 states: "Where at all possible and reasonable, appropriate opportunities should be taken to inform potential gift donors [that] Australia is not traditionally a gift giving country."

10. Philip Dorling, "Cost of Government Gifts for Foreign Officials Tops $3.4 m in Five Years." *Sydney Morning Herald,* 15 November 2014.

11. For example, see the Federal Register/Vol. 80, No. 227/Wednesday, November 25, 2015/Notices. Department of State, Office of the Chief of Protocol: Gifts to Federal Employees From Foreign Government Sources Reported to Employing Agencies in Calendar Year 2014.

12. Ibid.

13. NCC, "Management of the Prime Minister's Forfeited Gifts." Submission to the Advisory Committee on the Official Residences of Canada, September 2016. The remaining 30 gifts are preserved in the NCC's Crown Collection conservation center.

14. These low value thresholds for gifts may also expose heads of state, ministers, and public officials to attacks that attempt to exaggerate their potential to unduly influence officeholders.

15. "President Dwight Eisenhower greets Dzimbo, a 440-pound baby elephant, 1959." National Archives and Records Administration. https://www.whitehousehistory.org/photos/photo-4-10.

16. AFP, "Jumbo Row over Sri Lanka's Baby Elephant Gift to John Key." *New Zealand Herald,* 25 February 2016.

17. Wikipedia: "Panda Diplomacy." Since 1984 the pandas are not given away permanently by China but rather loaned for periods of ten years, with part of the loan fee directed to sustaining their natural habitats.

18. Natalie Lawrence, "The Prime Minister and the Platypus: A Paradox Goes to War." *Studies in History and Philosophy of Biological and Biomedical Sciences* 43:1 (2012): 290–297.

19. Guido Ruotolo, "Il regalo avvelenato di Putin Chiavette Usb con microspie A San Pietroburgo l' 'omaggio' dei russi ai leader: ma erano una trappola." *La Stampa Mondo* 29 October 2013; Nick Squires, et al. "Russia 'spied on G20 leaders with USB sticks.'" *The Telegraph,* 29 October 2013.

20. Mauss, op. cit., p. 62.

21. Ibid.
22. Wikipedia entry: https://en.wikipedia.org/wiki/Gift_basket_diplomacy (Visited: 3 July 2016).
23. W.H. Prescott, *The History of the Conquest of Peru*. New York: Cosimo, 2007. See Atahualpa's plea upon his death sentence: "you, who have met with friendship and kindness from my people, with whom I have shared my treasures, who have received nothing but benefits from my hands!" (p. 252).
24. A peculiarity of this gift offering was its veiled critique of Napoleon III's authoritarian outlook, reflecting the gargantuan statue's ideal of *liberté* back to France.
25. Wikipedia entry: https://en.wikipedia.org/wiki/Balbo_Monument (Visited: 3 July 2016).
26. http://cjournal.concordia.ca/archives/20081023/ceremony_rededi cates_place_bethune.php (Visited: 3 July 2016).
27. Will LeRoy, "Justin Trudeau's Official Gifts to China a Nod to His Father." *CBC News*, 31 August 2016.
28. Commonwealth War Graves Commission, American War Memorials Overseas (see http://www.uswarmemorials.org), In addition to state-funded monuments, there are hundreds of smaller memorials and monuments created through the independent efforts of many sub-national actors.
29. http://www.mercitrain.org/ (Visited: 3 July 2016).
30. See, for example, David Caute, *The Dancer Defects*. Oxford University Press, 2005; Graham Carr, 'Diplomatic Notes,' *Popular Music History* 1:1 (2004).
31. Danielle Fosler-Lussie, *Music in America's Cold War Diplomacy*. Oakland, CA: University of California Press, 2015. Annette Weiner's work with the Trobriand islanders is sensitive to Euro-centric attitudes toward reciprocity in anthropological literature. See Annette Weiner, *Inalienable Possessions: The Paradox of Keeping-While-Giving*. Berkeley: University of California Press, 1992. Her line of thought would make for an interesting re-reading of the literature on Cold War cultural diplomacy.
32. Sandys' sculpture is installed in close proximity to the Christopher Wren Church dismantled stone-by-stone in London and rebuilt, restored, and re-inaugurated in Fulton in 1965.
33. "Leifur Eiríksson Statue: Did You Know About the US Replica?" *Icelandic Roots*, 22 August 2013. A full-size twin of Reykjavik's Ericsson statue is located at the Mariners' Museum in Newport News, Virginia, one of 16 Ericsson statues in North America.
34. Sarah Jennings, *Art and Politics: The History of the National Arts Centre*. Toronto: Dundurn Press, 2009, p. 34.
35. Louise Sweeney, "Kennedy Center." *The Christian Science Monitor*, 10 September 1981.

36. Wikipedia; Cairo Opera website (Visited: August 2016).
37. See Wilton S. Dillon, *Gifts and Nations: The Obligation to Give, Receive and Repay*. Paris: Mouton, 1968; Robert Kowalski, "The Gift: Marcel Mauss and International Aid." *Journal of Comparative Social Welfare* 27:3 (October 2011): 189–205.
38. Kingsley Ighobor, "China in the Heart of Africa: Opportunities and Pitfalls in a Rapidly Expanding Relationship." *Africa Renewal*, January 2013. He points to the scope of previous Chinese donations: a hospital (Angola), a road (Zambia), stadiums (Sierra Leone and Benin), a sugar mill and farm (Mali), and a water supply project (Mauritania), among other projects: "In July 2012, Chinese President Hu Jintao listed yet more, including 100 schools, 30 hospitals, 30 anti-malaria centres and 20 agricultural technology demonstration centres."
39. Will Ross. "African Union Opens Chinese-Funded HQ in Ethiopia." *BBC News*, 28 January 2012.
40. Mauss, op. cit., p. 10.
41. Michael Phillips, 'HMS *Resolute*." 1998, http://www.cronab.demon.co.uk/Resol.htm (Visited: 3 July 2016); the desk's brass plaque reads "The ship was...sent as a gift to Queen Victoria by the President and People of the United States as a token of goodwill and friendship. This table was made from her timbers...and was presented by the Queen...to the President...as a memorial of the courtesy and loving kindness which dictated the offer of the gift of the 'Resolute'." As a grace note, Prime Minister Harold Wilson presented President Lyndon B. Johnson with the *Resolute*'s bell in 1965.
42. Andrew Burrows, "Restitution of Mistaken Enrichments." *Boston University Law Review* 92 (2012): 767–792.
43. Hans Bekker-Nielsen, "Icelandic Manuscripts in Denmark and Their Return to Iceland." Transl. Peter Foote. *Libri*. 23:3 (1973).
44. Sylvia Marchant, "Tale of Theatre Playbill." *National Library of Australia News*, December 2007; "Australians Delight in Canada's Gift of Historic Document." *News Release*, 11 September 2007.
45. Katharina Rietzler, "Before the Cultural Cold Wars: American Philanthropy and Cultural Diplomacy in the Inter-War Years." *Historical Research* 84:223 (February 2011): 148–164.
46. City of Atlanta, "City of Atlanta Celebrates 40th Anniversary of Atlanta-Toulouse Sister City Relationship." *News Release*, 22 April 2015. 30 people died and thousands were injured in the explosion at the AZF-Grand Paroisse chemical factory. Further strengthening the bond, a unique special loan arrangement between the High Museum and the Louvre was announced.
47. "French City Donates Items to Evacuees in Atlanta." *Athens Banner-Herald*, 27 January 2006. The report stated that, "the $50,000, 12-pallet

donation of items that include diapers, linens, shoes, clothes, school supplies and toiletries is just the latest example of more than 30 years of aid that has been shared between the two sister cities."

48. "De Gaulle and 'Vive le Québec libre.'" *The Canadian Encyclopedia*. Website: http://www.thecanadianencyclopedia.ca/en/article/degaulle-and-vive-le-quebec-libre-feature/ (Visited 12 August 2016).

49. Peter Ackroyd, *The Anniversary Compulsion: Canada's Centennial Celebrations, a Model Mega-Anniversary*. Toronto: Dundurn Press, 1992; Canadian Museum of History website: http://www.historymuseum.ca/cmc/exhibitions/tresors/treasure/174eng.shtml (Visited: 3 July 2016).

50. For more details see http://ncc-ccn.gc.ca/our-plans.

51. See http://www.ncc-ccn.gc.ca/planning/confederation-pavilions.

52. Ottawa was the only capital among World War II allies not to have built such a monument or memorial. See http://holocaustmonument.ca/.

53. Albie Sachs, "The Battle for the South African Constitution: Protecting Minorities Through Power-Sharing or a Bill of Rights?" Global Centre for Pluralism 2016 Annual Lecture, Toronto, 19 May 2016. http://www.pluralism.ca/images/APL2016/ASRemarksFinalEN.pdf (Emphasis added).

SELECT BIBLIOGRAPHY

Axworthy, Lloyd. "Canada and Human Security: The Need for Leadership." *International Journal* 52, no. 2 (1997): 183–196.

Bátora, Jozef. "Public Diplomacy Between Home and Abroad: Norway and Canada." *The Hague Journal of Diplomacy* 1 no. 1 (2006): 78–79.

Brooks, Stephen, ed. *Promoting Canadian Studies Abroad: Soft Power and Cultural Diplomacy.* London: Palgrave, 2018.

Bothwell, Robert. *Alliance and Illusion: Canada and the World, 1945–1984.* Vancouver: UBC Press, 2007.

Cohen, Andrew. *While Canada Slept: How We Lost Our Place in the World.* Toronto: McClelland and Stewart, 2003.

Cooper, Andrew F. *Canadian Foreign Policy: Old Habits and New Directions.* Scarborough: Prentice Hall, 1997.

Cooper, Andrew F. "In Search of Niches: Saying 'Yes' and Saying 'No' in Canada's International Relations." *Canadian Foreign Policy* 3 (Winter 1995): 1–13.

Cooper, Andrew F. "Stretching the Model of 'Coalitions of the Willing.'" In *Diplomacy and Global Governance: Worlds Apart?* Edited by Andrew F. Cooper, Brian Hocking and William Maley. London: Palgrave, 2008, pp. 257–270.

Copeland, Daryl. "Science and Diplomacy after Canada's Lost Decade: Counting the Costs, Looking Beyond." Canadian Global Affairs Institute, 2015. https://www.cgai.ca/science_and_diplomacy.

Cull, Nicholas J. *Public Diplomacy: Foundations for Global Engagement in the Digital Age.* Cambridge: Polity, 2019.

© The Editor(s) (if applicable) and The Author(s) 2021   231
N. J. Cull and M. K. Hawes (eds.), *Canada's Public Diplomacy*,
Palgrave Macmillan Series in Global Public Diplomacy,
https://doi.org/10.1007/978-3-319-62015-2

Cull, Nicholas J., and Geoffrey Cowan, eds. "Global Public Diplomacy." Special issue of *Annals of the American Academy of Political and Social Sciences* 616, no. 1 (March 2008).

Gienow-Hecht, Jessica, and M. C. Donfried, eds. *Searching for a Cultural Diplomacy*. New York and Oxford: Berghahn Books, 2010.

Goff, Patricia M. "Cultural Diplomacy." In *The Oxford Handbook of Modern Diplomacy*. Edited by Andrew F. Cooper, Jorge Heine, and Ramesh Thakur. Oxford: Oxford University Press, 2013, pp. 419–435.

Hawes, Michael K., and Christopher Kirkey, eds. *Canadian Foreign Policy in a Unipolar World*. Toronto: Oxford University Press, 2018.

Hawes, Michael K. "Managing Canada-U.S. Relations in Difficult Times." *The American Review of Canadian Studies* 34, no. 4 (Winter 2004).

Jessup, Lynda. "Art for a Nation?" In *Beyond Wilderness: The Group of Seven, Canadian Identity, and Contemporary Art*. Edited by John O'Brian and Peter White. Montreal: McGill-Queen's University Press, 2007, pp. 187–192.

Mark, Simon L. "Rethinking Cultural Diplomacy: The Cultural Diplomacy of New Zealand, the Canadian Federation and Quebec." *Political Science* 62, no.1 (2010): 62–83.

North American Cultural Diplomacy Initiative. *Cultural Diplomacy and Trade: Making Connections*. Kingston: North American Cultural Diplomacy Initiative, 2018.

Nye, Joseph S. *Do Morals Matter? Presidents and Foreign Policy from FDR to Trump*. Oxford University Press: New York, 2020.

Nye, Joseph S. *Soft Power: The Means to Success in World Politics*. New York: Public Affairs, 2004.

Olechowska, Elzbieta. *The Age of International Radio: Radio Canada International 1945–2007*. Oakville: Mosaic Press, 2007.

Paschalidis, Gregory "Exporting National Culture: Histories of Cultural Institutes Abroad." *International Journal of Cultural Policy* 15, no. 3 (2009): 275–289.

Potter, Evan H. *Branding Canada: Projecting Canada's Soft Power Through Public Diplomacy*. Montreal: McGill-Queen's University Press, 2009.

Potter, Evan. "Canada and the New Public Diplomacy." *International Journal* 58, no. 1 (Winter 2002–2003): 43–63.

Potter, Evan H. *Cyber-Diplomacy: Managing Foreign Policy in the Twenty-First Century*. Montreal: McGill-Queen's University Press, 2002.

Rasmussen, Rasmus Kjaergaard, and Henrik Merkelsen, "The new PR of States: How Nation Branding Practices Affect the Security Function of Public Diplomacy." *Public Relations Review* 38, no. 5 (2012): 810–818.

Sending, Ole J., Vincent Pouliot, and Iver B. Neumann. "The Future of Diplomacy: Changing Practices, Evolving Relationships." *International Journal* 66, no. 3 (2011): 527–542.

Siegel, Arthur. *Radio Canada International*. Oakville: Mosaic Press, 1996.

Tolksdorf, Domenik, and Xandie Keunning. "Trudeau's Foreign Policy: Progressive Rhetoric, Conventional Policies." *Green European Journal* (25 September 2019).

von Hlatky, Stéfanie. "The Gender Turn in Canadian Military Interventions." In *Canada Among Nations*. Edited by Fen Osler Hampson and Stephen M. Saideman.

INDEX

© The Editor(s) (if applicable) and The Author(s) 2021
N. J. Cull and M. K. Hawes (eds.), *Canada's Public Diplomacy*,
Palgrave Macmillan Series in Global Public Diplomacy,
https://doi.org/10.1007/978-3-319-62015-2